Orello Cone

Gospel-Criticism and Historical Christianity, a study of the Gospels
and of the history of the Gospel-Canon during the second century,
with a consideration of the results of modern criticism

Orello Cone

Gospel-Criticism and Historical Christianity, a study of the Gospels and of the history of the Gospel-Canon during the second century, with a consideration of the results of modern criticism

ISBN/EAN: 9783742874566

Manufactured in Europe, USA, Canada, Australia, Japa

Cover: Foto ©ninafisch / pixelio.de

Manufactured and distributed by brebook publishing software
(www.brebook.com)

Orello Cone

Gospel-Criticism and Historical Christianity, a study of the Gospels and of the history of the Gospel-Canon during the second century, with a consideration of the results of modern criticism

CONTENTS.

CHAPTER I.

	PAGE
THE TEXT	1
1.—The Autographs of the Gospels	1
2.—Copies	4
3.—Extra-Textual Witnesses	6
4.—The Manuscripts	9
5.—The Variants	12
a. Unintentional Changes	12
b. Intentional Changes	13
c. Dogmatic Changes	18
6.—Some Principles of Textual Criticism	19
7.—The Versions	22

CHAPTER II.

THE CANON	27
1.—The Apostolic Age	33
2.—The Post-Apostolic Age	37
a. Clement of Rome	41
b. The Epistle of Barnabas	45
c. The Shepherd of Hermas	48
3.—The Epistles of Polycarp and Ignatius	51
4.—Papias of Hierapolis and Hegesippus	60
5.—Justin Martyr's Gospels	65
6.—The Clementine Homilies, Basilides, and Valentinus	74
7.—The Canon of Marcion and Tatian's Diatessaron	85
8.—Dionysius of Corinth, Melito of Sardis, and Athenagoras	93
9.—Theophilus of Antioch and the Canon of Muratori	97
10.—Irenæus and Tertullian	102
11.—The Catholic Church and the Canon	108
12.—The Gospels in the Alexandrian Church	113

CHAPTER III.

THE SYNOPTIC PROBLEM	118
1.—The Hypothesis of Copying	125
2.—The Hypothesis of a Common Written Source or of an Original Gospel	130
3.—The Hypothesis of Oral Tradition	138
4.—The Course of More Recent Criticism	142
5.—Conclusions Regarding the Synoptic Problem	150

CHAPTER IV.

THE GOSPEL ACCORDING TO MARK 161

CHAPTER V.

THE GOSPEL ACCORDING TO MATTHEW 173

CHAPTER VI.

THE GOSPEL ACCORDING TO LUKE . . . 197

CHAPTER VII.

THE GOSPEL ACCORDING TO JOHN . . 210

CHAPTER VIII.

THE ESCHATOLOGY OF THE GOSPELS . . . 254

CHAPTER IX.

DOGMATIC "TENDENCIES" IN THE GOSPELS . . . 291

CHAPTER X.

THE OLD TESTAMENT IN THE GOSPELS; OR, THE HERMENEUTICS OF THE EVANGELISTS 306

CHAPTER XI.

THE GOSPELS AS HISTORIES 318

CHAPTER XII.

CRITICISM AND HISTORICAL CHRISTIANITY . . . 337

GOSPEL-CRITICISM
AND
HISTORICAL CHRISTIANITY.

CHAPTER I.

THE TEXT.

1.—THE AUTOGRAPHS OF THE GOSPELS.

IF the authors of the Gospels had a presentiment of the importance which later ages would attach to their writings, it does not appear in any words which they have left. The writer of the third Gospel is the only one of them who explicitly states the object for which his record was made, and he appears to have had in view primarily, if not solely, the instruction of a certain Theophilus. But any hope which the evangelists may be supposed to have cherished that their very words would be preserved as a sacred legacy by future generations, could not but be frustrated by the inevitable fortune to which their productions were subject by the conditions and circumstances under which they wrote. It was many years after the composition of their records before writings giving accounts of the life and work of Jesus came to be held in especially high regard, and to be preferred to the still living tradition handed down by word of mouth.

Accordingly, scrupulous care, either in their preservation or copying is not to be presumed on the part of those into whose hands they may have fallen. Besides, the autographs of the Gospels must have perished in a short time on account of the fragile nature of the material on which they were written. According to the custom of the time they were doubtless written upon papyrus* by means of a reed charged with ink,† instead of upon the more costly parchment. The best of the papyrus was fragile, and under constant use would be destroyed in a few years. Use or neglect must, however, be assumed in order to account for the early disappearance of the autographs of the Gospels, since there are examples of the preservation of papyrus-manuscripts through long periods of time in Egyptian tombs and in a villa of Herculaneum. But the reports of the discovery of wonderfully preserved originals of the Gospels, which were circulated by the Roman Catholics in the dark ages, must be put to the account of legend. It was said that the grave of Barnabas was opened in the fifth century in consequence of a "revelation," and that this saint was found to hold in his hands a splendid copy of the first Gospel in the handwriting of Matthew himself. This copy was held sacred, and preserved in Constantinople as a standard of the text of this Gospel. A similar legend was current respecting the marvellous preservation of an autograph of the fourth Gospel at Ephesus, where it was worshipped by the faithful. The time of the disappearance of the autographs of the Gospels cannot, of course, be accurately determined. No trace of them is found in the oldest Christian literature. Had they been in existence towards

---

* πάπυρος, or χάρτης.
† διὰ χάρτου καὶ μέλανος, II. John 12.

the end of the second century, when controversies were carried on which frequently turned upon readings of certain texts, they would doubtless have been appealed to as decisive authorities, especially since at that time the Gospels were beginning to enjoy high repute as oracles, and to be placed upon an equal footing with the Old Testament.

Of the manner in which the originals of the Gospels were written we may learn from the Italian and Egyptian papyrus-rolls of the same date which have been preserved. The text was written in columns upon the papyrus in the so-called uncials, or capital letters, and ran unbroken, *i.e.*, without division of words and marks of punctuation. The *iota* was not subscribed, nor was it always adscribed. Breathings and accents were not employed. That the authors of these writings gave them the titles which they now bear is improbable. Against the supposition that they entitled them "Gospels" is, according to Tischendorf, Justin Martyr's constant reference to the evangelistic records known to him as "Memorabilia of the Apostles,"* a designation to which he once adds, "which are called Gospels."† He could hardly have so expressed himself had these writings originally borne the formal titles by which they have been known since the formation of the canon. That part of the titles which indicates the reputed authors of the several works, the words, "according to Matthew," etc., has a so decidedly editorial look, as to leave little doubt that it was prefixed to the originals. The titles also presuppose a collection of Gospels, each one of which is distinguished from the others by a heading that is uniform except in the name of the evangelist to whom the writing is ascribed.

* ἀπομνημονεύματα τῶν ἀποστόλων.
† ἃ καλεῖται εὐαγγέλια.

2.—COPIES.

Not only have the autographs of the Gospels unhappily perished, but the earliest copies of them have had a similar fortune, and, like the originals, have left no trace of their existence. During more than two centuries the fate of these writings and of their earliest transcriptions is unknown. Of the care that was bestowed upon the preparation of these copies, and by whom and for what purpose they were made, history gives no information. If it could be shown that during the first century after they were composed the originals of the Gospels were held in veneration as writings inspired of God, the inference would be legitimate that the copying of them was regarded as a sacred office, to be performed only under a solemn sense of obligation to be painstaking and accurate. It will appear, however, when we come to study the history of the formation of the canon of the New Testament, that they were protected by no such sentiment. On the contrary, if Papias be allowed to have expressed the general opinion of his time * on the subject, the current oral tradition was even held in higher esteem as a source of information touching the life and works of Jesus than any written accounts of them. Whatever inferences may be drawn from the phenomena presented by the existing manuscripts of the Gospels to alterations and interpolations made in the first centuries, there is little that can be urged in favor of any radical changes from the originals effected during this period. The general agreement of the manuscripts which have been preserved and compared, in the most important parts of the narrative, and the remarkable similarity of the first three Gospels in plan and even in verbal expression, furnish a strong presumption against any theory which may be set up of ex-

* About the middle of the second century.

tensive modifications of the records by copyists. The vexing "synoptical problem" is a standing witness to the preservation of the essential integrity of at least a central and important portion of the first three Gospels. It is probable that single Gospels were copied separately at first for private use or for public reading in the religious assemblies. When the four Gospels were first wholly or in part written in one collection, or connected with copies of the Old Testament, is unknown.

Although many copies of the Gospels were doubtless made during the second and third centuries, yet owing to their destruction in the times of the persecutions of the Christians, to neglect, and to the natural dissolution of the material on which they were written, no manuscripts remain which are supposed to antedate the time of Constantine, or the first quarter of the fourth century. It is evident that, if the earliest Christian writers succeeding the evangelists had made numerous exact quotations either from the originals of the Gospels or from the first copies of them, such testimony to the condition of the text during an obscure period of its existence would have been of great importance. But information from this source is so meagre and untrustworthy as hardly to be worthy of consideration. Down to about the close of the second century the remains of Christian literature are inconsiderable. But they are sufficient to show us that there was not yet much quoting from the Gospels, or, indeed, from any part of the New Testament, in the proper sense of the word. Tischendorf finds that the citations made at about the time in question are of the sort that they agree with the variants handed down from a later time without on critical principles having any special claim to apostolical originality. The passages from the evangelic history which are found in the apostolical fathers and in Justin Martyr show that in the age of these writers the oral tradition had by no means yielded to written documents either in currency or authority. The character of the writings of this period was not such in general as to call for appeals to the text in order to ascertain precisely what had been taught by Jesus or the apostles. In the discussions, however, which were carried on between the so-called orthodox and heretical parties, it became important to know what was written in the records. Charges of corrupting the text in the interest of a doctrine were made from both sides. With the exception, however, of those brought against Marcion, the Gnostic, who did in fact omit some parts of the Gospel of Luke, these charges were generally groundless. The accusations are for the most part found on examination to have been founded on different readings of the text. Readings which can be shown to be wrong in the hands of the so-called heretics are found to have been widely diffused among writers opposed to them. With the exception just referred to, wilful changes and interpolations are rarely to be charged against either party. Even Marcion, like many another heretic, appears not to have been so bad as he was painted. For notwithstanding his conceded tampering with the Gospel of Luke, it is said of him that in the isolated readings which he is charged with having altered it happens not unfrequently that he has retained the right reading, and that his opponents are in error, while in very many cases the alleged corruption is a various reading more or less supported by the authorities.

3.—EXTRA-TEXTUAL WITNESSES.

If the writers who stood nearest to the evangelists fail us in contributing to a knowledge of the Gospels, their successors are found to be witnesses of more importance. Their testimony is, however, impaired negatively by our ignorance of their manner of quoting. Their citations would be of great importance if made carefully from a manuscript, but critically of little worth if made loosely from memory. It must also be taken into account that the text of their writings has been exposed to no little corruption by copyists who modified the citations according to the texts of the Gospels which they had before them. Clement of Alexandria furnishes many passages quoted from copies of the Gospels which antedate the oldest manuscripts now in existence. He complains, however, of a tendency prevalent in his own time to change the Gospel;* but it is not known precisely what kind of modifications he had in mind, whether those made by the Gnostics, or additions by such as thought they could improve the text, or arbitrary changes undertaken in the interest of harmonizing passages found in the different Gospels. He himself quotes two sayings of Jesus which are not found in the canonical text. Sometimes he makes citations freely from memory, not unfrequently mixing two narratives, while in very many places he has preserved the true reading.

Origen's contribution to a knowledge of the text of the Gospels as it was in the first part of the third century, is of greater importance than that of any of his predecessors among the early Christian writers. Many of his quotations are of considerable length, and appear to have been made from manuscripts, and not from memory. So numerous and extensive are they, that it has been said that almost the entire text of the New Testament might be transcribed from his voluminous writings. But his

* μετατιθέναι τὸ εὐαγγέλιον.

testimony is greatly curtailed by the loss of the original Greek text of many of his works, they existing only in a Latin translation, and is impaired by the corruption of the text of those that have come down in the language in which they were written. These latter, like the manuscripts of the New Testament, have suffered from the carelessness or the temerity of copyists. Origen's own testimony to the condition of the text of the Gospels in his time is worthy of especial consideration. "As the case stands," he says, "it is obvious that the difference between the copies is considerable, partly from the carelessness of individual scribes, partly from the wicked daring of some in correcting what is written, partly also from [the changes made by] those who add or remove what seems good to them in the process of correction." It is to be regretted that we have not, among the fruits of the great learning and industry of Origen, some considerable contributions to the criticism of the text of the Gospels. But while he gave his attention to the purification of the text of the Old Testament in the Septuagint version by a comparison of editions, he appears to have been deterred at least from making public any work of this kind on the text of the New Testament by the fear of giving offence to the Church. He did not think he could do it "without danger." It is evident that the sentiment of his time must have been very unfavorable to textual criticism. Several cases are, however, cited by Norton, in which Origen has expressly noticed various readings in the Gospels.* In three of these passages it is pointed out that the variations which he notices are no

---

* Matt. viii. 28 ; xvi. 20 ; xvii. 1 ; xxi. 5, 9, 15 ; xxvii. 17 ; Mark iii. 18 ; Luke i. 46 ; ix. 48 ; xiv. 19 ; xxiii. 45 ; John i. 3, 4, 28. To these Hort adds, Matt. v. 22.

THE TEXT.   9

longer found in our Greek copies; in several our copies are still divided; and in one, Matthew xxvii. 17, a few copies of no great age retain the interpolation which was found in his time "in very ancient copies." Westcott calls attention to the circumstance as remarkable that Origen asserts in answer to Celsus that Jesus is nowhere called "the carpenter" in the Gospels which were circulated in the churches, though this is undoubtedly the true reading in Mark vi. 3.*

4.—THE MANUSCRIPTS.

No complete description of the manuscripts of the Gospels can be undertaken here. A few of the most important will be mentioned with the letters designating them for convenience of reference in the course of this treatise. The number of uncial manuscripts of the Gospels now in existence is not great. Tischendorf reckons forty, of which five are entire; three nearly entire; ten contain very considerable portions; fourteen, very small fragments; and eight, fragments more or less considerable. To these must be added the Sinaïtic, which is entire, and two others. The following are the principal primary uncials:

a. *Codex Sinaiticus* (א), obtained by Tischendorf from the convent of St. Catharine, Mt. Sinai, in 1859. The Old and New Testaments are entire, and the Epistle of Barnabas and the Shepherd of Hermas are added. It was published under the editorial direction of Tischendorf at St. Petersburg in 1862 in four splendid folio volumes. It is generally regarded as of the fourth century.

b. *Codex Alexandrinus* (A), also a manuscript of the entire Greek Bible with the Epistles of Clement added;

---
* Orig. contra Celsum, v. 36.

now in the British Museum. There are some chasms in the Gospels: Matt. i—xxv. 6, ἐξέρχεσθε; John vi. 50—viii. 52, λέγει. Its date is supposed to be in the first half of the fifth century.

c. *Codex Vaticanus* (B), No. 1209 in the Vatican library, where it appears to have been almost from the founding of that library in about A. D. 1450. Besides the Old Testament in Greek it contains the New Testament entire to Heb. ix. 14. The rest of Hebrews, the pastoral Epistles, and the Apocalypse were added in the fifteenth century. It is assigned to the fourth century.

d. *Codex Ephræmi* (C), a palimpsest manuscript containing fragments of the Septuagint and of every part of the New Testament. From the fourth century.

e. *Codex Bezæ* (D), a Græco-Latin manuscript of the Gospels and Acts with a small fragment of III. John. It has many lacunæ. Referred to the sixth century.

f. *Codex Guelpherbytani* (PQ) two palimpsests of the sixth and fifth centuries respectively. Fragments of the Gospel of Luke.

g. *Paris Codex* (L), one of the most important of the late uncial manuscripts, contains the four Gospels with some lacunæ. The text agrees remarkably with B and with Origen. It is of the eighth century.

h. *British Museum Add.* 17,211 (R), a palimpsest brought to England in 1847 from the convent of St. Mary Deipara. The original text is covered by a Syriac writing of the ninth or tenth century. About 585 verses of Luke were deciphered by Tregelles and Tischendorf in 1854 and 1855 respectively. It is assigned to the sixth century.

i. *Codex Dublinensis rescriptus* (Z), in the library of Trinity College, Dublin, is a palimpsest containing large portions of Matthew. Assigned to the sixth century.

j. *Codex Basileensis* (E), contains the four Gospels with a few lacunæ, and was probably written about the middle of the eighth century. A secondary uncial.

k. *Codex Borgianus* (T), fragments of John and Luke. Fifth century.

l. *Codex Cotton* (N), twelve leaves of purple vellum four of which are in the British Museum. Thirty-three additional leaves containing fragments of Mark have recently been found at Patmos, and were used by Tischendorf in his eighth critical edition of the New Testament. Sixth or seventh century.

m. **Codex** *Sangallensis* (Δ) a manuscript of the Gospels with an interlinear Latin translation which corresponds rather with the Vulgate than the Greek text. From the ninth century.

n. The designations Y, N^b, T^b, O, Ξ, I (Tischendorf) are of less importance, as are the secondary uncials, F, G, H, K, M, S, U, V, Γ.

Tregelles has in his catalogue of manuscripts, which Westcott regards as the most complete and trustworthy yet made, thirty-four uncials of the Gospels and six hundred and one cursives. Uncial writing continued in use until about the middle of the tenth century. In the later manuscripts of this class a slight space between the words first makes its appearance.

The method of continuous writing employed in the earlier manuscripts has already been mentioned. The reading of the New Testament in the public assemblies, however, required a division of some sort, and to meet this want Euthalius published in the year 458 an arrangement of Paul's Epistles in clauses ($\sigma\tau\iota\chi\omicron\iota$). A similar division had previously been applied to the Gospels by an unknown hand. But the earliest extant division of the New Testament into sections is found in Cod. B. This division is elsewhere found only in the palimpsest fragment of Luke Ξ. Two other divisions of the Gospels exist, one into chapters (κεφάλαια, τίτυλοι, breves) which correspond with the distinct sections of the narrative, and are on an average about twice as long as the sections in B. This is found in A, C, R, Z, and probably came into use before the fifth century. The other division, made in the interest of a Gospel-harmony, originated with Ammonius of Alexandria in the third century. He took the first Gospel as the basis of his harmony, and grouped around it the parallel passages from the other Gospels. His work was completed by Eusebius of Cæsarea.

5.—THE VARIANTS.

Cicero loudly censures the copyists of his time, charging their errors to false seeing, false hearing, and misunderstanding. Mistakes of copyists are doubtless in the nature of the case to be expected, particularly when, as already remarked, the writings copied are not protected by a sentiment of veneration. Since the errors themselves are likely to be copied and fresh ones made in each copy, it is evident that with frequent transcribing the number of so-called readings must become very great. The various readings have been classified according to the causes from which they arise.

a.—Unintentional Changes.

These are very numerous, and are due to several obvious causes. From errors in hearing and possibly in seeing came the confusion of different I-sounds, called Itacism, by which η, ι, ει, ε, etc., are frequently interchanged, and less often ο and ω, ου and ω, etc. Almost all manuscripts contain errors of this kind.* Numerous errors arose from the repetition or omission of similar letters, and from a false division of words by which a part of one word was joined to another, so that in some places the true division still remains in doubt. In one manuscript the false divisions of words have been corrected by another hand than that of the writer, and the frequency of their occurrence is regarded by Westcott as an instructive illustration of the corruption to which the text was exposed from this source. Here belong errors in writing the breathings, as εἰς ἐλθών for εἰσελθών, ἐν τούτῳ for ἓν τοῦτο, etc. Not infrequent are errors from failure of memory, when a sentence may have been read and immediately written: the exchange of synonyms and particles and the omission of the latter; orthographic confusion, as in the manifold writing of Genesaret. Finally, the frequent insertion of connecting particles, καὶ, γὰρ, οὖν, may have been "as much due to an unconscious instinct to supply natural links in the narrative or argument as to intentional efforts to give greater clearness to the text."

b.—Intentional Changes.

These may have been made in good faith, says Holtzmann, who remarks that a thinking copyist may in some circumstances be more dangerous than a thoughtless one. There are found, then, "learned corrections" of a linguistic or grammatical nature and syntactical changes in the interest of what the copyist appears to have regarded as an improvement of the construction. Arbitrary

---

* Matt. xxvii. 60, κένος, empty, for καινός, new; John xv. 4, μείνῃ for μένῃ; Matt. xi. 16, ἕτερος, for ἑταῖρος; by dictation of the text, εἰ δέ for ἴδε, ἡμεῖς for ὑμεῖς and vice versa.

variations in the text often arose out of the endeavor on the part of copyists to bring parallel portions of the Gospels into harmony. An example of this tendency is furnished in the closing words of the Lord's prayer. Matthew closes the prayer with the words, " but deliver us from evil," and so reads Luke according to the usual text. This reading in the third Gospel has the very strong support of Codd. Alex., Ephr., Bezae, Basil., and many versions ; but Codd. Vat., Sinaït., and some later ones omit the words, and close the prayer with " not into temptation." Besides, Origen, Jerome, and Augustine mention the omission of them in Luke. How, then, came they to stand in so many manuscripts? The answer of textual critics is that they were written there by copyists in order to bring the third Gospel in this passage into harmony with the first, since their omission from such manuscripts as the Sinaïtic and Vatican cannot be accounted for if they were original, while the harmonizing tendency readily explains their appearance elsewhere. To the same motive must be attributed the reading in some manuscripts which changes " the sixth hour" to " the third " in John xix. 14, in order to bring the statement of this evangelist more into accord with Mark xv. 25 as to the hour of the crucifixion. According to the latter historian, Jesus was crucified at the third hour,* while the former says that it was about the sixth hour † when Pilate pronounced sentence upon him. Again, in Mark ii. 7 there appears, as some suppose, to be a combination according to certain manuscripts of the parallel passages in Matthew and Luke. In Matthew we read, "this one blasphemes,"‡ in Luke, " who is this that speaks blas-

---

* ἦν δε ὥρα τρίτη. † ὥρα ἦν ὡς ἕκτη.
‡ οὗτος βλασφημεῖ.

phemies?"* But Mark reads, "why does this one thus speak? he blasphemes," † in Codd. Vat., Sinaït., Bezæ, etc., while in Codd. Alex., Ephr., Basil., etc., we find, "he speaks blasphemies." ‡ In this case the judgment of criticism is that internal grounds do not appear to decide for the one reading **or** the other, and the external witnesses are divided. § Tischendorf has adopted the reading of Codd. Sinaït. and Vat. One more example **of this sort must suffice, out of the many which** might be adduced, and that is quite remarkable. **According to some of the best** authenticated manuscripts, Sinaït., **Vat., Ephr., the account** of the lance-thrust into the body of Jesus as he hung upon the cross, given in John xix. 34, is found also in Matt. xxvii. 49, with the difference that according to Matthew the body was pierced before, and according **to** John, after death had taken place. **It is said that** Pope Clement V. at the Council of Vienna in 1311 forbade the addition in **Matthew**; but not for this reason, certainly, nor indeed **on account** of the contradiction, has the reading in the first Gospel been rejected by the critical authorities. **It could** hardly have been wanting in any copies, had it been in the original, and the harmonizing tendency explains its appearance in some manuscripts of the first Gospel, even though the attempt at harmonizing results in a contradiction which probably escaped the notice of the copyists. Such an inadvertence is not, however, surprising.

Changes made for the purpose of reconciling an **evan**gelist with himself or with facts are sometimes found. **For** example, **in John** vii. 8 the reading, " do you go up to the feast, I go *not yet* (οὔπω) up to this feast," is found in manuscripts whose authority gives it strong support, as

* τίς ἐστιν οὗτος ὃς λαλεῖ βλασφημίας;
† τί οὗτος οὕτως λαλεῖ; βλασφημεῖ. ‡ λαλεῖ βλασφημίας.
§ Immer, Hermeneutik des N. T. 1886, p. 97.

Vat., Basil., and the most of the other uncials; but the οὔπω is omitted in Sinaït. and some others, and οὐκ (not) stands in place of it. Textual criticism decides against the οὔπω, not altogether, indeed, on the authority of manuscripts, but because its presence is accounted for by the interest of copyists to reconcile the declaration of Jesus that he would not go up to the feast with the fact that he did immediately go. The attempts of copyists to correct an error in referring a citation from the Old Testament to its author caused persistent and wide-spread variations. In Mark i. 2 the most of the uncials and some versions support the common reading, "as it is written in the prophets," and Irenæus sanctions it. But Tischendorf has adopted the reading, "in Isaiah the prophet," although the passage quoted, "behold I send my messenger before thee," is not found in Isaiah. The reading, "in the prophets," was evidently inserted by a copyist who, finding that the passage was not in Isaiah, wished to set the evangelist right by making a vague reference to "the prophets." Tischendorf's reading rests on the authority of the majority of the versions, of several of the fathers, and of the old manuscripts, Sinaït. and Vat. It is deemed more probable that the error should have existed in the original than that it should have been inserted in such manuscripts as those referred to. But the fact of well-attested attempts on the part of copyists or readers to correct an author in one interest or another has no little weight in determining the verdict of textual criticism in such cases as this. One might, perhaps, be justified in the observation that the well-known practices of copyists have established a presumption in favor of a reading which contains an error, and against one which is in conformity with facts, when such variants as the one in question are found.

Additions were sometimes made to the text by copyists by inserting into it explanatory words, or glosses, which some one had written in the margin of a manuscript. The Codex Bezæ is the most remarkable among the Greek manuscripts for the variety and singularity of these additions. Some of these glosses have passed into the text, and retained a place there until the critical revision of Tischendorf threw them out. The critical authorities are generally agreed in explaining the origin of many of these glosses from the use of the Gospels for public reading in the assemblies of the early Christians. Sometimes they are repetitions of solemn expressions found elsewhere in the Gospels, as, "He that hath ears," etc., and "Many are called, but few chosen." The addition of the doxology to the Lord's prayer in Matt. vi. 13 is regarded as liturgical. The words, "For thine is the kingdom," etc., are wanting in Codd. Vat., Sinaït., Bezæ, in several versions, and in some of the Greek and Latin fathers. The spurious character of this addition is the more evident from the fact that its origin is so easily traceable.

Interpolations of greater importance are the concluding verses of the Gospel according to Mark, the account of the angel at the pool of Bethesda, and of the woman taken in adultery.* The first of these is wanting in Codd. Vat. and Sinaït., while two Codd., D and L, give each a different text from the received text. Besides, Eusebius, Jerome, and others remark the absence of the section in the most accurate manuscripts. It is found, however, in several manuscripts and versions, and Irenæus is the first among the early Christian writers to mention it. It is probable, therefore, that these verses are not from the author of the second Gospel, but were added by a later writer or a

---

* Mark xvi. 9–20; John v. 4 and vii. 53–viii. 12.

copyist of the second century. They may have been taken from one of the many lost writings touching the life of Jesus which were in existence in the first centuries, and are mentioned by Luke in the prologue to his Gospel, or they may be a fragment of the oral tradition which found its way into the record, no one knows how or when. A comparison of this section with the Gospel to which it is attached, in respect to style and contents, shows how slight was the difference among the first generations of Christians between those narratives which we now accept as historical, and those which we reject as legendary. The interpolation in John v. 4 doubtless had a legendary origin. The words are wanting in Codd. Vat., Sinaït., Ephr., Bezæ, and in several old versions. The case is similar, so far as the testimony of manuscripts is concerned, with respect to the section, John vii. 53–viii. 12, containing the account of the woman taken in adultery. In addition to the external testimony, which is against it, criticism calls attention to the language as unlike that of the author of the fourth Gospel in the use of single words and phrases. That it found its way into the Gospel out of the oral tradition which, as we have seen, was held in high repute in the second century, seems highly probable.

c.—Dogmatic Changes.

A few readings are found which appear to have had their origin in a dogmatic interest, and to have been made in order to bring the teachings of the Gospels into accord with the customs of a certain period or with its prevailing opinions. Accordingly, it is thought by some that the reading in Matt. xxviii. 19, βαπτίσαντες, "having baptized," found in some manuscripts in place of βαπτίζοντες, "baptizing," was inserted in the interest of infant baptism, which was practised after the third century. The former reading is, however, supported by the high authority of the Vatican manuscript. On account of the similarity of the Greek forms of the two words, Immer is perhaps chargeable with drawing a too hasty conclusion, when he pronounces this "without doubt" a dogmatic change. The undoubtedly spurious πρωτότοκον, "first-born," in Matt. i. 25, may have been omitted from some manuscripts in the interest of the doctrine of the perpetual virginity of Mary. There can be no question, however, of the influence of a dogmatic interest in the reading, Luke ii. 33, "Joseph," for "his father," and in verse 43 of the same chapter, "Joseph and his mother," for "his parents." The latter reading in both the passages referred to has been adopted by Tischendorf.

6.—SOME PRINCIPLES OF TEXTUAL CRITICISM.

The process of textual criticism is not altogether governed by general rules. The true critic cannot be restricted by a mechanical method, but must move freely among his materials, under the direction of principle, indeed, but not the less of judgment and insight. The first and indispensable requisite to a sound criticism is a knowledge of the relative critical worth of the most important manuscripts. The weight to be allowed to a manuscript in deciding a critical question as to a reading depends partly upon its age and partly upon its relative accuracy in comparison with the others. The Vatican and Sinaïtic manuscripts, for example, not only date from a relatively high antiquity, but omit very many readings which are regarded as spurious in the later manuscripts. Besides, these two manuscripts agree in a majority of the readings. Among the chief guides in the procedure of textual criticism are the following general principles, recognized in the main by Tischendorf, and given according to Immer's classification: 1. No critical conjecture is to be admitted unless it is supported by at least one of the ancient witnesses. 2. The oldest readings, although supported by few witnesses, generally deserve the preference over the later, even when these latter are more extensively confirmed. 3. The oldest witnesses are so much the more assured as they are the better supported by witnesses of different sorts, as manuscripts, versions, and quotations from the fathers, or by testimony of different origins, for example, oriental and occidental. Every passage is to be regarded as a traditional addition which is omitted by the oldest witnesses, or designated as doubtful from a trustworthy source: when it presents a striking number of variants; when it shows a joining, breaks the connection, or at least when it may be omitted without disturbing the connection; when it shows a style deviating from that of the writer. Again, a word or a sentence is to be regarded as a gloss when the expression in question does not have the oldest and best witnesses in its favor, that is to say, is not established by the most trustworthy quotations and the most ancient and accurate manuscripts; when it appears to be intended to remove an ethical or dogmatic difficulty; and when it explains and relieves a thought hard to understand. In such cases the more offensive or harder reading is to be preferred to the less offensive and easier one, if the former has a strong external confirmation. The principle is accordingly followed which finds illustration in the example previously adduced of the reading, "in the prophets," for "Isaiah the prophet," that of two readings that one is to be rejected which betrays itself as intended to remove an offence, and that one to be retained which furnishes occasion for the scruple, provided that the supposed correct reading has a preponderance of critical testimony in its favor. But the reading which betrays itself as a correction is then only to be decidedly rejected, and that which is regarded as genuine on internal grounds to be preferred when the latter is supported at least by one, or still better by several witnesses, and, indeed, of different sorts, as manuscripts, versions, and quotations. The reading which removes a difficulty, being suspicious, is to give place to a more incorrect or harder reading when the latter has the support of the most important and oldest manuscripts. The critical judgment must always be grounded as well upon an appreciation of the external witnesses as upon internal probabilities. In case these two contradict each other, no general rule can be laid down. The one comprehensive rule in reference to the internal grounds is that the original reading is that one from which the origin of the other may be explained.

These principles are not to be regarded as arbitrary or as *a priori* in their origin. They are the result of a painstaking and learned study of the manuscripts, quotations, and versions of the New Testament, and are as nearly scientific in their nature as under the conditions they could be. They are the product of a careful induction from the facts and phenomena which are presented in the vast amount of materials which come into the hands of the textual critic. No presumption favoring a supposed exceptional character of the manuscripts of the Gospels has stood in the way of the rigorous application to them of the principles which govern the treatment of all ancient remains of the kind. Such a presumption, and, indeed, any *a-priori* theory which should attempt to remove them from the class of literature in general, and shield them from critical scrutiny as sacred, would defeat the very ends which textual criticism proposes to itself. Westcott has well remarked that, "if, indeed, there were any thing in the circumstances attending the first publication of the New Testament which might seem to remove it from the ordinary fortune of books, then it would be impossible not to respect the pious sentiment which accepts the early text as the immediate work of Providence. But the history shows too many marks of human frailty to admit of such a supposition. The text itself contains palpable and admitted errors in every way analogous to those which occur in the first classical texts. The conclusion is obvious, and it is superstition rather than reverence which refuses to apply to the service of Scripture the laws which have restored so much of their native beauty to other ancient writings."

7.—THE VERSIONS.

Only those versions will be considered which belong to the material of importance employed in the criticism of the text, that is to say, a few of the most ancient. It is a commonplace of textual criticism in reference to versions that so far as they admit of a re-translation into Greek they may serve as secondary witnesses at least for the original text. Literal translations are accordingly regarded as of the greatest importance. Since in particular the Latin version, *Itala*, and the Syriac, *Peschito*, are older than the oldest existing manuscripts, they would be of great weight in the critical determination of the text, were it not that their own text appears to have suffered much from corruptions and in some doctrinally important passages to have been conformed to the later Greek text or to the Vulgate. They are, then, only especially helpful to textual criticism so far as fragments of them have been preserved in citations which have come to hand in the early Christian writings. We have knowledge of the existence of a Latin translation of the Gospels at about the end of the second century. It is distinguished from the later Vulgate by the name of Itala. Of this Bianchini published in 1749 Codd. Veronensis, Vercellensis, and Brixianus, and Tischendorf, in 1847 Evangelium Palatinum, etc. The Codex Veronensis dates from the fourth or fifth century, the Vercellensis from about the middle of the fourth, and the Brixianus from the sixth. The translation is characterized as strictly literal, and the language as awkward and frequently offensive to Latin usage on account partly of its provincialisms and syntactical errors. The translator (or translators) appears not to have been well versed in Latin, and to have prepared a work which better served the needs of the common people than pleased the learned. It is not surprising that after two centuries the manuscripts of such a translation should present a "variegated mixture." This version probably originated in proconsular Africa, where after the Roman conquest the Latin language became dominant. The numerous citations made by the Latin writers of the Church from Tertullian to Gregory the Great furnish to some degree an apparatus for the restoration of this version, and in them our oldest documents for the Itala find some confirmations of their readings. But the loose manner of making quotations which prevailed in that time and the differences in the manuscripts in use render this source of information very untrustworthy. The difficulties of restoring an edition of the Itala by a comparison of all the fragments accessible are probably not too strongly stated by Holtzmann, when he says that their removal would require the labor of more than one human life.

The confused and corrupt condition of the Itala, whose

text suffered fresh distortions with every new copy which was made, caused the preparation of a more correct and homogeneous version to be felt as an urgent necessity. For this great task one man alone, perhaps, in his age was qualified, Jerome, "the most learned westerner of his own and many centuries." Commissioned by the Roman Bishop, Damasus, he undertook the work with many misgivings and no little apprehension and anxiety as to charges against his orthodoxy which were likely to be made. He expected, as he wrote in his *Prefatio in Evangelia ad Damasum*, that every one "*doctus pariter et indoctus*" would cry out against him, "*me falsarium me esse sacrilegum.*" Under the influence of this solicitude, which the event proved to have been only too truly prophetic, he proceeded cautiously, correcting only the most palpable errors, *ut his tantum quæ sensum videbantur mutare correctis reliqua manere pateremur ut fuerant*, and in 383 the Vulgate version of the Gospels was completed. Important for the Old Testament which he translated directly from the Hebrew, his work was of less worth for the New Testament, which he can only be said to have improved. For fear of giving offence he left unchanged many erroneous renderings which he thought to be harmless. Critically regarded, the Vulgate is important as a translation of the biblical text as it was at about the close of the fourth century. This version made its way to recognition against great and determined opposition. The African Church declared against it, and the Roman Bishops in undertaking its support entered upon "a conflict of two hundred years." Only in the sixth century did it appear to have gained ground, and not until the ninth was its victory won. Used for centuries side by side with the older translation, it was inevitable that its text should be even more corrupted than under ordinary circumstances it would have been. By command of Charlemagne a revision of the text was undertaken by Alcuin who in 801 presented him with the Gospels in an improved text. This emperor himself is said to have been occupied in his old age with correction of manuscripts of the Vulgate. The corrupt condition of the text remained, however, and in 1276 Roger Bacon complained that readings and corrupters were equal in number, "*quot sunt lectiones per mundum, tot sunt correctores seu magis corruptores.*"

A translation of the New Testament into Syriac was made at about the end of the second century, according to the best authorities.* It is met with in manuscripts since the ninth century under the name of *Peschito*, which according to Eichhorn means "the literal," according to others, "the translated," or again, "the simple," "the sincere." It does not appear to have gained wide recognition and to have displaced other translations before the year 350. A literal translation it is not, though in the main true. Its worth for purposes of textual criticism is questionable, since the text lies under the suspicion of having been modified by the Antiochian scholars in order to make it conform to their Greek manuscripts. Not only are some interpolations wanting, as John vii. 53–viii. 12, but also whole books of the minor Epistles. It is not of great importance apart from hermeneutical purposes, for the reason that no thorough critical investigation of the text has been made, and all editions of it are very defective. Fragments of the Gospels in Syriac, perhaps written in the fifth century, have been discovered in Egypt and brought to the British Museum. They were published in 1858 by Cureton under

---

* Tischendorf, **Wann** wurden unsere Evangelien verfasst, p. 9; Wichelhaus, De N. T. versione Syriaca antiqua quam Peschito vocant, p. 63.

the title, " Remains of a very Ancient Recension of the Four Gospels in Syriac."

It is evident from the foregoing brief survey of the fortune of the text of the Gospels that textual criticism has to do with facts and phenomena purely human and historical. Whatever may be the conclusion which men reach respecting the original composition of these writings and the inspiration of their authors, there does not appear to have been any divine intervention for the preservation of their words from the common fortune of ancient literary productions in rude and uncritical ages. Accident, carelessness, caprice, and dogmatism have contributed to embarrass the scholar in his unachievable task of restoring the original text. The influence of a mother-church upon its dependents, the fame of a copyist, of a copy itself, a prevailing taste in some province, have conspired to give a local coloring to the text. The influence of a single manuscript or version may be traced in others of even a remote origin. The surprising relationship of the text of ℵ to the Itala may, indeed, favor the theory of a text antedating both, which approached the original, and maintained a neutral relation to the locally determined differences ; but this is conjecture, and conjecture too of only an approximation. The oldest versions present a text so much corrupted that in the use of them there is imposed upon the critic the double task of making a critical recension of their texts and of that for the restoration of which he invokes their aid. Finally, when he has in a measure mastered the immense mass of material which his task brings to his hand, there still lies before him the unexplored and unexplorable *terra incognita* which occupies the period extending from the beginning of the second century to the time when the first express witnesses to the text appear.

CHAPTER II.

THE CANON.

THE history of the canon of the Gospels is a study of the early fortune of these writings as literature, of the use that was made of them, and of the estimation in which they were held from the time when they first came into the light of a literary period until they were united, to the exclusion of other kindred records, in the New Testament. More extensive and trustworthy historical materials are here at our disposal than in the study of the text. The literature of the Christian Church which immediately succeeded the Gospels, bears unconscious testimony to the use which was made of them and to the reputation which they had during the period of the formation of the canon, which may be said to have occupied the latter part of the second century and the beginning of the third. The manner, indeed, in which the Gospels were treated in the Christian and so-called heretical literature of this period is precisely the question to be considered. For the study of the Gospel-canon is not an inquiry into the nature of the Gospels with respect to their divine authority, nor should it be controlled by an interest to place them on a level with productions merely human. Whether their authors were inspired, or wrote as ordinary men, are questions with which this study is not concerned. If, as the result of the investigation on which we are entering, it shall appear that the Gospels were at one time regarded in the Christian communities as merely human productions, and at another as the infallible works of men under divine guidance and instruction, in each case we shall have nothing more than an external, historical fact, a matter of opinion, which may, indeed, be explicable in its genesis, but will decisively answer no questions respecting the internal character of the writings.

The inquiry in question, then, being historical, it is evident that its purpose would be defeated if its procedure should be controlled by traditional presumptions or dogmatic opinions. With traditions it has nothing to do except to investigate them historically. Whatever importance ought to be attached to them can be determined only by the results of an historical investigation. The aim should constantly be kept in mind to follow the earliest traditions respecting the Gospels to their sources, and critically to ascertain their worth by a study of the influences and environments by which they were determined. A tradition concerning the Gospels which arose in or near the apostolic age will naturally be deemed very important, since it may fairly be assumed to have been formed under the influence of their authors or of men who enjoyed intercourse with them. It must, however, be genetically studied, and subjected to critical examination, precisely as traditions of a later origin should be treated.

What, then, is precisely the idea of canonicity which must be kept in mind in this study, and alone comports with a truly historical examination of the canon of the Gospels? What, in a word, does it signify that certain biographies of Jesus have been selected out of the considerable number known to have been written and circulated, and have been honored with an exclusive authority as canonical? It is evident that an inquiry proceeding upon historical data will naturally, in the first place, establish the fact of such a selection, and show that certain writings began at a particular time to have a distinction and repute as accounts of the life and teachings of Jesus above all others of a similar character. So far as reasons may appear among the historical facts accessible to the student for this preference shown to any books, it plainly belongs to the task of the historian of the canon to set them forth to the advantage of such books. But it is just here that the limits of a purely historical investigation clearly appear. For the reason why men accord to some writings a preference over others must lie in their conviction of the superiority of those over these in point of literary excellence, trustworthiness, origin, or other similar considerations. History, however, can only record the acts and opinions of men, and determine their importance from the relation which the persons in question may be found to have held to the matters on which their judgments or actions proceeded. The history of the canon of the Gospels would, accordingly, go beyond its province, if it were to enter upon a critical examination of these writings, and pass judgment upon their divine or human origin or authority. Tradition may assign an apostolic origin to a certain book, and deny it to another. The historian of the canon must record this tradition, and may properly test its grounds. But what an apostolic origin may add to the worth of one book, or its absence detract from that of another, it does not belong to him to determine. The canonicity of the Gospels, then, so far as the present historical inquiry has to do with it, is simply the reputation in which they were held during a certain historical period as the best or most trustworthy among the current writings of a similar character. Just as certain writings of other ancient literatures have been preserved and honored as classical by the common judgment of men, so a few books on the life and works of Jesus were early regarded as most worthy of confidence and most excellent as literary productions, and were separated from others as canonical.* Classical and canonical from the historical point of view are substantially of the same import.

Even if we consider the term canonical from another point of view according to which the canonicity of a biblical writing is regarded as determined by its genuineness, or by its conformity to Christian doctrine as set forth in writings of undisputed validity and eminence, it will be found to have its origin in an act of judgment very similar to that by which some writings are called classical in distinction from all others. For the discussion of questions of this sort is always carried on with reference to a certain standard, conformity to which determines the canonicity referred to, just as conformity to a literary standard marks a writing as classical. It is doubtless from this point of view that the Epistle to the Hebrews and the Apocalypse are sometimes treated as if their canonicity were open to question, and that Luther called the Epistle of James an epistle of straw. Neither its supposed apostolical authorship nor the decree of an ecclesiastical council assigning it a place on the canonical

---

* Eusebius furnishes a confirmation of this view of the matter when, writing of certain books, the Gospels of Peter, Thomas, and the Acts of the Apostles by Andrew and John, and other writings "adduced by heretics," he says: "The character of the style itself is very different from that of the apostles, and the sentiments and the purport of those things which are advanced in them, deviating as far as possible from sound orthodoxy, evidently prove that they are the fictions of heretical men, whence they are not only to be ranked among the spurious writings, but are to be rejected as altogether absurd and impious."—Hist. Eccles. iii. **25.**

list can permanently establish the real canonicity of a writing. Very likely a feeling or judgment like that just referred to was an important if not a determining factor in the formation of the New-Testament canon in the early Church, and the recognition everywhere and by all, *ubique et ab omnibus,* of certain writings as canonical was the result of their supposed conformity to a standard which existed in the Christian consciousness of the time. The term canonicity, however, when applied to a biblical writing to mark it as infallible or inspired is dogmatic, and has no other foundation than an assumption of the infallibility of the writer. It is scarcely necessary to say that no one of the writers of the four Gospels has set up any such claim for himself as dogmatic theologians have gratuitously made for all of them. With this sort of canonicity it is evident that criticism can have nothing to do, since it admits of no presumptions of the kind as to the character of the Gospels, but requires that the results of the critical process be awaited as the only right ground of all judgments regarding their origin, purpose, and claims to be regarded as exceptional productions.

The historical treatment of the canon of the New Testament has never been regarded with favor from the dogmatic point of view, and is, indeed, of modern origin. For a long time the belief was entertained that the Church had always had the same canon. The old and even the new orthodoxy down to Augusti in 1832 [*] believed that John made a collection of the books of the New Testament, and put a seal upon it in the words in Rev. xxii. 18, 19, "If any one shall add unto these things God will add unto him the plagues that are written in this book," etc. The appeal to the authority of John is supposed to rest

[*] Versuch einer Einleitung in die heiligen Schriften.

on a misapprehension of a passage in Eusebius, Hist.
Eccl., iii. 24, to the effect that this apostle approved the
synoptical Gospels, and confirmed them for use in the
Church. Accordingly it is said in the verses in the library
of Eugenius of Toledo of the seventh century,

" Summus et egregius congessit cuncta Joannes." *

Notwithstanding the fact which the history of the canon
clearly shows that the early Church, at least after the
second century, exercised considerable critical discrimination regarding the canonicity of the New-Testament
writings, and that in the classical passage in Eusebius,
Hist. Eccl., iii. 25, the doubts respecting certain books
since accepted as canonical which prevailed as early as the
beginning of the fourth century are set forth in detail, it
was not until the first decade of the eighteenth century
that these doubts, already expressed thirteen centuries
before, began to be brought forward again. Even in 1707
Mill maintained that the Gospels were collected about
the year 100, and the Epistles about 110. But Semler's
thorough criticism showed that the canon of the New
Testament was a gradual growth which only reached a
relative completion towards the end of the second century. † He also called attention to the catholic tendency
towards a union of the opposing factions in the early
Church as an important factor in the process of the formation of the canon. Eichhorn showed the settlement of
the canon to have been the result of a long historical
development, and called attention to Marcion's collection
of New-Testament writings as marking a tendency in this
direction. ‡

* Holtzmann, Einleit. in das N. T. 2te Aufl. 1886, p. 91.
† Abhandlung von **freier Untersuch. des Kanons**, 1771–5.
‡ Einleit. in das N. T. 1804.

1.—THE APOSTOLIC AGE.

The apostolic age furnished few conditions favorable to the formation of a canon of such Christian writings as were then in existence, or, indeed, to embodiment in literary form of the ideas which were destined through literature to exert so vast an influence upon mankind. The spiritual vitality and persistence of the teachings and life of the great Nazarene are not more strikingly illustrated than by the fact that, unhonored by a great literary expression and committed to the fortune of oral tradition, they have survived to become the most fruitful agencies in human civilization. Had the impulse which came from the life of Jesus spent itself in a great Christian epic, there might never have been a Christian Church. The absence of a literary expression suited to the taste of the cultivated was the good fortune of Christianity. Its positive good fortune, too, it was that just as the common people heard gladly the teachings of its founder and the learned among his hearers took offence at him, so in the earliest course of its development it made its way among such common people and "broke its path from below upward." The learned and the scribes were not among the first disciples of Jesus. Perhaps no church in the middle of the first century was more cultivated than that at Corinth; yet Paul in writing to the Corinthians reminds them that not many of them are "wise men after the fashion of this world, not many mighty, not many noble."

Unfavorable also to the formation of a canon was the absence of a true historical perspective in the apostolic age. Christianity was not then looked upon as destined to an historical development and a world-conquering dominion extending through many centuries. Prophets there were, indeed, in that time, according to Paul; but no one of them appears to have been endowed with a vision far-seeing enough to forecast the wonderful history of eighteen Christian ages. On the contrary, the horizon was very limited which shut in the view of the men of those times. The "last days" were near at hand in which they expected the great Christophany, which to them was the only truly Messianic appearance of him who had ascended that he might come again in glory and power. * Under such conditions it were unreasonable to look for literary productions intended for the instruction of future ages or for the collecting of existing writings to be handed down for any remote result. That men like the apostles, drawn from humble avocations, † should in such a situation occupy themselves with matters of this kind is *a priori* improbable, except that under the spur of necessity and for immediate ends they might set down some things in a fragmentary way in writing. From Paul more than from any other man in the apostolic age might one look for a profound apprehension of the future fortune of the Christian religion. But even from him we have only writings for the occasion. His letters were called forth by the immediate needs of the communities to which they were addressed, and relate largely to affairs of the moment, to personal considerations, to business, or are occupied with the then important but really quite temporary question of the adaptation of Christian doctrines to the acceptance of Jewish inquirers and disputants. The permanent influence of writings like those of

---

* 1 Thess. i. 10; iv. 16, 17 and numerous other passages. An able treatment of the subject has been made by Dr. Forbes in Essays, etc. by Fifteen Clergymen, Boston, 1889.

† Acts iv. 13, "unlearned and common men," ἀγράμματοι καὶ ἰδιῶται.

Paul, which were called forth by local and temporary interests, and even their attainment of immortality as literature are one thing, and the author's own thought and intention respecting them are quite another. There is no evidence and scarcely a probability that Paul intended his Epistles to constitute a sacred canonical literature for appeal and citation by future generations. He sometimes, indeed, refers to them, but no less to his own spoken words and to the apostolic tradition as of equal authority.* His preaching he calls "the word of God," † and never pretends to a special spiritual charisma, or inspiration, for writing. Indeed, he places himself on the same footing with other believers of his time as to the gifts of the Spirit, such as speaking with tongues, and claims no difference from them in kind, but rather recognizes the endowment with the Holy Spirit as a common grace and privilege of all who had accepted Christ.‡ The Old Testament is the only writing to which he appeals as an authority. Passages from this he applies by a somewhat strained allegorizing to the circumstances of his time, as if their authors had written with express reference to its conditions and needs. §

Although in the apostolic age no need of a canon of the New Testament was felt, and no steps were taken to form one, tendencies in this direction may be traced in it. These show themselves in connection with some of the writings which are the oldest in our present canon. For a certain public recognition, or canonizing, may be allowed in the reading in the Churches to which they were written of certain of the Epistles of Paul. ‖ There

---

* 1 Cor. xv. 1–3 ; 1 Thess. ii. 11, 13.   † 1 Thess. ii. 13.
‡ Gal. iii. 2, 5 ; 1 Cor. iii. 16 ; Rom. viii. 9 f.
§ 1 Cor. ix. 9, 10; x. 11 ; Gal. iii. 8.   ‖ 1 Thess. v. 27.

is, however, no intimation of any such recognition of the Gospels, nor does the apostolic literature contain any reference to them. A sort of "oral canon" of the Gospel existed in the valued "words of the Lord," λόγοι κυρίου, and we cannot but find it surprising that Paul, writing soon after the middle of the first century, does not show more frequent points of contact with it. He does, indeed, frequently say that he writes certain things "by the word of the Lord," or that the Lord says them, and not he, whereby he probably refers to current traditions of the teachings of Jesus*; and in his account of the institution of the Lord's Supper he reproduces ostensibly the very words.† But in connection with the great events which held the foremost place in his thought, his teaching, and his philosophy of Christianity —the crucifixion and resurrection—there is an entire absence of the influence of any historical tradition upon his mind. With the earthly history of Jesus this man, who had been caught up into the third heaven, and seen unspeakable things, had little concern. He went his own way, and "did not confer with flesh and blood." It is not, indeed, improbable that some of the most important sayings of Jesus may have been committed to writing as early as the date of the composition of the great Pauline Epistles. An old tradition, in fact, runs to the effect that a writing ascribed to Matthew was early in circulation, in which were set down certain discourses or oracles of Christ‡ in the vernacular of the people.§ But there is no trace of its use in the apostolic age, and the date of its composition is altogether a matter of conjecture.

---

* 1 Thess. iv. 15 ; 1 Cor. vii. 10, 12 : ix. 14 ; xi. 24, 25.
† 1 Cor. xi. 23–25. ‡ λόγια κυριακά.
§ Euseb., Hist. Eccl. iii. 39.

2.—THE POST-APOSTOLIC AGE.

In the period extending from about the year 70 to 120 of our era there existed conditions and were at work influences of considerable importance to the formation of the canon. Here is to be found the prehistorical material for the history of the canon. In the conditions of this time are manifest the reasons why a collection of Christian writings was not earlier made, and the forces which were in operation to bring it about eventually. To one who is able to transport himself by imagination into this age, and realize its conditions and the life of the Christian communities in it, views of the writings composing the New Testament similar to those entertained at the present time by believers will appear unthinkable in those people, and much more a pressing interest and zeal in the formation of an exclusive, sacred collection. The oral tradition of the life and teachings of Jesus was still fresh and vivid, and was repeated by the preachers and teachers in the public assemblies of believers. Almost the whole literature of the time being epistolary, letters from prominent leaders in the Churches must have been frequently received and read to the congregations, and probably in some instances passed on to others. The Epistles of Paul were in existence, and can hardly have failed to be multiplied by copyists and circulated to some extent. Perhaps fragmentary narratives of the life of Jesus may have had a similar fortune. That many such existed appears from the prologue to the third Gospel, where writings of this kind are expressly mentioned. To these scattered writings no especial, exclusive sanctity appears to have been attached; and when our **canonical** Gospels were completed, and came into the hands of the people, there could **have been** no reason, either from their contents as compared with other writings of the kind in circulation, or from any claims put forth by their authors, for regarding them as possessing a divine sanction. Indeed, the author of the third Gospel makes it very apparent in the introduction to his narrative that he undertakes the work after the manner of an ordinary biographer who wishes accurately to instruct his friend. Besides, the reverence felt by the Jewish Christians for the Old Testament must have made them very reluctant to place upon an equal footing with it any other writings, particularly such as set up no claims to inspiration ; and the gentile Christians who had been under the teaching of Paul must have been imbued with a similar reverence for the ancient oracles. Add to this that we may reasonably assume that there was carried over from the apostolic age into this the belief in the gift of the Holy Spirit as common to all Christians,[*] and it becomes evident that any new writings must have made their way with no little difficulty to recognition as sacred scripture.

A canon in the sense under consideration is conditioned upon an agreement on the part of a large number of persons to accept certain writings and exclude others. Such an agreement implies communication and intercourse which cannot be supposed to have been practicable to any considerable extent during the period in question. The absence of an organization through which a general consensus might be promoted and at length find expression was also at this period a reason why the formation of a canon could not be effected. In such a condition of affairs there could not but be a considerable development

---

[*] Clem., Rom. 1 ad Cor. ii. 46 ; Barnab. ix. xvi. xix. See Reuss, Gesch. der heil. Schriften N. T., Eng. transl. by Rev. E. L. Houghton, 2 vols., Boston, 1884.

of individual freedom of opinion and independence in isolated Churches, and a corresponding narrowness and provincialism of judgment as well as decided predilections in favor of certain writings. Accordingly marked tendencies and preferences and tenacious adherence to opinions might naturally be looked for, which would operate unfavorably to the settlement of the canon. If we add to these considerations the fact that the age was uncritical, that is, not inclined in the nature of the case and not moved by any motives to undertake a recension of manuscripts and to examine the claims of writers to special authority, when none stood forth with pre-eminent claims to it, we shall find the critical selection and sifting of books and the distinguishing of them by a general consensus as exclusively authoritative the remotest of probabilities.

In the apostolic age there had already broken out a conflict between two opposed conceptions of Christianity, represented respectively by Paul, the apostle to the gentiles, and the so-called " Pillar-Apostles," a term applied by Paul himself to those who represented the Jewish tendency. The question at issue was one of the greatest moment, and it is not, perhaps, too much to say that on its decision depended the entire historical development and fortune of the Christian religion. A controversy which was of so great importance, and was conducted with so much earnestness that it left a marked impression on a considerable part of the early literature of the Church, could not at once be put to rest. Rather in the natural course of things we should expect to find it gradually brought to an end by compromises made in the interest and under the influence of the faith held in common by the opposing parties. The triumph of the great Pauline doctrine of the universal mission of Christianity in freedom from the galling yoke of Jewish legalism over the narrow opinions and tenacious prejudices of the original apostles is a fact of history. But this view did not prevail at once by the exclusion of all that opposed it ; and accordingly there stand side by side in the canon Gospels, Epistles, and other writings in which its doctrines, those which opposed it, and those of a mediating tendency are represented. But this conflict, carried over as it was into the post-apostolic age, could not but interfere with an early settlement of the canon. The situation in question is well stated by Reuss : " The parties, which had required some time to come to a full consciousness of the principles which separated them, were in the post-apostolic age in some respects still less disposed to be friendly than when the first preachers of the Gospel, now no longer living, had endeavored in vain to twine the bonds of one faith about the scattered members of the Church. Besides, the writings of these men were in many ways involved with the polemics of the day, so that they were to the one party a stumbling-block and to the other a refreshment of its convictions ; and a long time must have passed before those inclined to peace found a formula by which, upon middle ground and by means of mutual concessions, an actually common, catholic church could be formed, abandoning the extreme views on both sides, and gathering up for the common advantage whatever each party had inherited of apostolic literary treasure." * Another writer says to the same effect, that the circulation of some of the books of the New Testament for a while depended more or less on their supposed connection with specific forms of Christianity, and the range of other books was

---

* Gesch. d. heil. Schrift. N. T. § 288.

limited either by their original destination or by the nature of their contents.*

The important witnesses for this period are Clement of Rome, Barnabas, and Hermas. Their testimony is to be considered with regard to the current opinions in their time respecting the inspiration and authority of the Christian literature then in use, with particular reference to accounts of the life and teachings of Jesus, or so-called Gospels. In order to ascertain what were the earliest tendencies towards the formation of the canon, they must be questioned as to the nature of the writings in their hands and as to their manner of using them for quotation or illustration.

a. *Clement of Rome.*—Two Epistles attributed to Clement of Rome are appended to one of the oldest manuscripts of the Bible, Codex Alexandrinus. They are addressed to the Corinthians. The text is not entire, and some passages are supposed to be interpolations. The second of these is spurious, but the first is probably genuine, notwithstanding Schwegler's objections,† and was written at about the close of the first or the beginning of the second century. Clement appears from the testimony of Irenæus to have held a prominent place in the Roman Church, perhaps that of an overseer, or Bishop, and to have had intercourse with some of the apostles.‡ An early tradition ascribed to him the authorship of the Epistle to the Hebrews and the Acts. He has been thought also to have been a mediator between the contending Pauline and Petrine parties in the early Church, and this theory

---

* Westcott, A General Review of the History of the Canon of the New Testament, 6th ed., Cambridge and London, 1889.

† Nachapol. Zeitalter, 1846, ii. p. 125 f.

‡ Adv. Haeres. iii. 3, ὁ καὶ ἑωρακὼς τοῖς ἀποστόλους.

finds some confirmation in his Epistle, the peculiarities of the language showing, as some maintain, the influence of both Peter and Paul,* and the doctrine of justification by faith and of righteousness through works finding expression. The Epistle cannot be accorded a high rank as a literary production, and as an exposition of Christianity it is not worthy of mention beside the great letters of Paul. It betrays a mediocre personality without intellectual grasp and destitute of profound feeling. It abounds in homilies which are commonplace and flat, and there appears to be no reason for its survival apart from its antiquity and the position held by its author.

The words of Clement respecting the commission of the apostles and spiritual gifts in general are significant both for what they say and for what they leave unsaid. "The apostles have brought us the good tidings," he writes, "by the Lord Jesus Christ; Jesus Christ, by God. Christ was sent forth by God, the apostles, by Christ; and both [these things] were done in an orderly way by the will of God."† Again, "God having chosen the Lord Jesus Christ and us through him to a peculiar people," etc. And, "Have we not one God and one Christ and one Spirit of grace poured out upon us"; "a full pouring out of the Holy Spirit was made upon us all.‡ There is here no intimation of the doctrine of especial apostolic inspiration, but rather the contrary is implied. The apostles were sent forth by divine ordination to preach the Gospel, and the only distinction which they enjoyed appears to be that they were near to Christ and directly commissioned by him. One Spirit of grace was, however,

---

* Westcott, Canon, p. 24.
† 1 Ep. ad Cor. c. 42.
‡ Ib. c. 58, 46, 2.

poured out upon the believers in general, who must be regarded as designated by "us,"* in accordance with the doctrine of the general inspiration of Christians which we have seen to have been that of the apostolic age.†

Of quotations from the Gospels in the proper sense of the words there are no examples found in Clement. In chapter 13, after making a quotation from Jeremiah ix. 23, 24, which he introduces with the words, "let us do as it is written, for the Holy Spirit says," he proceeds: "Especially remembering the words of the Lord Jesus which he spake teaching clemency and long-suffering, 'pity, that you may receive pity; forgive, that you may be forgiven; according as you do it shall be done to you; as you give so shall it be given to you; as you judge, so shall you be judged; as you are merciful, so shall you obtain mercy; with what measure you mete, so shall it be measured to you.'" Again, in chapter 46, after quoting with the formula, "for it is written" ($\gamma\acute{\epsilon}\gamma\rho\alpha\pi\tau\alpha\iota\ \gamma\acute{\alpha}\rho$) some words which are not to be found in the Bible, he proceeds: "Remember the words of Jesus our Lord, 'woe to that man; it were well ($\kappa\alpha\lambda\acute{o}\nu$) if he had not been born, than that he offend one of my elect; it were better for him that a millstone be put about him and he be thrown into the sea than that he offend one of my little ones.'" It is to be noted in the first place that the words ascribed to Jesus in these passages are not quoted with the formula, "it is written," or, "the Scripture says," according to the custom of the time in taking words from the Old Testament; in the second place, that they are not correctly quoted at all, but appear to be either feebly remembered fragments of oral tradition or citations from

---

* $\kappa\alpha\grave{\iota}\ \acute{\epsilon}\nu\ \pi\nu\epsilon\tilde{\upsilon}\mu\alpha\ \tau\tilde{\eta}\varsigma\ \chi\acute{\alpha}\rho\iota\tau\sigma\varsigma\ \tau\grave{o}\ \acute{\epsilon}\kappa\chi\epsilon\upsilon\vartheta\grave{\epsilon}\nu\ \acute{\epsilon}\varphi'\ \acute{\eta}\mu\tilde{\alpha}\varsigma$.

† Credner, Beiträge zur Einleit. in die heil. Schr. 1832, i. p. 14.

written collections of the teachings of Jesus now unknown; and finally, that they are not attributed to any Gospel either by particular name or general reference, as if the writer were acquainted with or at least in the habit of using such records. It cannot, certainly, be fairly urged that the words are introduced "with a remark implying a well-known record * * * and in a way suggesting careful and precise quotation of the very words." Such striking inaccuracies in quoting could hardly be committed by a writer at all familiar with our canonical records, and Weiss' remark that the citation in chapter 46, 8 may be "fully explained" by a combination of Matt. xxv. 24 with xviii. 6* cannot be substantiated if by "combination" be meant a uniting of passages from a written page. Some of the sayings of Jesus which Clement quotes are not found in the Gospels, and others are apparently shattered echoes of actual words of Jesus. No one well acquainted with the Greek Gospels would be likely to employ in making quotations from them words totally unlike those used in the records.† The positive affirmation in chapter 44 that "our apostles knew through our Lord Jesus Christ that there would be contention concerning the episcopacy" could only be made by one who rather held in his mind some floating traditions of words of Jesus than made careful reference to the records afterwards accepted as Gospels. Besides, no one who could so carelessly make use of the reputed sayings of Jesus can fairly be supposed to have attached especial sacredness or even importance to written accounts of them, even if he was acquainted with such documents.

* Einleit. in das N. T. von B. Weiss, 1886, p. 29.
† As $περιτεθῆναι$, "put about," for $περίκειται\ περὶ\ τὸν\ τράχηλον\ αὐτοῦ$, "be hung about his neck." Many similar examples might be quoted.

b. *The Epistle of Barnabas.*—The early date of this Epistle cannot be successfully contested, although there are good reasons why it should not be ascribed to the "apostle" Barnabas, the companion of Paul.[*] The first quotation of it under the name of Barnabas is found in Clement of Alexandria who cites it frequently. Origen calls it a Catholic Epistle, and treats it with great consideration, "almost according it canonical authority.". Eusebius mentions it as well known and commonly circulated (φερομένη), though he reckons it among the antilegomena, or disputed books.[†] Jerome, while regarding it as genuine, classes it among the apocryphal writings, with which it appears to have been publicly read in his time. In the Sinaïtic manuscript of the Greek Bible it stands next after the book of Revelation. The Epistle is without address, and there exist no data for determining its original destination. Its date is also indeterminate, but a reference in it to the destruction of the temple at Jerusalem places its composition beyond question later than the year 70 of our era, while Norton's reasons for dating it as late as the middle of the second century are not at all conclusive. Its more probable date is between 100 and 110.[‡]

The doctrinal portion of the Epistle, which occupies the first seventeen chapters, has for its object to set forth the decadence of the Law and to separate Christianity and its believers from the Old-Testament economy and its rites and duties. The point of view is, accordingly,

---

[*] Acts iv. 26 ; xii. 25 ; xiii. 1.
[†] Hist. Eccl. iii. 25 ; vi. 14.
[‡] Westcott, Canon, p. 42. Lipsius, Barnabasbrief in Schenkel's Bibel-Lexicon, i. p. 363 f. Hilgenfeld dates the Epistle at about 97, Die apostolischen Väter, 1853, Einleit. in das N. T. 1874.

Pauline; but the manner in which the writer accomplishes his purpose shows his immense inferiority to the great apostle. In no way does a mediocre intellect so fully reveal itself as in the handling of a large theme. He adopts, indeed, the Pauline typological theory of interpretation in dealing with the Old Testament,—a theory which dominated the apostolic and post-apostolic ages,—but in applying it he descends to puerilities and absurdities which are nothing short of disgusting. It is, indeed, difficult for one who takes the trouble to read the Epistle not to sympathize with Norton's contemptuous judgment that "it might have been written as a task by a dull pupil in a rhetorician's school." The entire Mosaic economy in all its details becomes in his hands a series of prophetic figures which are gathered up hap-hazard and explained with a surprising subtlety, indeed, but without a dominating principle, in bad taste and with great paucity of ideas.* In his typologizing interpretation he employs some of the passages from the Old Testament which are treated in a similar way by various writers of the apostolic age, but in his daring and invention in applying this method he has furnished its most thorough refutation.

The author's use of New-Testament writings is confined within very narrow limits. He was acquainted with some of Paul's Epistles, and certainly used Romans, possibly also Galatians. If he had any knowledge of any one of our four Gospels he certainly does not betray it by mention or unquestionable citation. He makes a few quotations of sayings of Jesus which have some similarity to passages in the first Gospel, and Weiss is probably right in saying that we do not need to go beyond this

* Reuss, La Théologie Chrétienne au Siècle Apostolique, 1864, Livre VI.

record for their explanation. Their source cannot, however, be determined with certainty, and speculation about it is futile, while dogmatic affirmation, like that of Tischendorf, is entirely unwarrantable. The writer certainly did not confine himself to sources known to us for the words of Jesus, for he quotes as one of his sayings, "Let us resist all iniquity, and hold it in odium." * Great stress has been laid, particularly by Tischendorf, upon the fact that the words "as it is written," which in the Latin version of the Epistle were regarded by some as a gloss,† by some as an addition of the Latin translator,‡ and by others as introducing a quotation substantially taken from some prophetical writing,§ have been found in the Greek text in the Codex Sinaïticus.‖ They introduce the quotation in chapter 4, "Many are called, but few chosen," and since this Sinaïtic discovery they have been regarded by some as proving that Matt. xxii. 14 is here cited as canonical Scripture with the formula employed in quoting from the Old Testament. But apart from the consideration that a single instance of the use of this formula would prove nothing in view of the writer's manner of dealing with the evangelic material, there appears to be no good reason why the words might not be a gloss in a Greek manuscript of the fourth century. It is not improbable, as even Westcott admits, that the proverbial phrase introduced by the formula of Scripture-quotation may through a failure of memory have been referred by the writer to some scripture of the Old Testament. Several errors of this kind are found in the Gospels, the writer of the first Gospel

---

* "Sicut dicit filius Dei," etc., c. iv.
† Dressel, Pat. apostol. Opera, "glossam olent."
‡ Credner, Beiträge, i. 28.
§ Orelli, Selecta Patrum, p. 5. ‖ καθὼς γέγραπται.

confounding Zechariah with Jeremiah and Mark referring to Isaiah a passage from Malachi."* A similar confusion occurs several times in Justin Martyr.† The preponderance of historical evidence from this period is opposed to the probability of the quotation of a passage from one of the Gospels as Scripture by any writer in it. Hardly does Justin, who wrote from thirty to forty years later, show such consideration for any of the writings of the New Testament. In chapter 5 of this Epistle there is a strange application, or interpretation, of the words of Jesus recorded in Matt. ix. 13, "I came not to call the righteous, but sinners to repentance," by which they are supposed to find their explanation in his choosing the greatest sinners as his apostles! The absence of any reference to a written Gospel does not, indeed, exclude the hypothesis that this passage was quoted from our first Gospel, but so gross a misapplication of it indicates that it was only known to the writer out of its proper connection and as a fragment of the popular tradition.

c. *The Shepherd of Hermas.*—A certain Hermas is mentioned by Paul in Rom. xvi. 14, and to this man an ancient tradition ascribed The Shepherd. There are, however, good reasons for rejecting this tradition and for holding that the writing was composed in the first quarter of the second century. It is clearly indicated in the book not only that none of the apostles were living when it was written, but that many of the heads of the Church had departed. Christianity is represented as already widely proclaimed and as having suffered manifold and bloody persecutions. The internal evidences so decidedly indicate a date as late as the year 117 that they outweigh

---

* Matt. xxvii. 9 ; Mark i. 1.
† Dial. c. 14, Apol. i. 53. Scholten, Die ältesten Zeugnisse, p. 11.

the testimony of some eminent fathers who were inclined to regard it with great consideration as the work of Hermas. The writer himself evidently desired to have the book pass for such, since he mentions Clement of Rome as a contemporary. It is difficult to account for the high favor in which it was held by many in ancient times. Clement of Alexandria often quoted it with great respect, and even Origen regarded it as the work of the Hermas mentioned by Paul, thought it a very useful writing, and, indeed, divinely inspired, though his citations from it were sometimes made with reserve and qualifications. Tertullian implies that it had been regarded by some as having a claim to canonical authority, while after he became a Montanist he reprobated its teachings, and declared that it was rejected by the catholic Christians as "apocryphal and false." Eusebius speaks of it as reputed to be the work of Hermas, but reckons it among the "not genuine" scriptures, although admitting that it was thought by some to be "very necessary," and was in his day read in the churches. The date assigned to it in the canon of Muratori, that is, about 142, is hardly consistent with the high estimation in which it was held by the fathers.

The work, which consists of visions, commandments, and similitudes, is destitute of literary interest, and has been characterized by one who studied it much, and wrote a treatise on it, as "one of the most spiritless books that the ancient Church has handed down to us."* He regards it as of importance, so far as it shows the judgment and discrimination of those fathers of the Church who could hold in veneration a writing to which we find ourselves almost constrained to refuse respect. But the present

---

* Jachmann, Hirte des Hermas, p. 43.

concern is not so much with the literary character of the work, its Jewish-Christian tendency, its romance, and its defence of asceticism, as with its bearing on the history of the canon through its relation to the Gospels. With all its visions and apocalyptics, it has almost nothing to do with the facts of Christianity. Christ is mentioned but once, and his death and resurrection not at all. The great Pauline doctrine of justification through faith receives no notice, and Paul's letters are not quoted. There are no definite quotations from the Gospels, but certain frequent coincidences of language show the writer's familiarity with the Gospel-tradition at least. A confounding of two sayings of Jesus appears to be indicated in the remark that they who remain like little children will be the first to see God.* Certain admonitions against adultery may be reminiscences of Matt. v. 28. The divorce of a wife is allowed, and re-marriage forbidden as an act of adultery, in accordance with Matt. v. 22.† The injunction is laid down to fear the Lord (rather than Satan), because He is able to save and to destroy—probably a reminiscence of Matt. x. 28.‡ An allusion to Matt. xviii. 3, is made in the narrative and discourse on strife for precedence, and to Matt. xviii. 10, in the declaration that all little children are honored of God and regarded as first.§ Of the account of the rich young man there appears to be a reminiscence in the remark that the rich will with difficulty enter into the kingdom of God. Westcott, however, is evidently hasty in drawing the conclusion that the writer of Hermas was probably familiar with our Gospels, and even made allusions to the fourth.‖ Weiss more cautiously and correctly says that the work contains

* Sim. ix. 29.   † Mand. iv. 1.   ‡ Mand. xii. 6.
§ Sim. ix. 29.   ‖ Canon, pp. 201, 203.

no certain trace of them, and finds only an accord with Mark x. 24 in Sim. ix. 20.*

3.—THE EPISTLES OF POLYCARP AND IGNATIUS.

The authorship of an Epistle to the Philippians, ascribed to Polycarp by Irenæus and Eusebius,† has been much discussed by the learned, and many still contend that it is spurious. But since Polycarp died in 167, and the letter is supposed by those who contest its genuineness to have been written about the middle of the second century, there appears to be no external evidence against the trustworthiness of the tradition which ascribes it to him. The objection of Schwegler that "so extremely meagre, weak, and disconnected a compilation of passages from the Old and New Testaments; a trivial combination of commonplaces, liturgical formulæ, and moral admonitions; a letter without occasion and aim, without individuality and salient character, without peculiarity in language and ideas, is wholly unworthy of the great Asiatic prince of the Church," ‡ is founded upon a presumption regarding the Bishop of Smyrna, which this critic does not take the trouble to substantiate. Whether the entire Epistle should be pronounced spurious, on account of the reference which it contains to the letters of Ignatius, or whether this passage and some others should be regarded as interpolations, and the remainder as a genuine writing of Polycarp,§ may be here left undecided. The internal evidences, which presuppose the existence of doctrines that did not appear so early as the date as-

---
* Einleit. p. 29.
† Adv. Haeres. iii. 3 ; Hist. Eccl. iii. 36.
‡ Nachapost. Zeitalt. ii. p. 154.
§ According to Volkmar, Ursprung unserer Evangelien, 1865.

signed to it by some scholars, furnish a strong probability that it was composed about the middle of the second century.* The dogmatic point of view of the author is Pauline, with a mediating tendency in respect to the opposing parties. Rich in Pauline citations, it is, according to Schwegler, poor in Pauline ideas, and is confined almost exclusively to the domain of a dry moralizing. Among its moral admonitions and warnings there is a frequent and quite wearisome return to the perils of riches and the blessings of poverty. An Ebionite tendency has, accordingly, been by some critics attributed to the Epistle. An inculcation of orthodox doctrine and a vigorous polemic against heresies are also prominent characteristics. The greatest importance is attached to the hierarchical organization of the Church as a means of maintaining the desired dogmatic unity, and believers are admonished to obey the presbyters and deacons as God and Christ.†

There is no reference by the writer to any one of our Gospels by name. There is no reason for supposing that he was unacquainted with the synoptical records at least, but he shows them no marked consideration, and deals very freely, after the manner of Clement of Rome, with the evangelical material. Sayings attributed to Jesus are sometimes thrown together regardless of connection and with entire indifference as to their source, as follows: "Remembering what the Lord said, 'judge not, that ye be not judged; forgive, and it shall be forgiven you; be merciful, that ye may obtain mercy; with what measure ye mete it shall be measured to you; and, blessed are the poor and those persecuted for righteousness' sake, for

---

* Lightfoot argues against this in Essays on Supernatural Religion, London, 1889.

† ὡς θεῷ καὶ χριστῷ.

theirs is the kingdom of heaven.'"* Of these passages some are found in the Gospels, and others appear to be reminiscences of reported words of Jesus. The use in some cases of different Greek words from those in which the same or similar sayings of Jesus are recorded in the Gospels indicates either want of familiarity with a written record, or free quotation from memory, or, again, dependence on oral tradition.† One exact verbatim quotation occurs in the words, "As the Lord said, 'the spirit, indeed, is willing, but the flesh is weak.'"‡ Some coincidences of language occur, as, "According to the truth of the Lord who became a minister of all"§; and, "If we desire the Lord to forgive us, we ought also to forgive." ‖ None of the quotations in this Epistle are traceable to apocryphal writings, but one is hardly warranted on this account in excluding, with Westcott, the author's possible use of Gospel-records somewhat different from ours. In the absence of the slightest intimation in the Epistle that he regarded any Christian writings as sacred or as exclusive sources of information, there is no ground for affirming that he limited himself in making quotations to certain records, or to any records whatever, and did not draw from the abundant oral and written evangelic material of his time.

The Epistles ascribed to Ignatius, Bishop of Antioch, are involved in so much uncertainty as to their authorship and date, and have given rise to so much discussion, which has brought out the greatest variety of opinion among the learned, that a modest reserve is the only

* Chap. ii.
† The parallels are supposed to be Matt. vii. 1, vi. 14, v. 7; Luke vi. 38 (Matt. vii. 2); Luke vi. 20; Matt. v. 10.
‡ Chap. vii.   § Chap. v.   ‖ Chap. vi.

becoming attitude with regard to them, even in one who has given the most careful attention to the subject. There are in all fifteen Epistles ascribed to Ignatius, of which eight are generally admitted to be spurious. The seven over which the contest as to their genuineness has been waged are addressed to the Magnesians, the Trallians, the Philadelphians, the Smyrneans, the Ephesians, the Romans, and Polycarp. These exist in a twofold Greek recension, a longer and a shorter. The longer recension is generally rejected as a fabrication made at a comparatively late date, perhaps in the latter part of the fourth century,[*] so that there remains to be considered only the shorter form. This is called the Vossian recension, the Greek text having been discovered by Isaac Voss in the seventeenth century. The Ignatian problem was complicated when in 1845 three of the Epistles were discovered in a Syriac version and published by Cureton. These are those to the Ephesians, the Romans, and Polycarp, and are designated as the Cureton Epistles. The questions in discussion now are whether the Vossian Epistles were expanded by interpolations from the Curetonian, or the latter reduced from the former by excision and abridgment, and finally whether that one of the recensions which may be decided to be original is genuine or not. The important question then, is, whether the Ignatian Epistles were written by the Bishop of Antioch, as they purport to have been written, while he was on the way to Rome, under a guard of Roman soldiers, to suffer martyrdom, in the early part of the second century (about 115), or were forged in his name about forty years later.

The external testimony for these Epistles is not very

[*] Lightfoot.

favorable to their genuineness. Irenæus, Clement of Alexandria, and Tertullian, are silent regarding them. With their polemics against heresies, they could hardly have escaped mention by Irenæus, along with that of Clement of Rome and that of Polycarp in this connection, had he known of them, or knowing of them, had believed them to be genuine.* Origen, indeed, is supposed by some to have twice quoted them. But one of the quotations adduced is found in a work of which only the Latin translation by Rufinus exists, in which little confidence can be placed on account of the changes and interpolations which he introduced ; and the other is in a work of doubtful genuineness. Eusebius is the first writer who makes express mention of them, and he introduces his narrative of the journey to Rome, the halt at Smyrna, and the writing of the several Epistles in their order with the words, "It is reported," or "tradition says."†

External improbabilities against such a correspondence under the existing circumstances are urged by the opponents of the genuineness of the Epistles. If, however, it be granted that a prisoner under the escort of a band of soldiers to the place of execution would be permitted to receive delegations from sympathizers along the way, and have opportunity to write long letters to the churches which they represented, or to others, the character of the

---

* The quotation of a passage by Irenæus from the Ignatian letter to the Romans, without other mention of its authorship than that it was by a member of the Christian brotherhood, is futile as evidence of the genuineness of these Epistles, though urged by Lightfoot. At most it shows their existence in the last decade of the second century.

† Lightfoot does not appear to attach great importance to the testimony of Eusebius, and passes lightly over it, appearing to rest the case, so far as external evidence goes, mainly on Origen and Irenæus. Essays, etc., p. 82.

reputed letters may well be appealed to in order to determine whether or no they are such as the supposed author would naturally write in his situation. Neander, who does not admit that the letters are altogether spurious, but speaks of them as much interpolated, goes so far as to say that, "as the account of the martyrdom of Ignatius is very suspicious, so the Epistles, which throughout assume the truth of this doubtful legend, do not bear the stamp of a definite peculiarity and of a man of this time— a man who announces his last words to the churches"; and adds that a hierarchical intention is not to be denied. Schwegler is moved to say that, under the circumstances supposed by the theory of their genuineness the contents of the letters are "an absolute psychological improbability."* Norton, who disputes their genuineness on other grounds also, is very outspoken on this point. "There is," he says, "no natural expression of feeling. The sentiments ascribed to Ignatius present a rude caricature of a very weak, half-crazy, vainglorious bigot." Then referring to the conception on which the Epistles are founded, that of an aged bishop taken to execution, he says: "One could hardly imagine that the outline could be filled up, as it is, by the forger of these Epistles, so that not a feeling of interest or respect should be excited for the sufferer. No writer of fustian tragedy ever more grossly misrepresented human nature, or put more extravagant rant into the mouth of his principal personage." †

Apart from the consideration that the letters abound in references to heretical opinions which are supposed not to have been promulgated until a time considerably later than that of Ignatius, the hierarchical purpose men-

---

* Nachap. Zeitalter, ii. p. 160. Baur, Urspr. des Episcopats, p. 149 f.
† Genuineness of the Gospels, vol. i. Additional Note, p. clxvi.

tioned by Neander is very plainly marked in them. They appear to favor the tendency to a union of the Pauline and Petrine parties, and to the formation of a catholic church. "Do ye all follow your Bishop as Jesus Christ did the Father, and the Presbytery as the apostles, and reverence the deacons as the command of God," is the extravagant language of the Epistle to the Smyrneans. Now the ecclesiastical situation and tendency which find their "programme" in these Epistles did not exist before the latter half of the second century. Altogether the preponderance of evidence appears to place their composition in this period, rather than so late as the beginning of the fourth century, as Norton will have it.*

The writer of these Epistles appears to presuppose a written Gospel, or Gospels, to which, however, he is indifferent from his spiritualizing point of view. He hears some say, he writes, that "unless they find the Gospel in the archives, or ancient documents, † they will not believe;" but to him the archives (ἀρχεῖα) are Jesus Christ, and the cross is the authentic ἀρχεῖον. In accordance with this point of view he makes no mention of Gospels by name, although he appears to have some knowledge of the evangelic history. He speaks, indeed, of the Gospel in the abstract (τὸ εὐαγγέλιον), of the prophets as having preannounced Christ, and of the apostles as the presbytery of the Church. ‡ But there is no intimation here or else-

---

* Hilgenfeld, "Hardly before 166," Einleit. in d. N. T. p. 72; Volkmar, "About 170," Urspr. uns. Evang. p. 163; Scholten, "Perhaps not before 170," Aelteste Zeug. p. 52.

† Ad Philad. viii. ἐν τοῖς ἀρχείοις (ἀρχαίοις). The meaning is doubtful. Credner refers the words to the prophets of the Old Testament, and is followed by Reuss and Holtzmann.

‡ Ad Philad. v. προσφυγὼν τῷ εὐαγγελίῳ ὡς σαρκὶ χριστοῦ καὶ τοῖς ἀποστόλοις ὡς πρεσβυτερίῳ ἐκκλησίας. Καὶ τοὺς προφήτας ἀγαπῶμεν, κτλ.

where in his writings of a conception of a sacred canon of Gospels and Epistles. In fact there are traces of almost as frequent a use of Clement of Rome and Hermas in his Epistles as of the first Gospel.* That he was acquainted with Matthew in its completed form appears from his reference to the tradition of the miraculous conception of Christ, whom he calls, "Our God, Jesus the Christ."† He says that Jesus was baptized in order that he might purify the water—an idea which he certainly did not find in the Gospels as known to us. Not a quotation, but a reminiscence of Matt. xii. 33, or of Luke vi. 44, are the words, "The tree is manifest from its fruit." ‡ There is an almost exact reproduction of the words in Matt. xvi. 26, "What shall it profit a man if he gain the whole world and lose his own life?"§ A similar case occurs in the citation of the words, "He that is able to receive it, let him receive it," the variation from the canonical text indicating a free quotation. ‖ The anointing of the head of Jesus is mentioned, and treated as having a spiritual and general significance, Jesus having received the ointment in order that he might breathe incorruption upon the Church. "These are not a plant of my Father" is a reminiscence of Matt. xv. 13, "Every plant which my Father hath not planted," etc.

The question of the acquaintance of the writer of these Epistles with the fourth Gospel has been warmly discussed. Expressions certainly occur which are similar to phrases found in this Gospel, *e. g.*, "The prince of this

---

* Holtzmann, Einleit. p. 123.
† Ad Eph. xviii. Ὁ γὰρ Θεὸς ἡμῶν Ἰησοῦς ὁ Χριστός.
‡ φανερὸν τὸ δένδρον, Ad Eph. xiv.
§ Ad Rom. vi.
‖ The Epistle (Ad Smyrn. vi.) reads ὁ χωρῶν χωρείτω, Matt. xix. 12, ὁ δυνάμενος χωρεῖν χωρείτω.

world," "the living waters," and "the bread of God which
is the flesh of Jesus Christ."* There appears to be no
reason for denying to him an acquaintance with the fourth
Gospel which would not bear against his knowledge of
some of the first three, since his use of the synoptic histories is largely based upon reminiscence, and the fourth
Gospel seems to stand upon substantially the same footing
in his mind. Scholten's argument to the contrary, which
does not take account of all the facts, while ingenious, is
not conclusive.† Hilgenfeld, though formerly denying,
has in recent works conceded the probability of the use
of the Johannean record by the author of these Epistles.‡
In reference to the resurrection-body of Jesus there appears to be a quotation from a record different from our
Gospels. Jesus is represented as having come to Peter
and those about him after his resurrection, and to have
said to them: "Touch me and see that I am not an incorporeal demon §; and straightway they touched him, and
believed, being convinced by his flesh and his spirit."
There are here, it is true, points of contact with Luke
xxiv. 36, and with the account of the unbelief of Thomas
in John xx. 24; but the divergences from these records are
such as to make it very probable that an apocryphal Gospel furnished the citation. Eusebius remarks regarding
this quotation that he does not know whence it was taken.¶
Jerome, however, found a similar or the same account in
the Gospel of the Nazarenes, for he reports that, accord-

---

* Ad Rom. vii.; ad Phil. vii.   † Die ältest. Zeug. p. 53 f.

‡ In Kanon und Kritik des N. T., 1863, he concedes "a preponderating
probability"; in Einleit. in das N. T., 1875, pp. 72, 73, he says that the
fourth Gospel belonged to the εὐαγγέλιον of the writer, and that the entire theology of the Epistles is grounded upon it.

§ δαιμόνιον ἀσώματον.

‖ Ad Smyrn. iii.   ¶ Hist. Eccl. iii. 36.

ing to this Gospel, the disciples took Jesus for an incorporeal demon.* Origen also found in the writing *Petri Doctrina* that Jesus said to his disciples *quod not sit dæmonium incorporeale*. That the author of the Ignatian Epistles, who nowhere shows any well-defined conception of canonicity, should have quoted from an apocryphal Gospel, is rather to be expected than otherwise.

4.—PAPIAS OF HIERAPOLIS AND HEGESIPPUS.

Papias is reported by Eusebius to have written a work entitled "Exposition of the Oracles of the Lord,"† in five books. Irenæus says that he was a hearer of John and a companion of Polycarp, a statement which need not be discussed for the present purpose. The writing mentioned by Eusebius was probably composed not far from the middle of the second century, and the fragments of Papias' testimony which have been preserved are important for the history of the canon, since he was especially occupied with the evangelic literature and tradition. The fragment from Papias' book, preserved by Eusebius,‡ runs to the effect that he gave place in his "expositions" to everything that he learned from the elders; that whenever he met any one who had been a follower of the elders he inquired about the discourses of these; and that he did not think that he could derive so much profit from the contents of books as from the utterances of a living and abiding voice. It is important to notice that we have here at length a mention of books as records of the Gos-

* Demon in the good sense, of course, *i. e.*, "a spirit inferior to God, superior to men"; πᾶν τὸ δαιμόνιον μεταξύ ἐστι θεοῦ τε καὶ θνητοῦ. Plato.
† λογίων κυριακῶν ἐξήγησις.
‡ Hist. Eccl. iii. 39.

pel-tradition. What these books were, Eusebius proceeds to inform us: "Of Matthew he [Papias] stated as follows: 'Matthew composed the Oracles* in the Hebrew dialect,† and every one translated them as he was able.'" As to Mark, Eusebius reports that Papias said: "And John the presbyter also said this: 'Mark being the interpreter of Peter, whatever he recorded he wrote with great accuracy, but not, however, in the order in which it was spoken or done by our Lord, for he neither knew nor followed our Lord, but was a follower of Peter, who gave him such information as was necessary, but not to give a history of our Lord's discourses. Wherefore Mark has not erred in anything by writing some things as he has, for he was carefully attentive to one thing, not to pass by anything that he heard, or to state anything falsely in these accounts.'"

Without undertaking to determine here whether the Syro-Chaldaic Matthew and the Mark which Papias mentions were our canonical first and second Gospels or earlier writings which served as a basis for them, it is sufficient to observe that the books referred to are a sort of Gospel-writings, and that he speaks of only two works of the kind. His manner of introducing them is significant. He appears to regard their composition as the work of ordinary historians, whose records he proposes to supplement by such information as he may be able to collect. There is no intimation in his language that he believed them to have been inspired, or in any supernatural way guarded against mistakes. One simply "wrote"; the other was "carefully attentive not to pass by anything that he heard, and to state nothing falsely." Yet this one is chargeable, it appears, with defect in arrangement. Of writings as canonical—that is, as exclusively to be received

---

* τὰ λόγια.   † Probably Syro-Chaldaic.

—he betrays no conception. In fact, the books which he knows he thinks to be inferior as sources of the information that he is seeking for the purpose of making his "exposition" to the living voice of oral tradition. Yet that this "unwritten tradition" needed more careful sifting than it received from Papias may be inferred from the remark of Eusebius that he gathered from this source "certain strange parables of our Lord and his doctrine and some other matters rather too fabulous." His account of the death of Judas, for example, shows that he put confidence in sources which do not agree with our canonical records. He relates that Judas' body, "having so swollen that he could not pass where a chariot could easily pass, he was crushed by the chariot so that his bowels were emptied out."* Now it is evident either that the work by Matthew which he knew, did not contain the account of the death of Judas which is now found in our first Gospel, or that he preferred some other source of information. Again, according to Eusebius, "he relates a story of a woman accused of many sins before the Lord, which is contained in the Gospel according to the Hebrews."

Although Eusebius declares that he will "carefully show" what use the early writers of the Church made of the acknowledged writings and what opinions they expressed of them, he does not mention any reference by Papias to our third and fourth canonical Gospels. Hilgenfeld's inference that Papias knew the Gospel of Luke, because he speaks with disapproval of employing "many" witnesses with disparaging reference to the πολλοί in the prologue of this evangelist's record, appears strained.†

---

* Preserved in Œcumenius, Comm. in Acta Apostol.

† Kanon u. Krit. p. 14. I do not find this inference drawn in the later Einleitung.

Lightfoot's argument that Papias was acquainted with the fourth Gospel drawn from the silence of Eusebius as to any reference to it by him is trivial.* Having taken pains to quote what he said about the first two Gospels, the historian could hardly have omitted to mention a reference to the other two, or one of them, had it been found in Papias' work. As there is no reason, however, for supposing that he was not acquainted with our third Gospel, his omission of all mention of it, which must be inferred from Eusebius' silence, cannot be satisfactorily explained. It is reported that he regarded the Apocalypse as inspired, and his favorable opinion of this book accords with his millenarian tendencies. As a Jewish Christian and a millenarian it would not be strange that he should regard with little favor the Pauline third Gospel. In fact, he appears to have passed Paul by without mention and to have quoted none of his Epistles, although, according to Eusebius, he "made use of testimonies from 1 Peter and 1 John."† Altogether he is a poor witness for the doctrine that the Gospels were recognized as canonical or inspired in the middle of the second century.

Hegesippus, a Palestinian Jewish Christian, made a journey to Rome about the middle of the second century, visiting many churches on his way. A few years later he wrote "Memoirs, ‡ in five books, of the unerring tradition of the apostolic message in a very simple style." § Only meagre fragments of this work have been preserved by Eusebius. He found, it appears, on his way "the same doctrine," and especially in Corinth was he refreshed by finding the "true doctrine."‖ What this right doctrine

* Essays on Supernat. Rel. p. 49.   ‡ ὑπομνήματα.
† Hist. Eccl. iii. 39.   § Eusebius, Hist. Eccl. iv. 8.
‖ ὀρθὸς λόγος.

was to him is important for his relation to the canon. He is pleased to find prevailing everywhere "that which the Law and the Prophets and the Lord enjoin." Now we know very well what he must have meant by "the Law and the Prophets." In accordance with the prevailing views of his time, the canon of the Old Testament is covered by these words and recognized as authority. The first steps towards a New-Testament canon are indicated by joining with this ancient standard the words of the Lord, or the sayings of Christ. But the first steps only are visible here. Hegesippus does not mention any one of our four Gospels as a source of this doctrine of the Lord, and had he mentioned even one of them, it is not probable that Eusebius would have failed to record the fact. Of a series of canonical New-Testament writings he does not reveal any conception. On the contrary, Eusebius expressly states that he quoted from the Gospel of the Hebrews.* In the fragments of his writings which have been preserved, there are allusions to the Gospel-history which appear to support the opinion that he was acquainted with our first and third Gospels. It is true that the reminiscences might have had their source in the oral tradition or in the Gospel of the Hebrews, but since our Gospels were undoubtedly in existence when he wrote, there is no good reason for supposing him to have been ignorant of them.† The important fact is, he did not

---

* Hist. Eccl. iv. 22. The conclusion of the author of Supernatural Religion, 4th ed., vol. i. p. 437, that Hegesippus used only this Gospel is quite unwarranted.

† The author of Supernatural Religion is needlessly strenuous on this point, and complains unreasonably that "an able and accomplished critic like Hilgenfeld" should conclude that Hegesippus knew the third Gospel. Another "able and accomplished critic," Holtzmann, concedes that he knew our first two Gospels. Einleit. in das N. T. p. 125.

ascribe to any Gospel or Gospels of our New Testament exclusive canonical authority or inspiration, nor even mention them by name. This fact is incontestable so far as accessible evidence is concerned. There is no evidence of his acquaintance with the fourth Gospel.*

5.—JUSTIN MARTYR'S GOSPELS.

Justin, of Greek descent, a student of Grecian philosophy, a convert to Christianity, "the only true and useful philosophy," was the author of two defences of the Christian religion and a dialogue with a Jew, Trypho, which were written about the middle of the second century. The other works ascribed to him are probably spurious. It promoted the attainment of his object in writing to make extensive quotations from the early records of Christian history, and on this account his works are of the greatest importance to the study of the canon. The controversy about the records which he used and his manner of using them, which has been carried on for more than half a century, constitutes a considerable literature. This controversy cannot be said to have solved all the difficulties of the problem, but it has brought to light facts of great importance. Justin frequently informs us that his quotations as to the life and teachings of Jesus are taken from a work or works which he calls "Memoirs of the Apostles,"† but he does not designate the authors

---

* Even Tischendorf does not claim this. There is a phrase preserved in Eusebius' fragment, ii. 23, concerning the death of James, "the brother of the Lord," to the effect that some one asked James, "Who is the door of [or to] Jesus?" (τίς ἡ θύρα τοῦ Ἰησοῦ;). Westcott, although conceding that the phrase may mean "door to Jesus" instead of "door spoken of by Jesus," yet hangs on this slender thread his argument for Hegesippus' acquaintance with the fourth Gospel! Canon, p. 208.

† ἀπομνημονεύματα τῶν ἀποστόλων, i. e., Memoirs [written] by the Apostles.

of these Memoirs by name. The number of citations is very large, embracing the most important events in the life of Jesus and many of his teachings, and their resemblances to and differences from their parallels in our Gospels render the question of their source very difficult. Various theories have been advocated: That Justin drew from an original or originals, from which our Gospels were derived; that his Memoirs were the Gospel according to the Hebrews; that he used a harmony, or combined narrative; and that our canonical Gospels furnished the greater part of his materials. It is not consistent with the plan of this treatise to enter into a minute examination of this question. A few of the prominent facts regarding the citations and Justin's relation to his sources will be sufficient to determine his evidence in the matter of the canon of the Gospels.

The way in which Justin speaks of his sources arrests attention. "Memoirs of the Apostles" appears to be a somewhat inexact term, if it was intended to apply to our four records, only two of which were ostensibly written by apostles. Once he adds to the term the explanatory words, "which are called Gospels," and once he quotes words which he says are "written in the Gospel." It is impossible to determine what Gospel or Gospels he had in mind, since, with the single exception of a Gospel of Peter mentioned once, he does not connect any particular authors with his sources. It is well known that many writings ascribed to apostles and others were early in circulation purporting to be Gospels,* and it would be a

---

* The Gospels according to Peter, James, the Twelve, Nicodemus, the Nazarenes, Thomas, etc. Eusebius, Hist. Eccl. iii. 25; Origen, i., in Lucam, in Matt. x. 17; Tischendorf, Evang. Apocr.; Nicolas, Les Evangiles Apocryphes.

begging of the question under discussion to assert that, whenever Justin mentioned Gospels in general, **he had in mind** just our four Gospels. Again, Justin says that the Memoirs of the Apostles or the writings of the prophets were read in the **assemblies** of the Christians on Sundays.*
This fact, however, unfortunately throws no light on the character of the Memoirs, or the estimation in which **they were held with regard to canonicity or** authority. **Many of the early Christian writings** which **did not attain** canonical **rank when critical discrimination in** this regard came to be applied **to them were** publicly **read** in these assemblies. Such were **an** Epistle **of Clement of Rome,** the Shepherd of Hermas, the Apocalypse of Peter, and others.† What Justin does **not** say about his sources **is** also **of importance.** He not only does not give the names **of** their **authors, but** omits to mention or imply that they were **regarded** as **canonical,** *i. e.,* as exclusively recognized, **or as** inspired. **He** cites **them** simply **as** historical documents. Yet **he** was **by no** means unfamiliar with **a doctrine of** inspiration, as applied to writers, for he held a very rigid theory of the inspiration of the authors **of** the Old-Testament books. Inspiration, he teaches, dispenses with the necessity for rhetoric or dialectics, and the subjects of it have simply **to abandon** themselves to **the action of the Spirit.** The divine *plectrum* comes down **from heaven, and uses** them as a harp to reveal celestial knowledge. He has been called the Doctor of Inspiration, and the originator of the doc**trine of** plenary inspiration.‡ It is, however, significant

---

* Apol. 67.

† Eusebius, Hist. Eccl. iii. **3,** iv. 23; Hilgenfeld, Die Evangelien Justin's, p. 19; Volkmar, Ursprung uns. Evang. p. 91; Schwegler, Das nachapost. Zeitalter, i. **p.** 228.

‡ Reuss, Histoire du **Canon,** 1863, **p. 50.**

that he puts faith in the statements of his Memoirs, because the events related in them had been foretold by the prophets of the Old Testament.* The highest certainty, he says, respecting incidents in the life of Jesus, is to be attained by regarding "what was foretold." † The presumption shows itself throughout his writings that his historical Christian sources are to be credited, because in them the words of the "spirit of prophecy" are confirmed. It is not open to question that his Memoirs, whatever writings they may have been, were not put by him upon an equality with the Old-Testament books as products of inspiration.

While some of Justin's citations from his Memoirs present no deviations from our Gospels which are not explicable on the hypothesis of a free quotation of them from memory, others show marked divergences from the parallels in these records, and furnish a strong presumption that he used other documents. His quotations from the Old Testament are also often inexact, and passages are sometimes referred to the wrong authors. Hence mere carelessness of quotation is not sufficient to establish the theory that his Memoirs were not our Gospels. The mention, however, of incidents in the life of Jesus which are not recorded in our Gospels presents difficulties which are not easy of solution on the hypothesis that he did not make use of other records. The statement, for example, that Jesus was born in a cave near Bethlehem ‡ can hardly be accounted for by the hypothesis of erroneous quotation from memory. The supposition favored by Semisch, that this variation crept in from oral tradition, might be allowed if the writer were Papias, who declared, as has been shown, a preference for tradition.

---

* Apol. i. 33.   † Apol. i. 35.   ‡ Dial. 78.

But Justin expressly states that the sources of his information are written, and he should not be interpreted on any other theory except for the most cogent reasons. That there is no need to resort to tradition in this case appears from the fact that several uncanonical Gospels record this tradition of the birth of Jesus in a cave.* The tradition was widespread, and if he did not quote it from some one of the existing records which contain it, the presumption is very strong that he found it in his Memoirs. Justin further relates that at his baptism Jesus was regarded as the son of Joseph, the carpenter, and himself as a carpenter, "for he was in the habit of working as a carpenter among men, making plows and yokes, by which he taught the symbols of righteousness and an active life." † The expression thrice recorded, that Jesus *sat* by the Jordan, can hardly be accounted for except on the supposition that it was contained in a written Gospel which Justin used. Justin reports that when Jesus went into the water for baptism a fire was kindled in the Jordan, and that when he came out of the water a voice came from the heavens: "Thou art my beloved son, this day have I begotten thee." ‡ These incidents are all wanting in our Gospels, and the task of criticism is to account for their appearance in Justin. The hypothesis of a traditional origin is, as we have seen, tenable if these accounts are not found in written records which he may be supposed to have known, and may have had as a part of his Memoirs. The legend that Jesus made plows and yokes as symbols, etc., is only implied in the Gospel of

---

* The Protevangelium of James, the Arabic Gospel of the Infancy of the Saviour; Tischendorf, Evan. Apocr. i. pp. 105, 171 ; Nicolas Les Évang. Apocr. p. 54. Tischendorf thinks that Justin probably derived this account from the Protevangelium.

† Dial. 88. ‡ *Ib.*

Thomas, where it is written that his father was a maker of these implements. But the story of the fire kindled in the Jordan is found in the fragments of the Gospel according to the Hebrews. Here also are the words said to have been heard from heaven in the form in which Justin has them, *i. e.*, "this day have I begotten thee," instead of "in thee am I well pleased," as in our Gospels. The legend of the fire in the Jordan is also found in the writing called "The Preaching of Paul." Some manuscripts of Luke, but not the oldest, contain it, and it is found in Cod. D and the Itala version of Matthew.

Justin also reports that in the time of Christ the people attributed his miracles to magic, "for they ventured to call him a magician and a deceiver of the people.* This might be regarded as a reminiscence of the account in our records of the charge that Jesus cast out demons by Beelzebub; but apart from the probability that had he depended solely on our Gospels he would have stated the matter in their language, which is striking, and not easily forgotten, the consideration is of no little weight that his version of it is contained in the uncanonical Gospel of Nicodemus to which he in another place refers by name.† The statement that after the crucifixion of Jesus all the apostles fled, "having denied him," is contrary to our Gospels, which mention only the denial of Peter. An incident of the crucifixion is very differently reported from the account in our Gospels. According to Justin, those standing about said, "Let him who raised the dead

---

* Dial. 69, καὶ γὰρ μάγον αὐτὸν ἐτόλμων λέγειν καὶ λαοπλάνον.

† λέγουσιν αὐτῷ γόης ἐστίν, Evang. Nicod. Tischendorf, Evang. Apocr. i. p. 208; Credner, Beiträge, i. p. 255; Hilgenfeld, Die Evang. Justin's, pp. 207, 258. The reference to tradition by Semisch is open to the objections previously mentioned.

deliver himself." Again, "Those who saw him crucified also wagged their heads each one of them, and distorted their lips, and screwing their noses one to another spoke ironically these words which are written in the Memoirs of the Apostles: 'He declared himself the son of God; having come down, let him walk about; let God save him.'"* The divergences in this account from our canonical records are so great that it cannot fairly be claimed that the quotation was made from them. The exactness of the reference is striking: "words which are written in the Memoirs of the Apostles." This is the language of one who is conscious of speaking by the book. It is futile to plead aberration of memory to account for such divergences as these, and a traditional oral source is excluded by the pointed reference to the document.

In a very few instances Justin's citations agree very nearly with parallel passages in our Gospels. These have been pointed out by Tischendorf and De Wette, and two or three of them are here subjoined: Matt. viii. 11, 12, "*Many* shall come from the east and the west, and shall sit down," etc.; Justin, "*They* shall come from the west and from the east," etc., three times with the same variations. Matt. xii. 38, 39, "Then certain of the scribes and Pharisees answered him saying, 'Master, we would see a sign from thee.' But he answered and said unto them, 'An evil and adulterous generation seeketh after a sign and there shall no sign be given to it but the sign of the prophet Jonah'"; Justin, "It is written in the Memoirs that some of your nation questioning him said, 'Show us a sign,' and he answered them, 'An evil and adulterous generation seeketh after a sign, and no sign shall be given

* Dial. 101.

to them but the sign of Jonah.'" Matt. v. 28, "Every one that looketh on a woman to lust after her hath committed adultery with her already in his heart"; Justin, "Whosoever may have gazed on a woman to lust after her hath committed adultery already in the heart."

It is needless to continue the examination of these quotations. The problem of Justin's Gospels does not admit of an exact and unquestionable solution; yet it appears to have exercised a strange fascination upon students of the canon, who have devoted to it hundreds of pages and one or two entire treatises. Rather than to go on and examine in detail the hundreds of quotations—a procedure which, as Reuss says, has somewhat the appearance of cavilling *—it is perhaps better to conclude this study with a statement of the results which have been reached by two of the most distinguished scholars who have given the subject a very thorough and conscientious study. Credner thus substantially sums up the results of the extended and minute investigation which he made of the subject in his Beiträge in 1832: Justin was acquainted with our canonical Gospels, but used them little or not at all immediately. The basis of his quotations was a writing different from them, which can hardly have been any other than his own recension of the manifold Gospel according to the Hebrews, the same which often appears also as the Gospel of Peter, and must have arisen from a harmonizing combination of the evangelic history.† Hilgenfeld, who in 1850 published an extended treatise on Justin's Gospels,‡ thus presents his conclusions in sub-

---

* Histoire du Canon, p. 57.

† Geschichte des neutest. Kanon, herausgeg. von Volkmar, 1860.

‡ Kritische Untersuch. über die Evang. Justins, der Clement. Homil. und Marcion's.

stance: Justin knew Matthew, Mark, and Luke, but his acquaintance with John's Gospel is still in doubt.* He advances beyond Papias, and marks a certain contrast to him in that he totally excludes the oral tradition as a source of the knowledge of the life of Jesus, and has every thing which relates to the Saviour in written Gospels. These apostolical Memoirs Justin reckons among the writings which belong to the Christians (ἡμέτερα συγγράμματα), and reports that they were read along with the writings of the prophets in the Sunday-assemblies for worship. Thus in him we approach nearer in every respect to the conception of a collection of the sacred writings of Christianity. Yet with all the approximation it cannot be denied that Justin limits the conception of holy Scripture to the Old Testament, and does not transfer it to the Christian writings. Everywhere, whether he contend with Jew or heathen, only the books of the Old Testament are recognized by him as holy Scriptures or γραφαί. Justin agrees entirely with Papias in holding exclusively to the *twelve* Apostles. Besides the Gospels he recognizes the Apocalypse as the work of the Apostle John. But no mention of the Apostle Paul and his letters is found in Justin; rather they are directly excluded. Accordingly, the Epistles of Paul are not reckoned by him among ἡμέτερα συγγράμματα. The Gospel of John might possibly have found admission into his original Gospel-harmony on account of the name of the apostle. But in the evangelic quotations of Justin we find much that is so peculiar as to require reference to an uncanonical Gospel.†

* But in his Einleitung, 1875, Hilgenfeld says that it is hard to deny Justin's use of John's Gospel.
† Kanon und Kritik, p. 27 f.

The attempt to explain Justin's quotations by the entire exclusion of our Gospels, by the author of Supernatural Religion, and that of Westcott and Norton by the exclusion of all other sources than these except oral tradition, are both extreme and hardly tenable. The essential facts in the case are, however, independent of the vexed question whether Justin was acquainted with our Gospels or not, and are rather that, granting that he knew and used them, he nowhere intimates that they are to him anything more than ordinary historical documents; that he does not regard or treat them as exclusive sources of information, but draws freely from another source or other sources, probably written; that he fails to identify any of the records which he used by giving the names of their real or supposed authors; that the only sacred Scripture that he recognizes is the Old Testament; that the supposed prophecies of the Old Testament relating to events in the life of Jesus are to him paramount and conclusive evidence of the significance of these events for the divine mission of Christ; that for him the credibility of certain things as facts related of Christ in the evangelic histories is conditional not upon the veracity of these histories, but upon just this prophetic foretelling; and that finally he does not reveal in his writings any well-defined discrimination as to canonical and uncanonical writings, but is apparently unconscious of such a distinction.

6.—THE CLEMENTINE HOMILIES, BASILIDES, AND VALENTINUS.

A strange and interesting product of the controversy between the Jewish-Christian and Pauline parties in the early Church is the Clementine Homilies,* a work which

* Clementis Romani quæ feruntur Homiliæ, etc., A. Schwegler, 1847; Clementis Rom. quæ feruntur Hom. xx. nunc primum integræ, etc., ed. A. R. M. Dressel, 1853.

was written in the interest of the former or Ebionite sect, and represents a contest of arguments between Peter and one Simon Magus, supposed to personate Paul, "the enemy whose lawless and foolish teachings the gentiles accepted."* The exact date of this "apocryphal religious romance" cannot be determined, but it should probably be placed in the latter half of the second century. Credner judges it to have been written before the middle of the second century,† Ritschl and Tischendorf about the middle,‡ Volkmar and Baur from twenty-five to forty years later,§ and Hilgenfeld, 160-180.|| It was forged in the name of Clement of Rome in accordance with the very common practice in that age of perpetrating pious frauds. The book possesses interest not as a literary production, but because it throws light on a momentous controversy in the early Church and on the question of the use and repute of the Gospels at the time when it was written. It is certainly not unimportant in this latter respect, even though it be, as Westcott remarks, "the product of an isolated speculator." For the author should be presumed not to speak for himself alone, but rather to represent the general opinions and tendencies of his time, at least so far as the particular sectaries in question are concerned.

The relation of the writer of the Homilies to the evangelic history is very similar to that of Justin Martyr, with the exception that while Justin expressly mentions that his sources are Memoirs of the Apostles, this writer refers

---

* Baur, Vorlesungen über Dogmengesch. i. 1, p. 155 ; Westcott, Canon, p. 285.

† Beiträge, i. p. 28.

‡ Ritschl, Entstehung der altkath. Kirche ; Tischendorf, Wann wurden, etc.

§ Volkmar, Ursprung ; Baur, Vorlesungen, etc.

|| Einleit. in das N. T. p. 43.

to no sources whatever in a general way, and does not quote any Gospel by name. Of a large number of references to sayings and acts of Jesus throughout a work of considerable extent only three or four are exact quotations from our Gospels. The most of his quotations present divergences more or less marked from the corresponding passages in the canonical records, and some are not found in them at all. Passages occur which are combinations of elements that are in our records and of material foreign to them. A very good illustration of the last-mentioned class is furnished in Hom. ii. 19 compared with Mark vii. 24-30. It runs as follows: "Justa, who is among us,* a Syrophœnician woman, whose daughter was affected by a sore disease, came to our Lord crying out and supplicating that he would heal her daughter. But he, being also asked by us, said: 'It is not meet to heal the gentiles, who are like dogs from their using divers meats and practices, while the table in the kingdom has been granted to the sons of Israel.' But she, hearing this and desiring to partake, like a dog, of the crumbs falling from this table, having changed, *i.e.*, leading the same life as the sons of the kingdom, she obtained, as she asked, the healing of her daughter." Here not only do the striking variations from Mark's account point to a different source, but the mention of the woman's name is a detail much more likely to have been preserved in a written form than to have been orally transmitted through a period of more than a hundred years.

Of words ascribed to Jesus which are not found in our Gospels two examples must suffice: "Be ye approved money-changers" and "Why do ye not discern the good reason of the Scriptures?" The conclusion of Hilgen-

---

* The representation of the Syrophœnician woman as still living accords with the writer's intention to pass his work off for a very early composition.

feld, who has made a very thorough study of the Homilies, is that the author used our four canonical Gospels along with an uncanonical one. He may have been more favorably disposed towards Luke's Gospel on account of its difference from Marcion's recension of it, and he may have admitted among his sources that of John by reason of the name of the Apostle. But this gradual recognition of these two Gospels on the part of the Jewish-Christian sect **indicates the weakening of the** original opposition **to writings of a** Pauline tendency. **The historical** influence which removed this opposition **was** catholicism, **or the** union of Christians into a catholic, united Church. This had as its result the acceptance of the Pauline "apostolicon" and the entire apostolic Scripture-canon.* In the spirit of an unbiassed critic this writer acknowledges that since the discovery, in **1853, of the** latter part of **the** Homilies he is constrained to admit that their author was acquainted **with the fourth** Gospel.† **The author of** Supernatural Religion undertakes too much in supporting the theory that the **writer of the Homilies did not make** use of our Gospels, but drew entirely from other sources.‡ Sanday concludes that **"the** facts do not permit us to claim the exclusive use of **the** canonical Gospels. * * * But that they were used mediately **or** immediately and to a greater or less degree is beyond question." § With this opinion Westcott substantially agrees.‖

* Kanon und **Kritik, p.** 30.
† *Ib.* p. 29, Anmerk. **3,** Einleit. pp. 43, 44. The most important passage is Hom. xix. 22: "Whether did this man sin or his parents, that he was born blind?" compared with John ix. 2 f.
‡ The passage, *e.g.*, in xix. 22, he regards as taken from a source which the author of the fourth Gospel also used. This is certainly very arbitrary. The citation of a Gospel by name is not **necessary** to establish its existence at least.
§ The Gospels in the Second Century, p. 186.
‖ Canon, p. 287.

The distinction, however, between knowing and using the Gospels, and recognizing them as an exclusive source of information regarding the life and teachings of Christ, cannot be too sharply drawn. When we have shown that our four Gospels were quoted by a writer in the middle of the second century, who also quoted from other similar writings without making any discrimination between these different sources, we are far from having established the doctrine that the Gospels now regarded as canonical were then so regarded. Rather we have established a fact precisely the opposite to this doctrine. When, again, we find a writer using our Gospels simply as ordinary historical records and giving no intimation of special regard for them as sacred or inspired, it is unwarrantable to argue that he had attained the conception of canonicity. Finally, if the writer in question does not mention any one of our Gospels by the name of its reputed author, it is manifest that no inference as to their genuineness can be drawn from his use of them.

The Ebionitism which was represented by the Clementine Homilies, although regarded by some as the purest form of original Christianity, has passed into history as a heresy. The great Pauline conception of the universal mission of the religion of Jesus enjoyed the fortune of victory which, in the course of human affairs, generally comes to broad ideas in conflict with ideas that are narrow. The heresy of Gnosticism also had its day, and because it was a narrow philosophy its day was short. Descended from the Platonic philosophy, developed in the allegorizing school of the Alexandrian Philo, Gnosis assumed peculiar forms in the early Church. A mixture of elements contributed by Jewish theology, oriental theosophy, and the idealism of Plato, dominated by the principle of dualism, and appropriating in an eclectic way certain doctrines of Jesus, was the Gnosticism of the second century. It was occupied with some of the great problems which speculative thought has always struggled with, and has never solved, such as the origin of the world, the reconciliation of its imperfections with the assumed perfection of God, how and why evil is in the world, and its relation to the divine goodness. It was a religious philosophy constructed upon the fundamental principle that matter is essentially evil. Accordingly, it was based upon dualism, and is thereby seen to have been a product of heathen modes of thought rather than of Christianity.* The world as material and evil could not, according to this philosophy, have proceeded from the Supreme Being, who is the Inconceivable, the Abyss, the Unnamable. The maker of the world was a subordinate power, the Demiourgos, sometimes apprehended as dependent on the Supreme Being, sometimes as hostile to Him. Judaism was subordinated, and regarded either as a very inferior and defective revelation of God, or as wholly the work of the Demiourgos. Christ held a most important place in the Gnostic systems, with all their variations in other respects. He was regarded as a higher Æon, or emanation from the Divine Being, who came forth from the kingdom of light for the redemption of the world from the power of darkness. With his name is connected everything which tends to maintain the connection of the totality of things, to unite what has been torn asunder, to bring back what has fallen away, to attain the upper world out of the lower, and to lead to the perfection of the entire world-order. He is the goal towards

* Baur, Das Christenthum, etc., in den drei ersten Jahrh., 1860, p. 183.

which the development of the world moves. What originally was salvation only in an ethical and religious sense is in the Gnostic systems the restoration and completion of the whole order of things.*

That these philosophizers undertook to bring their speculations into some sort of agreement with Christian doctrines there can be no doubt. Wishing to pass for Christians *par excellence*, they sought a support for their doctrines in the traditions and literature of Christianity. It is probable that of all the systems which their syncretism had put under contribution to build up new doctrines on the origin of evil, on the relations of the infinite and the finite, and on the means of elevating man to God, Christianity furnished then the most numerous and most precious elements, and that the Church offered them at the same time the audience most inclined to hear them. †

No little controversy has been carried on over the question whether or no Basilides, a leader of one of the Gnostic sects, who lived in the first quarter of the second century, used our canonical Gospels. His writings have not come down to us, and we have no knowledge of them except what is derived from the writers who controverted his teachings, principally Hippolytus, Irenæus, Clement of Alexandria, and Origen. An examination of the alleged quotations shows his relation to the evangelic history and tradition to have been very similar to that of the author of the Clementine Homilies. He is reported, furthermore, to have written a Gospel and called it after his own name.‡ Neander thinks that this was the Gospel according to the

---

* Baur, Das Christenthum, etc., p. 189.
† Reuss, Histoire du Canon, p. 65.
‡ Ausus fuit Basilides scribere evangelium et suo illud nomine titulare, Orig. Hom. ii. in Lucam.

Hebrews, and that Basilides brought it from Syria to Egypt. Eusebius states, on the authority of Agrippa Castor, that he composed a commentary on "the Gospel" in twenty-four books.* But it does not appear what this Gospel (τὸ εὐαγγέλιον) was. His own definition of "the Gospel" implies that he meant by the term a certain abstract, philosophical conception rather than such concrete realities as our records; for he says that it is "the knowledge (Gnosis) of supermundane things." †

The statement of Hippolytus that the followers of Basilides regarded "all things concerning Christ to have happened as they are recorded in the Gospel," has, of course, no necessary reference to Basilides himself, and even if it had it would not establish his recognition of our Gospels as canonical. Papias undoubtedly believed as much, yet he does not appear to have known our present Gospels, and such as he did know he subordinated to tradition. Indeed, what Irenæus says of the Gnostics of his time may fairly be supposed to apply to Basilides: "They boast that they have more Gospels than there are."‡ Again, the same writer charges that when they are refuted from the Scriptures, they retort by accusing the Scriptures themselves as without authority.§ Tertullian also says that the heretics of his time did not receive certain Scriptures.‖ The actual state of the case is doubtless well summed by Reuss: "The exegesis of the Gnostics attached itself above all to the words of Christ in order to bring out of them their own dogmas. But these

---

* Hist. Eccl. iv. 7.
† ἡ τῶν ὑπερκοσμίων γνῶσις, Hippol. Refut. omn. Haeres. vii. 37.
‡ Adv. Haeres. iii. 11, 9.
§ Adv. Haeres. iii. 2, 2.
‖ Praescr. Haeres. 17; Credner, Gesch. des neutest. Kanon, p. 24.

words either circulated still in a purely traditional form or were embodied in various writings more or less different, more or less circulated, but not yet sorted by an ecclesiastical authority, and all serving equally according to the occasion the use which one wished to make of them. Now nothing was easier than to form new collections of this sort, either by making extracts from those that one had at hand, or by combining several books, or by composing one's self accounts under the direct influence of the preoccupations of the system. There are famous examples of each one of these methods."* But whatever writings Basilides may have employed as sources of information for the support of his system, he did not, it appears, confine himself to them, but appealed to the authority of a certain Glaucius whom he declared to have been an interpreter of Peter, and made use of certain traditions of Matthias who, it was claimed, had had private intercourse with Jesus.†

Valentinus, the head of a Gnostic sect, who lived about the middle of the second century, appealed directly to one Theodas, a reputed follower of Paul.‡ Of direct appeal to the Gospels there is no example in the few fragments of his writings which have been preserved in quotations from homilies and letters. The charge is preferred against him of introducing alterations, corrections, etc., in some of the Epistles. Origen says that his followers acted with greater boldness, and altered the form of the Gospel. Irenæus charges this sect with bringing forward their own compositions as Gospels and entitling one of their books "The Gospel of Truth," "though it ac-

---

* Histoire du Canon, p. 70. † Hippol. Haeres. vii. 8.
‡ Clem. Alex. Strom. vii. 17, 106.

corded in no respect with the Gospels of the apostles." A distinction must be drawn between the use of our Gospels by the later followers of Valentinus and other Gnostic leaders, who were nearer to those who wrote in refutation of this heresy, and that of the leaders and founders themselves. It is not always clear to which these writers refer. The charge of Irenæus, however, is significant, that they (the Gnostics) neither consent to Scripture nor to tradition. All the evidence goes to show that the Gnostics, wishing to be regarded as Christians and to make their speculations pass for the only true Christian ideas, followed the custom of the orthodox believers in appealing to the current writings and traditions of the time to substantiate their tenets. But, instead of subordinating their opinions to the Gospels as authoritative, they exercised the greatest freedom in dealing with the documents, whatever they may have been, accepting such parts of them as furnished support for their speculations and rejecting the rest. The preceding investigations having shown that the orthodox Christians themselves had no canon, in the proper sense of the word, down to the middle of the second century, it is futile to argue from such a sort of recognition as the heretics gave to the current literature to the canonicity of any part of it.*
When we consider, furthermore, that no one claims that either Basilides or Valentinus quoted any one of our

---

* Valentinus, however, might have used all these writings [the Gospels] for his purposes without therefore according to them canonical authority. For he is reported not only arbitrarily to have altered the canonical Gospels, but to have used others besides these, and to have put one of them at the head of all; for such a rank is signified by the name which it bore, *evangelium veritatis*, by which only a purified Gospel can be meant. But if there was need of such a Gospel, the rest could not (in his opinion) have contained the pure, true Gospel. Credner, Beiträge, i. p. 38 f.

Gospels by name, it is evident how little significance is to be attached to their use of a few passages which are very similar to some in these records, and to Holtzmann's opinion that the latter argued from the Gospel, according to Matthew.* In view of the considerable number of Gospels which were in circulation in the second century, the use by these writers of isolated passages which are found in our Gospels, without reference to the particular source, does not go far towards establishing the genuineness of these records.

Credner has well stated the circumstances and conditions of this period: " The early Church saw come forth from its bosom a multitude of the most contradictory asseverations and systems which were more or less foreign to the true sense of the Christian doctrine, and were afterwards rejected and condemned by the orthodox as heretical. It was not intentional hostility to Christianity by which these so-called heretics were animated. It was rather, at least in the case of the majority, an honest seeking for truth, and the inborn striving of the thoughtful and intelligent man to bring an earlier mode of thought, in which he had been reared and perhaps grown gray, into accord with a new and, to him, acceptable doctrine. But these strivings would certainly have turned out quite differently, certainly there would have been no Cerinthians, Valentinians, Marcionites, and other sects of heretics of whatever name, at least not in the form which they took on, had the doctrines of Christianity been then laid down in divinely attested writings, and not in mere tradition. This assertion will be established if we are able to show that all these heretics sought to confirm their doctrines not by an appeal to certain writings au-

* Einleit. p. 136.

thorized in the Church, but to the oral and written tradition, just as we have found to be the case with the orthodox Christians."* The establishment of this fact may be regarded as one of the assured results of historical investigation into the condition of the Church in the second century, to which no one has perhaps contributed more than the learned and candid scholar from whom the preceding quotation is taken.

7.—THE CANON OF MARCION AND TATIAN'S DIATESSARON.

About the middle of the second century there appeared in Rome the son of a Bishop of Sinope in Pontus, who, although he called himself a Christian, and aspired to the first place in the Roman Church,† was refused communion there on account of his theological opinions. This was the great Gnostic heretic, Marcion, whose name holds a prominent place in the history of the second century as that of one of the most illustrious of its ecclesiastical leaders. In spite of all the calumniation and abuse which his orthodox opponents have heaped upon him, the verdict of history declares him to have been a man of a noble nature and a pure life. An Asiatic by birth and familiar with oriental philosophy, he believed that Christianity in its purity was in conflict with Judaism, and that the Hebrew elements which he found in it ought to be removed. He brought this opposition of the two faiths into relation with his oriental dualism by the theory of a just God and a good God. The former was the creator of the world and the author of the Old-Testament revelation.

---
* Beiträge, i. p. 36.
† Eph., Haeres. xlii. 1, first place, $\pi\rho o\varepsilon\delta\rho i\alpha$, perhaps a seat in the college of elders, $\pi\rho\varepsilon\sigma\beta\upsilon\tau\varepsilon\rho o\iota$, Westcott, Canon. Some think, however, that he aimed at nothing less than the bishopric.

On the other hand, the good God, the God of love, had remained unknown until the appearance of Christ, in whom, out of sympathy with man, He had revealed Himself, and attacked the kingdom of the just God, so that the doctrines of the Old and the New Testaments were placed in the relation of opposites to each other. Believing that the object of Christianity was the abolition of the teachings of the Old Testament, Marcion declared war against Hebraism and Judaism. Looking through the writings which set forth the current Christian tenets, he discovered in them, as in the teachings of the apostles, certain antithetic tendencies, some being freer and more independent, and others more limited and inclined to Judaism. Now, since both these tendencies, attachment to Judaism and separation from it, could not, in his opinion, represent the teachings of Christ, he was led to the conclusion that the twelve apostles, having come out of Judaism and being prejudiced in its favor, had not received and handed down the teachings of Jesus without an admixture of Jewish doctrines,* an opinion which he believed he could defend out of Paul's Epistle to the Galatians. He was led by this opinion to the bold undertaking to restore the original unity and purity of Christian doctrine, and in pursuance of this end he selected out of the existing Christian literature those writings which had remained least affected by Judaism, taking considerable liberty with them in the way of change and excision.† According to him, Paul was the only genuine apostle, and he accordingly accepted Pauline writings alone. Of these he acknowledged as the

---

* Apostolos adhuc quae sunt Judaeorum sentientes annunciasse evangelium, Irenæus, Adv. Haeres. iii. 12, 12.

† Credner, Beiträge, i. p. 41 f.

sources of his Christian doctrine ten Epistles, which he placed in his collection in the following order: Galatians, the two to the Corinthians, Romans, the two to the Thessalonians, Ephesians (which, according to Tertullian, he entitled "to the Laodiceans),* Colossians, Philippians, and Philemon. One Gospel alone he recognized which no longer exists in precisely the form in which he used it, and concerning which our only information is derived from the writings of those who undertook to controvert his teachings. He divided his collection into two parts, "The Gospel" and "The Apostolicon."

The precise character of Marcion's Gospel is one of the problems of history and criticism which do not admit of satisfactory solution. The question has been the subject of learned controversy since the latter part of the eighteenth century, and no general agreement has yet been reached among those best qualified to form a judgment upon it. On the authority of Tertullian it was generally believed, until the time of Semler, about 1783, that Marcion's Gospel was a mutilated copy of Luke's. Semler, after making a careful study of the problem, concluded that it was derived from an earlier one, of which Luke's was likewise a version. Griesbach also denied the relation usually supposed to exist between the two Gospels. Eichhorn, repudiating Tertullian's statement as untrustworthy, maintained that Marcion's Gospel was the more original, and one of the sources of Luke. Berthold and Schleiermacher held that it was not a mutilated copy of Luke,† but an independent original Gospel. Gieseler

---

* Adv. Marc. v. 11, 17.

† Schleiermacher, however, expressed himself cautiously: "Perhaps Marcion's Gospel was an earlier edition of Luke's, in which parts of the beginning and end were wanting." Einleit. in das N. T. p. 65.

adopted this view, but afterwards, influenced by Hahn's criticism, abandoned it in favor of the traditional one which was defended or acquiesced in by Neander, De Wette, Olshausen, Credner, Bunsen, Ewald, and Bleek, to mention only the most prominent critics. Much more extended and thorough studies of the subject were made by Ritschl, Baur, Köstlin, Volkmar, and Hilgenfeld, who, by reconstructing as far as possible the text of Marcion's Gospel from the statements of Tertullian and Epiphanius, appear to have gone to the limits of an exhaustive analysis of the data. The preponderance of opinion in this group of brilliant critics seems to be in favor of the traditional view and against the theory of the originality and independence of the Gospel of Marcion. Schwegler, however, holds that its relation to our Luke is similar to that of the Gospel according to the Hebrews to our Matthew. He thinks it far more probable that the Marcionite Gospel was one of those source-documents of Luke's Gospel, mentioned in the prologue of that record, an old, even if somewhat fragmentary, record of evangelic discourses and facts which originated in Pauline circles, than that it was a falsified and mutilated Luke.*

The limits which this work imposes do not admit of entering upon a discussion in detail of the question whether Marcion's Gospel was Luke's, with alterations and excisions, or some other. Indeed, so far as the matter of the canon is concerned, the solution of this problem is not of vital importance. The task before us is to determine the estimation in which the Gospels were held, and how they were regarded and treated in Marcion's time. His procedure furnishes the desired information on this point, whether he adapted to his purpose

* Das nachapost. Zeitalter, i. p. 261.

our third Gospel or an independent work, which may or may not have been one of Luke's sources. Only two or three important and conclusive facts need to be considered. Marcion does not ascribe his Gospel to any author, at least we have no information from his opponents that he did so. He called it simply "The Gospel" (τὸ εὐαγγέλιον). He admitted that he changed the original text, and gave reasons for doing so.* Now the taking of such liberties with a writing is irreconcilable with a belief in its infallibility or inspiration. While it must be admitted that his procedure was bold and violent, and that such a treatment of the evangelic records would have wrought great harm if extensively practised, it should be borne in mind that a just judgment on his motives and actions in the case can only be formed from the point of view of his age. He would, as Credner very justly remarks, have deserved the severe censure and condemnation which have been pronounced upon him, if, proceeding as he did, he had either attributed divine authority or inspiration to the Gospels which he pronounced defective, or had claimed the same for his own ostensibly purified Gospel.† But he lived at a time when, as has been shown, no trace can be found of a belief in the divine inspiration of the writings afterwards united in the New Testament and regarded as canonical. Accordingly, his treatment of a Gospel, his reception of some Epistles and exclusion of others were in accordance with the opinions and practices of his age, in which Christians were accustomed to rely upon oral tradition and to quote writings, since rejected as uncanonical, as if they were as authoritative as those finally accepted. It has

* Tertull., De Carne Christi, c. 2.
† Credner, Beiträge, i. p. 44.

been remarked that the general laxity of belief and usage regarding canonicity is evident from the fact that there does not appear to have been an objection raised against Marcion's procedure in his own time. It was unfortunate for his fame that he took a Gospel which was afterwards received as canonical, and treated it with so much freedom. But had such an opinion of its sanctity as could alone justify a condemnation of him existed in his time, it is certainly unaccountable that his contemporary, Justin Martyr, who frequently brings charges against the Marcionites, did not raise his voice against such a profanation of sacred documents.*

The question whether or no Marcion knew and rejected the fourth Gospel does not, from the testimony accessible, admit of so decisive an answer as Tischendorf gives it. Tertullian, writing at a time when the four Gospels were recognized, or about half a century later than Marcion's time, may very naturally have believed that any Gospel not acknowledged by the great heretic was known and rejected. But the fourth Gospel offers so many points of contact with the doctrines of Marcion that it is extremely improbable that if he had been acquainted with it he would have found it objectionable. It is even very likely that he would have preferred it to that of Luke.† But however this may be, it is particularly worthy of note that in the Evangelicon and Apostolicon of Marcion an important step is seen towards the formation of a canon of the New Testament, which could not have been without influence in orthodox Christian circles, where the exigencies of the contest with the Gnostics must have

* Credner, Beiträge, i. p. 44.
† Tertull., De Carne Christi, 2, 3. ; Hilgenfeld, Einleit. p. 50 ; Scholten, Die ältesten Zeugnisse, p. 76.

caused to be keenly felt the need of an authoritative list of writings, both for public reading in the churches and for appeal in discussion.*

Prominent among the heretics of the second century was Tatian, an Assyrian by birth, who in Rome was a disciple of Justin Martyr. After the death of his teacher in the persecution excited by Crescens, he left Rome, and joined the ascetic sect of the Encratites, of whose doctrines of abstinence he became a leading advocate. Of his writings there remains only an Oration to the Greeks, which was probably written about 170. The claim that in this writing there are any quotations from our Gospels rests on very questionable grounds, and is hardly worthy of consideration.† There are traces in it, however, of the first, third, and fourth Gospels,‡ but without ascription of them to their reputed authors. His chief importance as a witness for the Gospels rests on a work ascribed to him, called Diatessaron,§ or "By Four," which is assumed to have been a harmony of our four Gospels.∥ Critics are by no means unanimous regarding the character of this work, some holding that it was a harmony of our canonical Gospels, some that it was composed of our first three Gospels and that according to the Hebrews, and others that it did not contain any of our Gospels, but was a harmony of that according

---

* This is generally maintained by the critical school, Holtzmann, Einleit. p. 139.

† Even Tischendorf does not make this claim.

‡ This is contested, of course, by the author of Supernatural Religion, but conceded by Holtzmann, Einleit. p. 129, and Scholten, Aelteste Zeug. p. 93.

§ διὰ τεσσάρων.

∥ Eusebius, συνάφειά τις καὶ συναγωγὴ τῶν εὐαγγελίων.

to the Hebrews and three others unknown, or was simply the former alone, since Epiphanius says that it was called by that name in his time. The earliest mention of it is made by Eusebius, who writes of it as one ignorant of its character in detail. He says: "Tatian * * * put together a certain amalgamation and collection of the Gospels, I know not how,* and named it the Diatessaron, which even now is current with some." The testimony of Theodoret, Bishop of Cyros, about the middle of the fifth century, is important for the relation of this work to the history of the canon. He, it seems, had seen it, and he says of it: "Tatian also composed the Gospel which is called the Diatessaron, excising the genealogies and all the other parts which declare that the Lord was born of the seed of David according to the flesh. This was used not only by those of his own sect, but also by those who held the apostolic doctrines, who did not perceive the evil of the composition, but made use of the book in simplicity on account of its conciseness. I myself found upwards of two hundred of such books held in honor among your churches, and collecting them all together, I had them put aside, and introduced the Gospels of the four evangelists."† It is worthy of note that Theodoret does not tell of what writings Tatian "composed" his Diatessaron, and no inference can fairly be drawn in favor of any particular writings of the many in circulation in the early Church. It is not even certain that the name Diatessaron was always attached to the work, for Victor of Capua says that it was called Diapente ($\delta\iota\grave{\alpha}\ \pi\acute{\epsilon}\nu\tau\epsilon$), "By Five." Theodoret does not assure us that it was really composed of four Gospels, but only that it was "called" Diatessaron. The nature and sources of the

---

* οὐκ οἶδα ὅπως συνθείς.   † Haer. fab. i. 20.

work are, in fact, too little known to warrant any positive assertion concerning it, and Donaldson has well said that we know no more of it than Eusebius who never saw it knew. The absence of the genealogies, which Theodoret accounts for by excision, has been explained by the hypothesis that the Diatessaron was composed either from Justin's Memoirs or the Gospel according to the Hebrews, neither of which contained the genealogical matter and the reference to the Son of David. But even if it be granted that this writing was a harmony of our four Gospels, the omission in a dogmatic interest of certain parts of some of them is irreconcilable with the theory that Tatian regarded these books as authoritative. Historical documents without especial sanction he might, indeed, treat in this way, but records believed by him to be inspired and infallible he would rather have undertaken to bring into accord with his theories by means of a violent exegesis after the manner of all dogmatists since his time. All the evidence, then, goes to show that, as we cannot properly apply the term "canon" to Marcion's collection of a mutilated Gospel and certain Epistles, so Tatian did not appear to have any well-defined conception of a Gospel-canon, as that term came to be understood in the third century. Both men were in this respect in accord with the prevalent conceptions of their times, however widely their Gnostic tenets may have separated them from the orthodox believers in general.

8.—DIONYSIUS OF CORINTH, MELITO OF SARDIS, AND ATHENAGORAS.

Dionysius was Bishop of Corinth at the time of Justin Martyr's death, about 175, and was the author of a letter to Soter, Bishop of Rome, and of several other letters. A few fragments of the former are all that remains of his writings. Eusebius relates that in some of his Epistles he gives expositions of holy Scripture,* an expression by which the historian may have intended Scriptures of the Old Testament or of the New. It is important to observe that the words are those of Eusebius. In the fragments of the Epistle to Soter there is a complaint that certain "apostles of the Devil" had taken the liberty to change some of his letters by additions and excisions, and the writer adds that "it is not surprising if some have recklessly ventured to adulterate the Scriptures of the Lord, when they have corrupted these which are not of so much importance." These "Scriptures of the Lord" † were probably Gospel-narratives, the words being frequently employed, as Credner remarks, in the writings of the time in that sense.‡ The attempt of the author of Supernatural Religion to show that they designate writings of the Old Testament is futile.§ It should be considered, however, that no particular writings are mentioned, and that Westcott is accordingly too hasty in drawing the conclusion from these words that the "writings of the New Testament were at this time collected, that they were distinguished from other books, that they were jealously guarded," etc.‖ The most that can fairly be inferred from this fragment is that a sharp line of distinction is drawn between the writer's own productions and evangelic writings in general; but there is no intimation in it that a canon of the New Testament yet existed or had been thought of. This is, indeed, the first instance

---

* γραφῶν θείων ἐξηγήσεις.
† γραφαὶ κυριακαί, Euseb., Hist. Eccl. iv. 23.
‡ Beiträge, i. p. 52. See Clem. Alex., Strom. vi. 2, vii. 1; Iren., Adv. Haeres. ii. 35.   § Vol. ii. 3d ed. p. 165.   ‖ The Canon, p. 191.

in the second century of the application of the word Scriptures (γραφαί) to the evangelic writings; but it should be borne in mind that not only were many Gospels which have not been received into the canon freely quoted at about this time and, indeed, as will be shown hereafter, much later, but other apocryphal writings were regularly read in the churches, and some of these almost attained canonical rank, the Shepherd of Hermas having been quoted as "inspired" by Irenæus.* Dionysius informs the Romans that the Epistles of Clement and Soter, their bishops, were read in his church; and since the Epistles of Paul to this church can hardly have been neglected in the religious services, the inference is very natural that no exclusively sacred or canonical character was accorded to the latter. It is worthy of note that with all the accounts of the reading of Epistles in the churches there is no mention of this use of the Gospels.

Melito, Bishop of Sardis, who lived in the last quarter of the second century, has been quoted as furnishing evidence for the canon. In a fragment preserved by Eusebius he says, that having been requested by a certain "brother Onesimus" to furnish an account of the "Old books, how many they are, and what is their order," he undertook a journey to the East, and having obtained the desired information, he sends a list of the books of the Old Testament, and then he adds the names of the books, omitting, however, that of Esther.† Now the strange inference has been drawn that the mention of the books of the Old Testament implies the existence of a

---

* Adv. Haeres. iv. 20, 2.
† Eusebius, Hist. Eccl. iv. 26.

written canonical New Testament. But in making this assertion it seems to have been forgotten that the distinction of an Old and New Covenant by no means implies the existence of a canon of the latter, since it appears in the writings of the New Testament itself. In the account of the last supper Jesus is represented as having used the terms, "blood of the New Testament" and "this is the cup of the New Testament"; and Paul speaks of the Old Testament in contrasting the old and new dispensations. Yet no one will claim that a canonical collection of writings could have been implied in these words. But if it be granted that a New-Testament canon is implied in this fragment, there is no evidence to show what writings among the many Gospels and Epistles in existence and use in his time Melito would have included in his collection. The zeal of those who draw from such premises the conclusion that he knew anything of a New-Testament canon surpasses their discretion.*

Of Athenagoras no mention is made by Eusebius or Jerome. His principal work was an Apology, or Embassy, concerning Christians, addressed to certain Roman Emperors,† and written probably about 176. Westcott claims that in this writing there are "certain though tacit references to Matthew and John," and Tischendorf finds "several quotations from Matthew and Luke." An examination of the passages in question shows a resemblance to parallels in one or two of the synoptical Gospels, but does not establish "quotations," and as to "references," there are none in the way of a mention of the

---

* Westcott, Canon, p. 221.   On the contrary, Reuss, Hist. du Can. p. 43.

† πρεσβεία περὶ χριστιανῶν.

sources. Not even is the name of Christ introduced as the speaker, but the vague "he **says**"* precedes the passages. There is also one apocryphal **saying ascribed to** the "Logos" to the effect that if any one kiss a second time because it gives him gratification [**he** sins], and the writer **adds** that the kiss, or salutation, must be used **with care, as, if it be** defiled even a little by thought, it excludes **us from life eternal.** The conclusion of Dr. Donaldson regarding Athenagoras appears to be drawn from a correct apprehension of the facts: "Athenagoras makes no allusion **to the inspiration of any of** the New-Testament writers. He does not mention **one of** them by name, and one cannot be sure that he quotes from any except Paul. All the passages taken from the Gospels are parts of our Lord's discourses, **and** may have come down to Athenagoras by tradition."† It is evident that he **cannot fairly be quoted as** teaching **that our four** Gospels **were recognized in his time as an exclusive** authority, as genuine **and canonical.**

9.—THEOPHILUS OF ANTIOCH AND THE CANON OF MURATORI.

Theophilus **of Antioch was a heathen by** birth, and, according to Eusebius, the sixth **Bishop of** Antioch in the time of Marcus Aurelius. His three books to Autolycus, written in the latter part of the second century, are devoted to convincing a learned heathen of the truth of the Christian religion, and are preserved entire.‡ He quotes a passage contained in Matthew as of "the evangelic voice," and is the first writer in whom is found an ascription of the fourth Gospel to John, whom he designates as

* φησί.
† Hist. Christ. Doct., etc. iii. p. 172.
‡ Otto, Corpus Apologet. vol. v.

one of those who were "vessels of the Spirit," * quoting from the prologue to this Gospel. It is to be noted, however, that he makes a distinction between "the holy word" in general † and "the evangelic voice."‡ But he places all "vessels of the Spirit" on an equality with the holy Scriptures, thus probably according to the evangelists canonical rank and authority.§ "This," he says, "the holy Scriptures teach us, and all the vessels of the Spirit, one of whom, John, says, 'In the beginning was the Word, and the Word was with God.'" He even accords to the announcement in Matt. v. 18 superiority to the Old Testament.‖ According to Jerome he was the author of a commentary on the four Gospels.¶

In the latter part of the seventeenth century Muratori discovered in the Ambrosian library at Milan a manuscript of the eighth or ninth century which has been the subject of much investigation and discussion in the interest of the history of the canon of the New Testament. The writing is anonymous, and is defective and mutilated both at the beginning and the end. It appears to have been originally a list of the sacred books accepted by the Roman Church, although the first two canonical Gospels are wanting at the beginning, and is the oldest list of the kind that is known, since it claims to have been written by a contemporary of the Roman Bishop Pius, and mentions the writing of the Shepherd of Hermas as recent and

---

* $\pi\nu\epsilon\upsilon\mu\alpha\tau\acute{o}\phi\rho\rho\sigma\iota$. † $\acute{o}$ $\mathring{\alpha}\gamma\iota\sigma\varsigma$ $\lambda\acute{o}\gamma\sigma\varsigma$. ‡ $\mathring{\eta}$ $\delta\grave{\epsilon}$ $\epsilon\mathring{\upsilon}\alpha\gamma\gamma\acute{\epsilon}\lambda\iota\sigma\varsigma$ $\phi\omega\nu\acute{\eta}$.

§ The failure of the author of Supernatural Religion to acknowledge this fact is by no means an indication of fairness.

‖ Ad Autol. iii. 13.

¶ Quatuor evangelistarum in unum opus dicta compingens, Ep. 121 ad Algasiam.

the **author of** it as a brother of the Bishop.* Great uncertainty exists as to the date of this fragment, the episcopate of Pius being variously given from 127 to **157, and the composition of the writing from 160 to the beginning of the third century.**† The character **of** the writing is also in dispute, Credner maintaining that it **is merely a list of the books accepted and not a fragment of a larger work,** ‡ while **Westcott regards it as having formed part of an apocalyptic work, perhaps a dialogue with some heretic, unless it is composed of detached pieces of a** considerable composition. There **is** also uncertainty as **to** the language in which it was originally written. The Latin in which it was found, a sort of barbaric or rustic dialect, is thought by some to be **a** clumsy translation from Greek,§ by others as indicative of a North-African origin. The authorship is a matter **of pure** conjecture. Some assign it to a **writer of the fourth century, and** others doubt its authenticity **altogether.** Credner, whom Westcott **pronounces "a most impartial judge,"** regards it as a **genuine list of the latter part of the second century.** This point may be regarded **as settled** by the preponderance of critical judgment,¶ although some of the questions just mentioned **do not admit** of **a satisfactory** settlement.

* Pastorem vero nuperrime temporibus nostris in urbe Roma Herma conscripsit sedente cathedra urbis Romæ ecclesiæ Pio episcopo fratre ejus.

† Tischendorf, 160-170; Westcott and Wieseler, **about 170; Credner and Harnack, 170-190;** Volkmar, 190-200; Hilgenfeld, **time of Irenæus and Tertullian;** Keim, time of Tertullian.

‡ Gesch. d. neutest. Canon, p. 143.

§ Bunsen, Tregelles, Westcott, **Volkmar, Hilgenfeld (who has restored the Greek text in Kanon u.** Kritik, and Einleitung), and others.

‖ Credner, **Hesse, Reuss,** Bleek, and **many others** reject **the theory of a** translation from Greek.

¶ Hilgenfeld: "The conception of holy Scriptures of the New Testament appears here already fully formed."—Einleit. p. 99.

The first words of the fragment are the conclusion of a sentence, " at which (quibus) nevertheless he was present, and he so placed [it]." This sentence is supposed to relate to the Gospel of Mark, and the preceding, which is wholly absent, to that of Matthew. Then follow the words: "Third book of the Gospel according to Luke. Luke, that physician, after the ascension of Christ, when Paul took him with him as studious of the right, wrote it in his name as he deemed best; nevertheless he had not himself seen the Lord in the flesh, and followed him according as he was able, beginning thus from the nativity of John." The text then proceeds to narrate some strange circumstances connected with the origin of the fourth Gospel, which it ascribes to John " of the disciples," as follows : " Being entreated by his fellow-disciples and his bishops, John said, 'Fast with me for three days from this time, and whatever shall be revealed to each one of us, let us relate it to one another.' On the same night it was revealed to Andrew, one of the apostles, that John should relate all things in his own name, aided by the revision of all," etc. Then follows a mention of Acts, containing a record by Luke, and of thirteen Epistles of Paul, with an arrangement different from that in our canon and with reasons assigned for the writing of some of them. An Epistle to the Laodiceans and one to the Alexandrians* forged under the name of Paul and several others it is declared cannot be received in the Catholic Church, " for gall ought not to be mixed with honey." †
The Book of Wisdom is said to be received, written by

---

* Perhaps the **Epistle to the Hebrews**. Credner, Kanon, p. 161.

† " Fel enim **cum melle misceri non congruit."** This play upon words is adduced as evidence **that the writing was** originally in Latin, an argument **which appears** quite as trivial as the **trifle** on which it is founded.

friends of Solomon in his honor, also two Apocalypses, that of John and that of Peter. The Epistles of Peter, one of John, and that to the Hebrews are not included. The fragment closes with the mention of Hermas already referred to, and the rejection of some heretical writings. The conclusion is abrupt, in the midst of an unfinished sentence.

The canon of Muratori admits of several interpretations as related to the history of the New-Testament canon. It may be thought to indicate that the progress towards a real formation of the canon was well under way in the latter part of the second century; the extension of the canon of the original apostles so as to include the Pauline writings may be interpreted as the last act of the reconciliation of parties;* its special reference to certain heretical works may suggest that it was the result of the Gnostic and Montanistic storms when all non-apostolic ballast was thrown out of the ship of the Catholic Church.† In forming a judgment regarding it we need to be on our guard against the bias of a too strong apologetic interest. It must be borne in mind that the author is wholly unknown; that the Manuscript dates from the eighth or ninth century; that, as Donaldson suggests, it may have been interpolated, although the presumption of interpolation should not have weight in the absence of evidence; ‡ and finally, that in the light of the conclusions of the preceding investigations, the fragment would present a strange anachronism at any time before about the end of the second century. The writer does not give his own opinion regarding the books mentioned, but professedly

---

* Hilgenfeld. † Harnack.
‡ Donaldson thinks that the passage regarding the date shows signs of tampering.—Hist. Chr. Doct. and Life, iii. p. 209.

the general sentiment of the Church. If now, in writings of undisputed date and genuineness, we do not find that prior to the end of the second century the books of the New Testament are mentioned and massed after the manner of this fragment of uncertain date and unknown authorship, this fact ought certainly to have great weight in determining our judgment regarding its importance for the history of the canon.

10.—IRENÆUS AND TERTULLIAN.

Irenæus, Bishop of Lyons, is an important witness for the canon, since he speaks not alone for the Western but also for the Eastern Church, from which he went to Gaul. In his work against the heretics, written about 190, he appeals to the most of the New-Testament writings as holy Scripture,* and puts them on an equality with the Old Testament. He holds the following language respecting the Gospels: " Matthew produced his Gospel among the Hebrews in their own dialect, while Peter and Paul were preaching the Gospel and founding the Church in Rome. After the departure [death] of these, Mark, the disciple and interpreter of Peter, also transmitted to us in writing what had been preached by Peter; and Luke, the companion of Paul, committed to writing the Gospel preached by the latter. Afterwards, John, the disciple of our Lord, the same that lay upon his bosom, also published the Gospel while he was yet at Ephesus, in Asia," † The quaternity of the Gospels is distinctly recognized, or rather the four Gospels are referred to as one fourfold

---

* γραφαί, θεῖαι γραφαί, γραφαὶ κυριακαί, Adv. Haeres. ii. 5, 20; 27, 1.

† Adv. Haeres. iii. 1, 1.

Gospel.* We do not, however, find the critical point of view represented in Irenæus. Rather he appears unconscious of it, and writes as one who merely records current traditions. He is satisfied with reporting after Papias that Matthew wrote a Gospel in the dialect of the Hebrews, but as to the important question of the relation of this to the Greek first Gospel he is most uncritically silent. He proceeds with so little critical discrimination that he does not consider, as Scholten remarks, how much the recognition of a Hebrew original of Matthew stood in the way of the canonical validity of the Greek Matthew.† It is clear that the worth of his testimony must be determined by his point of view, and that so judged, he furnishes us nothing more than the fact that in his time our four Gospels were uncritically accepted, and ascribed to the writers whose names were traditionally associated with them.

The " fourfold Gospel " appears to be accepted as an article of faith without reasons sought and found in history or criticism, but for trivial reasons quite foreign to the subject: "But neither can the Gospels be more in number than they are, nor on the other hand can they be fewer. For as there are four quarters of the world in which we are, and four general winds, and the Church is disseminated throughout all the world, and the Gospel is the pillar and prop of the Church and the spirit of life, it is right that she should have four pillars on all sides, breathing out immortality and revivifying men. From which it is manifest that the Word * * * has given us the Gospel four-formed, but possessed by one spirit; as David also says supplicating his advent: 'Thou that sit-

* τὸ εὐαγγέλιον τετράμορφον
† Die ältesten Zeugnisse, p. 114.

test between the cherubim, shine forth.' For the cherubim also are four-faced, and their faces are symbols of the working of the Son of God, * * * and the Gospels therefore are in harmony with these, among which Christ is seated. For the Gospel according to John relates his first effectual and glorious generation from the Father, saying: 'In the beginning was the Word. * * * But the Gospel according to Luke, being, as it were, of a priestly (!) character, opened with Zacharias, the priest, sacrificing to God. * * * But Matthew narrates his generation as a man. * * * This, therefore, is the Gospel of his humanity. * * * But Mark makes his beginning after a prophetic spirit coming down from on high to men. * * * Such, therefore, as was the course of the Son of God, such also is the form of the living creatures * * * and such is the character of the Gospel [*i. e.*, quadriform]. Therefore, vain, ignorant, and audacious are those who set aside the form of the Gospel, and declare the aspect of the Gospels to be either more or less than has been said."* Such are the grounds which Irenæus finds for believing in the canonicity of the four Gospels, when cutting loose from tradition he trusts himself to reason. His position was not, however, uncontested in his own time, for he admits that the fourth Gospel was disputed by some.

Irenæus marks the transition from tradition to a New-Testament Scripture. The appeal to the latter predominates, while he cannot entirely break with the former. Addressing a friend of his youth, Florinus, who had adopted heretical doctrines, he says: "These doctrines were not delivered to thee by the presbyters before us, those who were the immediate disciples of the apostles.

* Adv. Haeres. iii., 11, 8, 9.

For I saw thee, when I was yet a boy, in Lower Asia with Polycarp. * * * I can tell the very place where the blessed Polycarp was accustomed to sit and discourse * * * his familiarity with those who had seen the Lord; how also he used to relate their discourses and what he had heard from them concerning the Lord, his miracles, his doctrine; all these were told by Polycarp in consistency with the holy Scriptures, as he had received them from the eye-witnesses of the doctrine of salvation."* Although the work of the Spirit is fully recognized by him in the apostles, he by no means regards the divine powers as absent from his own age. He claims that in cases where a whole church has united in fasting and prayer to bring a dead man to life, "the spirit has returned to the reanimated body, and the man has been granted to the prayers of the saints." He testifies also that "some have knowledge of things to come * * * others heal the sick by the imposition of hands, and even the dead have been raised, and continued with us many years."† That he did not regard the Gospels as self-authenticating, but rather as needing the support of prophecy, is apparent from the words in immediate connection with those just quoted: "But if they say that our Lord also did these things [miracles] only in appearance, we shall refer them to the prophetic declarations, and shall show from them that all these things were strictly foretold." We find him in this respect at the point of view of Justin Martyr. ‡ But apart from this support invoked from the Old Testament, he recognizes the Gospels as independent sources of evidence for the doctrines of the

---

* Eusebius, Hist. Eccl. v. 20.

† *Ib.* v. 7.

‡ οἶς ἐπιστεύσαμεν, ἐπειδὴ καὶ τὸ προφητικὸν πνεῦμα ἔφη. Apol. i. 33, "whom we believed, since also the prophetic spirit said it."

Church and decisive documents of Christianity, which possess the same authority for those of the New Covenant as the Old Testament for the Jews.* The Old and New Testaments are placed upon the same footing, the former having come forth from the prophets, the latter from the apostles.† The apostles, and they alone, have handed down true Christianity not only orally, but also in writing. The Gospels they have delivered to us in our Scriptures by the will of God to be the foundation and column of our faith.‡ The Gospels are quoted as "Scripture" with the same formula as the writings of the Old Testament, and Matthew is referred to as "inspired."§ Mark and Luke are brought into connection with an apostolic source by being associated, as previously shown, with Peter and Paul.

Tertullian, whose activity extended into the second decade of the third century, may be regarded as a witness for the canon of the African Church. His scientific method renders him a very valuable witness, because with him the Scripture-citations do not present themselves sporadically, without order and succession, as with Irenæus; but when he treats a special point of morals or of dogma, he aims to pass in review the different parts of sacred Scripture according to the order of the books.∥ He gives his testimony as the judgment of the Church: " I say, then, that not only among the apostolic churches,

---

* Holtzmann, Einleit. p. 152.

† Universæ scripturæ et prophetiæ et evangelia.

‡ Per Dei voluntatem in scripturis nobis tradiderunt fundamentum et columnam fidei nostræ futurum.

§ With the formula of Scripture ($\gamma\rho\alpha\phi\eta$) he also quotes the Epistle of Clement and the Shepherd of Hermas.

∥ Reuss, Histoire du Canon. p. 113.

but among all the churches which are united with them in Christian fellowship the Gospel of Luke, which we earnestly defend, has been maintained from its first publication. And the same authority of the apostolic churches will uphold the other Gospels which we have in due succession through them and according to their usage, I mean those of Matthew and John, although that which was published by Mark may also be maintained to be Peter's, whose interpreter Mark was; for the narrative of Luke also is generally ascribed to Paul, [since] it is allowable that that which scholars publish should be regarded as their masters' work." "These are, for the most part, the summary arguments which we employ when we argue about the Gospels against heretics, maintaining both the order of time which sets aside the later work of forgers, and the authority of churches which upholds the tradition of the Apostles, because truth necessarily precedes forgery, and proceeds from them to whom it has been delivered."*

Tertullian employs "*scriptura*" and "*scripturæ*" as Irenæus employs γραφή and γραφαί of the New Testament as an inspired document in two parts, "*Evangelicum*" and "*Apostolus*," or "*evangelicæ et apostolicæ literæ*." His favorite expression, however, for the Gospel is "*Evangelicum Instrumentum.*" He also uses the word "*Testamentum*," and speaks of the "*totum instrumentum utriusque testamenti*," the whole instrument of both testaments, as containing all the ordinances and commandments of God. It does not appear, however, that he assumes a critical attitude either towards the Gospels or the traditions by which he believes them authenticated, but rests his belief in their genuineness on the tradition of the churches, his maxim being that "That has been derived

* Adv. Marc. iv. 5.

by tradition from the apostles which has been preserved inviolate in the churches of the apostles." We are not surprised, accordingly, at his uncritical acceptance of the tradition that "the narrative of Luke is generally ascribed to Paul." The "summary arguments" in the preceding quotation indicate his point of view and the limitation of his inquiries. Previously to his acceptance of Montanism he used the Shepherd of Hermas, which as a Montanist he rejected, apparently for purely dogmatic reasons, as "that apocryphal Shepherd of fornicators," * while saying a good word for the Epistle of Barnabas.

11.—THE CATHOLIC CHURCH AND THE CANON.

In the absence of means of easy communication between the different and often widely-separated Christian communities in the second century, the conception of unity and a common bond of faith and fellowship among them must have been slowly developed. The journeys, however, of prominent teachers among the various little communities, and the letters occasionally sent from the leader of one of them to the brethren in another, must have tended to generate the idea of a whole church, or a church throughout all; that is, a catholic or universal church.† The Gnostic controversy, however, probably contributed more than any other influence to bring the churches to a consciousness of historic unity. The appeal to tradition was not, indeed, unknown apart from the exigencies of this controversy, in the midst of which it became the very natural and general resort of

* Illo apocrypho Pastore mœchorum.

† ἡ καθ' ὅλου ἐκκλησία, Eusebius, Hist. Eccl. v. 16. The term "catholic church," ἡ καθολικὴ ἐκκλησία, first appears in the Ignatian Epistle to the Smyrneans, viii.

the defenders of the orthodoxy of the times. It was deemed the best answer to the speculations of the heretics to set forth the fundamental doctrines of primitive Christianity as they had been handed down from Christ through the apostles and their successors. The creed was simple and in few words. There was one God, who had created the world by His Son, the Word. This latter had inspired the prophets, had finally become flesh, and preached the new kingdom of God; had been crucified, raised from the dead, and was seated at the right hand of God, whence he sent forth the Holy Spirit upon believers. At length he would return in glory in the great Parousia to take them to himself, and punish the unbelievers. This was the Rule of Faith* which had been handed down, and was deemed essential to the integrity of the Church and the soundness of the individual believer Above all questions of mere interpretation of Scripture, it appeared to the orthodox contestants to be of supreme importance to determine the grounds of the authority of the writings themselves; and it is natural that in proportion as the conception of canonicity was formed and defined, the tendency in this direction should become more pronounced and positive, particularly in the exigencies of controversy with heretics. To minds untrained in critical investigation, the appeal to the venerated tradition of the Church furnished the most congenial source of confirmation. What Christ had taught and the apostles preached could be determined in no way so well as through the churches in which the living word had been preached and handed down. We have seen that to Papias "the living voice" was that of individual teachers. It is not surprising that with the

---

* Regula Fidei, Canon of the Church, κανὼν ἐκκλησιαστικός.

consolidation of the Church a change should take place in the form of the appeal to tradition; and in Tertullian a change is, in fact, observable. For he finds the standard of right knowledge and belief, as well as of all true interpretation in the tradition of the churches from the apostolic age down through the entire succession. When the heretics denied the infallibility of the apostles, and claimed that these were incapable of comprehending the profounder sense of the teachings of Jesus; when they referred to the disagreement between Peter and Paul, it was maintained by the defenders of the faith that only among themselves, the real descendants of the apostles, was the genuine tradition to be found, on which the true faith could alone be established, and in accordance with which alone a right interpretation was possible.

It was but a step from this appeal to the tradition of the churches, which derived its chief worth from its apostolical source, to an appeal to writings of a supposed apostolical origin, so as to meet the heretics with weapons drawn from the armory of Scripture-texts. Their denial of the participation of the Supreme God in the revelation of the Old Testament could not be more effectively answered than by an appeal to apostolic writings recognized as equal in authority to that, as inspired—in a word, as holy Scripture. The ground of their validity was their supposed connection with the apostles in their origin and their conformity in doctrine with what was believed to be the genuine apostolic tradition as held in the churches. A striking illustration of this point of view is furnished in a proceeding of Serapion, a Bishop of Antioch, at the end of the second century. It appears that a division had arisen in the church at Rhosse in reference to the Gospel of Peter. Serapion, in order to appease the strife, at first permitted the Gospel to be read, presumably because of its supposed apostolic origin. But having learned afterwards that it contained some **heretical** teachings, he forbade its use. He declared the principle on which he acted to be that Peter and the other apostles are to be accepted as Christ himself, **but that the writings which falsely go under their names are to be rejected.***

The consolidation of the catholic Church, then, was the condition of the settlement of the canon of the Gospels. As the Church came to **a consciousness of itself;** as the instinct of self-preservation **in** the conflict with heresy more and more united it; **as** the appeal to apostolic tradition preserved in its various branches and to writings believed **to be** of apostolic origin became a necessity; **as an** authority held **to be** above question could **not be dispensed with in the exigencies of its development, it found itself constrained to hold fast to its revelation contained in** the teachings of **the apostles, to** exclude all writings which **deviated from the traditional** catholic faith, and to collect the documents of this revelation **in a canon, or** rule of **faith and** practice.† Apostolic in origin, that is, written **by** apostles or by men **who had been in intercourse** with **them,** and apostolic in doctrine **according to the** tradition **of the** churches must all writings be which were accepted as canonical. The **chief promoters** of canon-forming were **probably** the Bishops, and it is likely, as Holtzmann maintains against Tischendorf, Bleek, and others,‡ that the process of establishing the canon would have been much **slower** than it was, if **it had** been obliged to wait upon the agreement

---

* Eusebius, Hist. Eccl. vi. 12.   † κανών, canon, rule.
‡ Einleit. in das N. T. p. 143.

of the churches through general enlightenment and mutual understanding. The Bishops, tracing their succession from the apostles, would naturally regard the writings of these as the true standard of catholic orthodoxy. The procedure of Serapion, previously mentioned, is a good illustration of the fact and the necessity of episcopal supervision in the matter of accepting and rejecting the current writings. Clothed with authority in matters of doctrine, it would naturally fall to them to decide what books should be read in the churches, and thus receive a sort of canonical recognition.

It would doubtless be a great error to suppose that the leaders in the Church during the latter part of the second century engaged, after the manner of modern theologians, in critical researches to establish a canon of sacred New-Testament Scripture. As little are we justified in thinking them to have been preoccupied with the absolute and exclusive authority of the supposed apostolic writings. True representatives of the catholic tendency, which has remained essentially the same to the present day in the Roman Church, their predominant interest was ecclesiastical. They were far from being protestants in their attitude towards Scripture or tradition. According to one of them, the Spirit of God comes to individuals only through the Church, so that one may say not only that the Church is where the Spirit is, but also that the Spirit is where the Church is.* They taught that the depositaries of tradition, the chiefs of the different communities, especially of those founded by the apostles, above all of that at Rome, were the best teachers of the truth.†

---

* **Ubi enim ecclesia** ibi et spiritus Dei, et ubi spiritus **Deii bi** ecclesia, * * * cujus non participant omnes qui non currunt ad ecclesiam.—Irenæus.

† Discere oportet veritatem apud quos est ea quæ est ab apostolis ecclesiæ successio.—*Ibid.*

12.—THE GOSPELS IN THE ALEXANDRIAN CHURCH.

The Alexandrians treated the conception of canonicity with greater freedom and in a more spiritualizing way than did the Western Church. Clement (170-211) not only took into account the external, apostolic origin of writings, but their spiritual derivation from the apostles, or the question of their contents as worthy or unworthy of their authorship. So purely subjective a point of view as this latter undoubtedly has its perils. But it was controlled by a regard for testimony, and also, it appears, modified somewhat by philological criticism.* In a work which is lost, "Hypotyposes," Clement gave, according to Eusebius, an abridged account of all the canonical scriptures, not even omitting those that were disputed, such as the Epistle of Barnabas and the Revelation of Peter. In the "Stromata" he quotes Clement of Rome and Barnabas as apostles,† and the Shepherd of Hermas as a divine revelation.‡ Besides, he quotes the Gospels according to the Hebrews and the Egyptians, and although he distinguishes these from the four Gospels,§ his distinction between canonical and uncanonical books does not appear to be drawn with a very firm hand. In the writing previously mentioned, the "Hypotyposes," he gives the tradition respecting the order of the Gospels, as derived from the oldest presbyters, as follows: "Those which contain the genealogies were written first; but the Gospel of Mark was occasioned in the following manner: When Peter had proclaimed the word publicly in Rome, and declared the

---

* The Epistle to the Hebrews, attributed in the Western Church to Barnabas, was regarded by Clement as the work of Paul, because worthy of an apostle. It was thought to have been written in Hebrew, and the translation was attributed to Luke because of a similarity in its style to the Acts.—Eusebius, Hist. Eccl. vi. 14.

† Strom. ii. 6, sec. 31, iv. 17.   ‡ *Ib.* i. 29.   § *Ib.* 93.

8

Gospel under the influence of the Spirit, as there was a great number present, they requested Mark, who had followed him from afar, and remembered well what he had said, to reduce these things to writing; and after composing his Gospel, he gave it to those who requested it of him. Which when Peter understood, he neither hindered nor encouraged it. But John, last of all, perceiving that what had reference to the body of the Saviour was sufficiently detailed, and being encouraged by his familiar friends, and urged by the Spirit, wrote a spiritual Gospel."* It is noteworthy that this tradition proceeds upon the assumed priority of Luke to Mark, and that it represents the composition of the Gospels as undertaken in a quite human way and without divine impulse or guidance, with the single exception of the fourth Gospel, to the writing of which the author was " urged on by the Spirit."

Origen, whose life extended to the middle of the third century, drew more sharply than Clement the distinction of canonical and uncanonical. With him the historical interest predominates, and the internal character of the Christian writings is subordinated to their recognition and use in the churches. He was the first to distinguish the current Gospels, Epistles, and other works, as "accepted"† and "doubted"; ‡ but from the manner in which he was able to carry out this distinction is apparent the great difficulty of establishing a clear and secure result. § So far as the Gospels are concerned, however, he unhesitatingly declares that our four canonical ones are alone to be accepted, although he uses and quotes that according to the Hebrews, and mentions the Acts of Paul. His language concerning the Gospels is: "I have learned by tradition

---

* Eusebius, Hist. Eccl. vi. 14. † ὁμολογούμενα.
‡ ἀμφιβαλλόμενα.   § Hilgenfeld, Kanon und Kritik, p. 47.

concerning the four Gospels, which alone are uncontroverted in the Church of God spread under heaven,* that that according to Matthew, who was once a publican but afterwards an apostle of Jesus Christ, was written first; * * * that according to Mark, second; * * * that according to Luke, third; * * * that according to John, last of all."

As to other Gospels, they were all rejected by Origen, and excluded from use, especially from public reading. There might, indeed, he thought, be much in them that was unobjectionable and even right, but they were to be regarded as apocryphal.† While all that was contained in the four Gospels rested upon divine inspiration, and was therefore genuine, the contents of others were doubtful. In regard to these apocryphal Gospels, however, we find him sometimes holding a tentative and even wavering attitude, which might, perhaps, be expected in a man who held the Epistles of Barnabas and Clement of Rome in high esteem, and thought the Shepherd of Hermas very useful and even inspired.‡ In one passage he appears to be undecided whether the book called "The Preaching of Peter" is genuine, spurious, or mixed,§ while in another place he excludes it definitely from the canon.‖ In general these Gospels had for him an unequal worth, or very little, or none at all, and he quotes few of them, rejecting others entirely with the remark that they were not written at the impulse of the Holy Spirit. But if Origen was unable without some wavering to draw the line between

---

* ἃ καὶ μόνα ἀναντίρρητά ἐστιν ἐν τῇ ὑπό, etc.

† εὐαγγέλια ἀπόκρυφα.

‡ Quæ scriptura valde mihi utilis videtur, et ut puto divinitus inspirata. In Ep. ad Rom. x. c. 31.

§ πότερον γνήσιον ἢ νόθον ἢ μικτόν. In Joh. xiii. 17.

‖ De Prin. Pref. § 8.

canonical and uncanonical writings, he spoke without reserve of the necessity of closing the canon of holy Scriptures according to the principle that those documents must be held as sacred which had been regarded as holy Scripture in the Church down to that time, and that the number of them must be neither increased nor diminished. These are called "the books in the Testament," or Covenant,* or so far as there was no doubt as to their admission in the Church, " the generally acknowledged, the Scriptures which are current, and believed in all the churches of God to be divine." The acknowledged writings ($\delta\mu o\lambda o\gamma o\acute{u}\mu\epsilon\nu a$), in regard to whose admissibility a general agreement existed, he placed in the first class of holy Scriptures. From these he distinguished a second class, which comprised the writings in respect to whose origin and genuineness doubts existed in the Church. In view of what has already been said it is evident that none of our four Gospels were placed in the second class.

A period in the history of the canon of the Gospels has now been reached at which the study of the subject for the purposes of this treatise may be terminated. Our four Gospels, after having remained unnamed and undistinguished in the mass of the early Christian literature for about one hundred years, are found to have made their way by the beginning of the third century to a general recognition in the Church as exclusive historical sources for the life and teachings of Jesus. They are clearly distinguished from other similar writings. They are believed to be of apostolic origin, that is, to have been written by apostles or their immediate followers. They are regarded as "inspired," and are quoted as such along with the

* $\tau\grave{a}$ $\dot{\epsilon}\nu$ $\tau\tilde{\eta}$ $\delta\iota a\theta\acute{\eta}\kappa\eta$ $\beta\iota\beta\lambda\acute{\iota}a$, or simply $\dot{\epsilon}\nu\delta\iota\acute{a}\theta\eta\kappa a$.

writings of the Old Testament. In other words, they are recognized as the Christian classics of the Church, and have accordingly attained to canonical rank in the sense of that term which was set forth at the beginning of this chapter. The inquiries which are here terminated, it should be borne in mind, are historical, and have resulted only in establishing certain facts of history. To what extent the judgments which the Church held of these writings in the third century are tenable on critical grounds it will be the task of the succeeding investigations to determine.

CHAPTER III.

THE SYNOPTIC PROBLEM.

ALTHOUGH a difference between the first three Gospels and the fourth was early observed, and expressed in the tradition that John wrote "a spiritual Gospel," it is due to the critical tendency in modern times that, in the investigation of these writings, the former have been kept quite distinct from the latter, and considered as a special type of the evangelic history. So long as the mechanical theory of inspiration prevailed, the study of the Gospels in their relation to one another exhausted itself in the futile endeavor to harmonize the four records, in order by all sorts of arbitrariness and violence to bring them into accord. But when they could no longer be regarded as written after the dictation of the Holy Spirit, the study of them as literature resulted in giving to the critical interest its due influence and importance, and not only in distinguishing them more sharply into the two classes previously mentioned, but also in subjecting the first three to a thorough examination in their relation to one another. The conclusion has been reached that these present the biography of Jesus from the point of view of the popular tradition, while the fourth Gospel is controlled, in a less degree, by a historical purpose, and much more by a theological interest. The tendency in the study of the Gospels during the last fifty years, has not been towards an investigation of them by the process of criticism alone, but by means of historical inquiry as well. According to this historico-critical method of examining them, they are studied not simply as literature, but as products of the time in which they were written, that is, as works which in no small degree reflect the ideas and discussions, the hopes and fears, which prevailed in Christian circles towards the end of the first century and the beginning of the second. Whatever defects and limitations may be charged against this method, it is certain not only that nearly all the results of importance which have been attained in this field of investigation are due to it, but also that it is destined henceforth to prevail, and that a return to the old dogmatic point of view is not likely ever to become general.

The first three Gospels, in their relation to one another, present a unique phenomenon in literature. Their accounts of the life and teachings of Jesus are so similar in outline and contents, and present agreements in conceptions and forms of expression so striking, that they offer a common view of the history, and accordingly received from Griesbach the designation of "Synoptics." Not only, however, do they thus to a certain extent cover one another, but they also present remarkable differences, which often amount to discrepancies, and even contradictions, in words, in names, in forms of expression, and in the sequence of events. The similarity appears in a very striking form in the general conception and order of the whole narrative. The public ministry of Jesus is connected in all three with the preaching of John the Baptist, is chiefly confined to Galilee, and is set forth in certain epochs, as the feeding of the five thousand, Peter's confession, and the tragic conclusion in Jerusalem. This last series of events, the discourses spoken here, the passion, death, and resurrection, are set forth with a greater agreement than is found in any other extended part of the narrative. A remarkable similarity is also evident in the method of constructing the history and of using the materials composing it. Instead of that consecutive sort of narrative, which results from a complete grasp and fusing of the subject-matter, these Gospels present a succession of little accounts, which isolate themselves by peculiar beginnings and formulas of closing, as if they were put together by the writers like mosaics. Sixty such small sections have been distinguished which, a few differences apart, are found in all three. Matthew and Luke have about forty sections in common; and Mark has twenty in common partly with Matthew and partly with Luke.*

The extent of the agreement of the three synoptists also appears to be determined by a uniform choice of material, which can hardly be explained by a reference to an "objectively identical background of history." Out of the great amount of historical material, which must have been at the disposal of each of them, all appear to have confined themselves to the same small group of incidents. It can hardly be supposed that Jesus pronounced no other discourses than those reported by these three narrators. It is expressly related that he healed vast numbers of the ill of various diseases; but why are no cases given except those in which all the three evangelists agree? Of the "many wonderful works" which he performed, why do these historians present almost the same, and no others? A woe is pronounced upon Chorazin and Bethsaida, according to Matthew and Luke; but as to the occasion which called it forth, why

---

* Holtzmann, Einleit. p. 348.

are all silent? It appears from such phenomena that the connection of the accounts, the extent and choice of the material, cannot have been determined by the historical data actually existing, and probably within reach of any writer who might be inclined to seek them, but rather by some influence in their sources which affected all the narrators. It is inconceivable that three historians, who should have made independent researches in the abundant materials for a life of Jesus which must have existed towards the end of the first century, would have produced three writings presenting such phenomena as those of our three synoptics. Remarkable agreement in details, along with slight variations, is illustrated in the sections reporting the baptism, the temptation, and the return to Galilee, in the accounts of the storm on the lake and of the Gadarenes, of the paralytic and the publican, Matthew, of the teachings regarding fasting, the plucking of the ears of corn and of the cure of the withered hand, of the woman with an issue of blood, of the daughter of Jairus, of the first prophecy of the passion, of the transfiguration, of the blind man at Jericho, and of Jesus' entrance into Jerusalem. The agreement of all three, or more frequently of two, narrators is often remarkable in passages where it extends to the very words with only slight variations, as in the account of the feeding of the five thousand.* Sometimes this sort of agreement runs through a considerable section, as in the accounts of the cure of the paralytic which are regarded as furnishing " a classical example." †

Parts of the discourses of Jesus appear in all three narrators, and more frequently in two of them almost

* Matt. xiv. 19, 20; Mark vi. 41, 42; Luke ix. 16, 17.
† Matt. ix. 2-8; Mark ii. 3-12; Luke v. 18-26.

literally alike in the Greek text. This is the more surprising, as Jesus spoke in Aramaic. An example of this is found in the eschatological prophecies.* Quite remarkable is the use of unusual words and expressions by the three, as, "The bridegroom shall be taken from them"; the figure, "taste of death"; † the middle voice $ἀπεκρίνατο$ in the essentially parallel passages, Matt. xxvii. 12, Mark xiv. 61, Luke xxiii. 9, while in all other places where the word is used, with one exception, the passive is employed; the use of the unusual word $δυσκόλως$ precisely in three parallel passages.‡ It is quite significant that some citations from the Old Testament common to the three records are found to differ from the Hebrew text in the manner of the Septuagint, and yet to have certain peculiarities which are the same in all of them.

These phenomena are manifestly inexplicable on the hypothesis that the three evangelists wrote independently of one another. Criticism, then, could not but undertake the task of explaining the relation of the three records in their origin to ascertain how such facts as they present can be accounted for, or, in other words, to furnish a solution of the synoptic problem. The problem is complicated, as has already been remarked, by the fact that in the same passages which indicate a close relation of the records in their sources, striking differences often appear which sometimes amount to contradictions. In the account of the cure of the paralytic, previously referred to, a variation appears at the conclusion after

* Matt. xxiv., Mark xiii., Luke xxi.

† Matt. ix. 15; Mark ii. 20; Luke v. 35; Matt. xvi. 28; Mark ix. 1; Luke ix. 27.

‡ Matt. xix. 23; Mark x. 23; Luke xviii. 24. Holtzmann, Einleit. p. 350.

much that is remarkably similar. According to Matthew, the people glorify God *who had given such power to men;* according to Luke, they say, "We have seen strange things to-day"; according to Mark, "We never saw it in this fashion." But the accounts of the appearances of Jesus after the resurrection, by Matthew and Luke, are mutually exclusive and irreconcilable. According to Luke, Jesus appeared to his disciples after his resurrection only in Judea; according to Matthew, only in Galilee. This is one of many examples which might be quoted of a peculiarity of these narratives. They sometimes give accounts of the same event in almost entire agreement, then suddenly separate, and disagree in their statements, only soon perhaps to come again into harmony.* Again, there are sections in one which are entirely wanting in one or both of the others. The discourses of Jesus in Mark are few in comparison with those in Matthew and Luke, and Luke has some important ones which are not given in the other two, the parables of the prodigal son and of the good Samaritan, for example. Much that Luke has in common with Matthew appears in a different historical setting. The accounts of the call of Peter in Matthew and Mark are totally irreconcilable with that given in Luke.† Differences in the grouping and succession of events are not uncommon, one evangelist scattering material which by one or both of the others is given in a mass. Lexically regarded the records present considerable differences. The words common to all three are found to be in Matthew and Luke 14 per cent.; in Mark 23 per cent. Matthew has of words peculiar to

* Compare the story of the Centurion, Matt. viii. 5-10 with Luke vii. 1-10.
† Matt. iv 18-22; Mark i. 16-20; Luke v. 1-11.

himself 56 per cent., Mark 40 per cent., and Luke 67 per cent. About half the words in Mark are found in Matthew, but only a fourth of those of Luke, while a third of the words of Mark are in Luke.* Lexically the first two are most alike, the first and third most unlike.

The foregoing very meagre outline of the relation of the first three or synoptic Gospels will perhaps suffice to give a tolerable idea of the general nature of the critical problem to be solved. This synoptic problem, however, is not concerned merely with a mechanical solution of the relation of the synoptics to one another, but must necessarily include the more important question of the origin of these writings. The hypothesis which proposes to explain their likenesses and differences can be no other than a hypothesis as to their composition. The subject is, accordingly, of great importance, and it has been in accordance with a right insight that for more than a hundred years critical researches in the study of the Gospels have concentrated upon it. No thorough treatment of the Gospels can avoid this problem, and its importance to their exegesis is not likely to be overestimated. Holtzmann shows a correct apprehension of the matter when he says that where doubt arises as to the correct exegesis of a passage, the right view is obtained in very many cases only from a comparison of the two- or three-fold form in which it appears in the different synoptical narratives; and that the formation of a competent judgment on the contents of the narratives depends largely on a right insight into the origin and dependence of the different forms in which they lie before us.† Davidson's remark that it would be a waste of time at the present day

---

* Holtzmann, Einleit. p. 351.
† Hand-Commentar zum N. T., 1889, p. 1.

to discuss the various attempts which have been made to solve the synoptic problem may be true in reference to the learned, but the general reader can hardly be better introduced to the study of the Gospels than by a brief review of the principal hypotheses which have been offered for its solution. These with some modifications are the following: 1. That the later evangelists copied from the earlier. 2. That a common written source (or sources) was used by all. 3. That all drew from an oral tradition which had assumed a fixed form. These proposed solutions will now be considered briefly without strict regard to historical sequence.

1.—THE HYPOTHESIS OF COPYING.

The theory that the similarities in the first three Gospels may be accounted for by supposing that the later writers used the work of their predecessors is perhaps the most natural. It is also the oldest, and was essentially, though not at all in detail, set forth by Augustine,[*] who taught that the evangelists wrote with reference to one another in the order, Matthew, Mark, and Luke, and that the differences among them are due to their not having remembered the history in the same way, so that the parallel course of the three lines was disturbed by purely subjective influences. This order, according to which Mark was the slavish follower and abbreviator of Matthew,[†] held sway until the end of the eighteenth century, when it was broken by Koppe and Storr,[‡] the former contesting the doctrine that Mark was an epitomator of

---

[*] De Consensu Evangelistarum, i. 2, 4, 12.
[†] Marcus Matthæum secutus tamquam pedisequus et breviator.
[‡] Koppe, Marcus non Epitomator Matthæi, 1792; Storr, Ueber den Zweck der evangel. Gesch. Joh., 1786; and De Fontibus Evangel. Matt. et Lucæ, 1794.

Matthew, and the latter maintaining that he was first in the order of time, and the Greek translation of Matthew the latest. The priority of Luke was defended as early as 1776 by Büsching,* and a little later by Evanson.† But the most celebrated work upon the subject in the interest of the copying-hypothesis is that of Griesbach, who attempted to account for the synoptic phenomena by the theory that Mark was founded upon Matthew and Luke, and that its writer stood to these Gospels in the relation of a copyist and abbreviator.‡ De Wette followed Griesbach in making Mark dependent on Matthew and Luke, leaving the way open for the assumption of several media between any two of the evangelists.§

The test of this hypothesis, in whatever form it may be maintained, does not lie in accounting for the similarities in the three records, but in explaining the differences and discrepancies which they present. Verbal coincidences and agreements in matters of fact and in the sequence of events very naturally suggest the use of one or two of the records by the writer of another; and while it is true that a slavish copying need not be assumed by the terms of the hypothesis, it is equally true that wide divergences present insuperable difficulties on the presumption that a copyist respected the record which he used. At any rate, a rational explanation of the differences in the records is necessary to the establishment of the hypothesis. The three accounts of the calling of Peter furnish an illustration in point.‖ Now, on the supposition that Mark copied

---

* Die Evangelien, etc., 1776.
† The Dissonances of the Four Evangelists, 1792.
‡ Commentatio qua Marci Evangelium totum e Matth. et Lucæ commentariis descriptum esse monstratur, 1789–90.
§ Lehrbuch der hist.-krit. Einleit. in das N. T. 7te Ausg. 1852.
‖ Matt. iv. 18–20; Mark i. 16–20; Luke v. 1–11.

from Matthew, or *vice versa*, this section would not be entirely free from difficulties. The expressions, "two brethren, Simon who is called Peter and Andrew, his brother," and "Simon and Andrew, his brother," are hardly related to each other as original and copy. But the difficulties become insuperable when Luke's narrative is taken into account. To suppose this to have been an original for the other two, or for one of them, is absurd. It has all the features of an independent composition, and the others are equally independent with regard to it. A similar difficulty appears in comparing the three accounts of a healing of blindness at Jericho. Matthew relates that as Jesus was *going out* of the city, two blind men cried out to him to have pity on them, and he healed them. Mark records the incident as if there were but one blind man, and gives his name, with special detail, as the son of Timæus, Bartimæus, entering into particulars in his usual graphic way as to his throwing off his garment, leaping up, and coming to Jesus. On the other hand, Luke says that the incident occurred as Jesus was *approaching* the city. He differs from Matthew, and agrees with Mark in reporting but one blind man, but contradicts the latter in saying that Jesus ordered the man *to be brought to him*. According to Matthew the blindness was healed by a touch,* but according to Mark and Luke by a word only.† Again, Matthew relates that two demoniacs were restored by Jesus among the Gadarenes, while Mark and Luke mention but one, and enter into many details not given by Matthew.‡ In the account of the cursing of the barren fig-tree Matthew represents its withering as the immediate

* ἥψατο τῶν ὀμμάτων.
† Matt. xx. 29–34 ; Mark x. 46–52 ; Luke xviii. 35–43.
‡ Matt. viii. 28–34 ; Mark v. 1–20 ; Luke viii. 26–39.

consequence of the curse: "And the disciples seeing it were struck with awe, and said, 'How suddenly this fig-tree has withered.'" But Mark's account runs to the effect that the curse was pronounced on one morning, and the withering of the tree was first observed on the following morning.* Luke omits the story. These facts are quite irreconcilable with the hypothesis of the dependence of the synoptists on one another as copyists in whatever form it may be presented.

A favorite illustration of Mark's dependence on the other two evangelists is furnished in the following parallels:

Matt. viii. 16.	Mark i. 32.	Luke iv. 40.
And when evening came they brought to him many that were possessed by demons, etc.	And in the evening when the sun was set they brought to him all that were sick and those possessed of demons.	And when the sun was setting all who had any sick with divers diseases brought them to him, etc.

The fact that Mark here appears to combine from Matthew and Luke the expressions, "And when the evening came" and, "When the sun was setting" into, "And in the evening when the sun was set," was regarded as evidence that his Gospel is an epitome of the other two. But it has been pointed out that double expressions of this kind are in several other places used by Mark, who seems to have had a predilection for them, for example, "Early, long before day," i. 35, and "Very early . . . at the rising of the sun," xvi. 2. Besides, in the case referred to, Mark had said in verse 21 that the day was a sabbath, and on that day the sick could be brought only after sunset, so that the double expression is not necessarily referable to a careless epitomizing. But conclusive against the hypothesis that Mark used the other two records is

* Matt. xxi. 18–22; Mark xi. 12–25.

the fact that his text does not contain the lexical and stylistic peculiarities which are found in these.*

This hypothesis of a copying by the later evangelists of the writings of their predecessor or predecessors, although supported in some of its protean forms by many eminent scholars, has not well stood the test of time, and now finds little favor. Weiss says of it that it appears as a pure aberration, so far as it only leads to a mistaking and obscuring of the actual situation, while all other hypotheses proceed from considerations which are partly right, and so have a relative justification.† Reuss remarks that by all the combinations to which the hypothesis has given rise are easily explained the agreement of one writer with another and the pure additions which have been borrowed from other sources either oral or written. But the deviations in detail give rise to difficulties, because they show that a preference was given to those other sources over the evangelist (or evangelists) who by the hypothesis was used, so that actually the relation of dependence did not exist. This concerns especially the beginning and end of the history. But wholly inconceivable is the omission of entire sections of importance.‡ To Mark must be attributed the intention of only giving excerpts from the history, if he is supposed

---

* He does not take from Matthew the peculiar words, ἄγγελος κυρίου, μαλακία, καιρῷ, παρουσία, ὁ λόγος τῆς βασιλείας, ἡ βασιλεία τῶν οὐρανῶν, etc.; nor from Luke, λίμνη, ἐπιστάτης, ὁ κύριος (of Christ), χάρις, χαρίζεσθαι, σωτήρ, σωτηρία, δὲ καί, μετὰ ταῦτα, ἐφιστάναι, ὑποστρέφειν, παύεσθαι, ὑπάρχειν, etc.; nor finally, from both, words which would most naturally force themselves upon his attention, as πορεύεσθαι, καλεῖν (to name), which last he uses only once in a quotation, xi. 7, ἄξιος, ἕτερος, etc., Holtzmann, Einleit. p. 361.

† Leben Jesu, i. p. 39.

‡ Of Matt. xiv. 22–xvi. 12, xix. 1 f. xx. 1 f. in Luke; of Luke vii. 11 f. x. 25, and the greater part of chapters xii.–xvii. in Matthew.

to have written later. The lesser differences in the common sections are such that it is not always the same evangelist who has the more complete, accurate, and vivid narrative; these differences cannot, therefore, be regarded as thorough-going emendations, or signs of individual negligence and haste. But as one is compelled to explain them as due to other causes, the hypothesis falls on account of its untenableness, since it must assume that one of the evangelists had the work of another before him, and line by line copied, corrected, abridged, interpolated, transposed, etc. But the narrative certainly does not give the impression of such careful, studied labor. Besides, the consideration has been disregarded throughout that still other books, in like manner similar and dissimilar, were in existence, and must also in any case have been taken into the series of sources.*

2.—THE HYPOTHESIS OF A COMMON WRITTEN SOURCE OR OF AN ORIGINAL GOSPEL.

The celebrated author of the hypothesis of an original Gospel as a solution of the synoptic problem believed himself, to employ his own language, to have accomplished the first essay of a higher criticism of the New Testament, the writings of which he in his Introduction proposed to investigate according to the rules of criticism as they are applied to other human writings. Eichhorn, in the learned work in which his theory of an original Gospel was set forth,† undertook a purely literary and historical treatment of the Gospels, which exerted a powerful influence on the thought of the century which it introduced. Already in the study of the canon it

* Gesch. der heil. Schr. N. T. § 180.
† Einleit. in das N. T., 1804.

has been seen that contemporaneous with, and perhaps anterior to, our Gospels there existed a considerable Gospel-literature, and the third evangelist expressly declares that the work of writing accounts of the life of Jesus had been taken in hand by many before he attempted it. The existence of such writings, some of which appear to have been held in high regard in the early Church, could not but suggest an inquiry as to the relation which they may have sustained to the canonical Gospels, and whether some other writings of the kind of which no trace remains may not have been very near to the latter in their origin. The peculiar phenomena of the synoptic Gospels still further provoked investigation, and it was with reference to them to the exclusion of the fourth Gospel that Eichhorn's hypothesis of Gospel-formation was propounded.

The synoptic phenomena of agreement and difference are accounted for on this theory by the hypothesis that the basis of the narratives was an original Gospel * which was a sort of guide, or book of elements, for the preachers who assisted the apostles in the earliest teaching of Christianity. It was supposed to have been written about the year 37 or 38 and to have been a rough outline in the popular language and mode of thought of Judaism to serve as a proof that Jesus was the promised Messiah. From this sprang the numerous Gospels which were in circulation in the second century, and were rejected in favor of our four canonical Gospels, as well as other translations and revisions of the original writing. For the solution of the problem which our synoptics present Eichhorn supposed that these were written independently of one another, thus rejecting entirely the theory of copy-

* Urevangelium.

ing or dependence in all its forms. The sections in them which are common to all are on this hypothesis to be regarded as the original biography of Jesus, but the differences which are found along with the similarities are to be explained by supposing that the original Hebraic outline which was the basis of the synoptic narratives underwent many revisions, of which each of the writers had a different one. Since the similarities of expression in many passages of the three records cannot be accounted for on the supposition of three independent translations of the original Gospel by each of the three evangelists, it is supposed that a translation of it into Greek was made before it had received additions. This translation was used by the three independent translators of three different copies of the revised and enlarged original Gospel in the preparation of Greek editions of them. Thus the differences and verbal agreements of our synoptics are supposed to be accounted for, the latter being traced to one translator and the former to the three translators who could not escape from the influence of their predecessors.

But there remain to be accounted for whole sections in one evangelist which are not in either of the others, or in two which are not in the third. These are regarded as incompatible with the theory that one evangelist wrote with the work of another before him, and there remains, according to Eichhorn, only the supposition that when two of these writers have common sections they derived them from the same original source. These sections were originally composed in the Hebrew language, and the two writers had two different translations of them into Greek. It is also necessary to assume, in order to carry out the theory, that the documents used by the three evangelists had gone through many hands, and had received various

additions from the current tradition of the life and teachings of **Jesus.** Many important changes may also have **been** made by the evangelists themselves, but it is, **of** course, impossible to determine what they **are.** The Gospels, then, are in a certain sense **distortions of the** original biography **of** Jesus. What is really original in them constitutes only that part in **which they agree.** All **else is the result** of alteration, difference in translation, **addition, interpolation, transformation.** The genuineness **of the Gospel of Matthew can, of course, according to this** theory, be maintained only in a very **unusual sense.** Of apostolical origin it contains nothing but those sections which are common to all three, and passed into it from the original Gospel. But the portions which are peculiar to it **and,** indeed, many which the other two have in **common** with it are regarded as unhistorical and unapostolical on account of their legendary character. **The first Gospel,** Eichhorn says, may be regarded **as Matthew's, but not in** the sense **that it came from him in its present form,** but because an original Gospel **lay at** the basis of it which was **by** him transformed and in some places corrected.* **By** means of this separation of the unapostolical (the accounts of the birth, childhood, and temptation) from the apostolical portions, **or all** that had an apostolical confirmation, Eichhorn thought that he was establishing the credibility **of** the evangelic history, because the original Gospel did, indeed, contain accounts of miracles, but only in harmless adaptation to the lower popular speech and the ordinary Jewish ideas.† "If no angelic host greeted the **birth of** Jesus with a song **of** praise, if no graves were opened at the crucifixion, and no saints were sent from **them to ap-**

---

* Einleit. i. p. 457.
† Hilgenfeld, Kanon und Kritik, p. 134.

pear in Jerusalem, and no guardians watched the tomb of Jesus; how much remains of the objections with which thirty years ago [in the Wolfenbüttel Fragments] the Gospel-history was shaken in its foundations? And where would be found its new fortifications which might hitherto have been successfully undertaken? Through this separation of the apostolic from the unapostolic which the higher criticism, if one will only not scorn its gift, recommends with the weightiest grounds, are to be found the means of securely establishing the inner credibility of the evangelic history."* The Gospel according to Matthew, in which there are many additions, did not receive its present form until after the destruction of Jerusalem. The Gospel according to Mark is a Greek edition of the Hebrew original Gospel, with a few additions made for the purpose of elucidation. The third Gospel was written by Luke, the travelling-companion of Paul, for the use of a distinguished man, Theophilus. It is a similar edition of the enlarged original Gospel, and its credibility depends on the excellence of the sources, which are given for the most part word for word, and on the capacity of the evangelist for critically judging them. "Eichhorn, then, put the one original Gospel, whose changed and enlarged emanations our first three Gospels were assumed to be, in the place of the one and identical history of Jesus upon which the old harmonistic view distributed the Gospels."

Eichhorn did not share the doubts concerning the genuineness of the fourth Gospel which had been entertained before his time. He did not relate it to the original Gospel in the same way as the synoptics, but thought it to be an independent work of an illuminated apostle who wished to establish the Messianic dignity of Jesus not from the

* Einleit. i. p. 459.

Palestinian point of view, as derived from the Holy Spirit, but rather after the Palestinian-Hellenic mode of thought, as from the fulness of the Logos. It was a Gospel written with reference to the Hellenic culture of the period which, in accordance with the philosophy of Zoroaster, Plato, and the Stoa, apprehended the Logos as the expression of the power and wisdom of God. As a sort of "correcting supplement" to the original Gospel, it derives the proof of the Messiahship of Jesus not from his miracles, but from his teaching, in which he attributes to himself all the wisdom of God, and appeals to the pure truth of his doctrine, while the miracles are only mentioned as a secondary matter. For Eichhorn, then, there were really only two Gospels, one of the Jewish popular belief and one of illuminated Christianity.[*]

Although the elaboration and defence of this hypothesis were accomplished with great ingenuity and learning, it is so complicated and mechanical, and rests on so many arbitrary assumptions, that it was unable to secure general or lasting acceptance. There appears to be no good reason for the assumption that personal peculiarities, arbitrariness, and independence in the writers of our Gospels might not as well be supposed to account for the phenomena which these writings present, as like qualities attributed to unknown authors, translators, and manipulators of assumed documents from which the existing evangelic literature may have been formed. The supposition that our Gospels are mere aggregates of an indefinite plurality of materials for history cannot explain why out of so large a supply three historians should hit upon substantially the same. Nor is it probable that they would have arranged and grouped the materials so that almost

[*] Hilgenfeld, *ut supra*, p. 137.

always where one of them suspends the sequence of events both the others hold it fast.* Again, the question naturally arises whether there is any reason for supposing that such a work as the assumed original Gospel ever existed at all. There is no evidence offered for its existence, but it should at least be made to appear that the circumstances and needs of the time called for such a writing, or rendered its production probable. It ought to be shown that within six or seven years after the death of Christ an apostle should have thought it necessary to prepare a bare outline of his life in writing, intended to show that he was the promised Messiah, and to serve as a book of elements for the early preachers. It is necessary to overcome the presumption that at a time when the oral tradition was fresh in the minds of all the need of writings embodying it would not be felt at all, even for those who might be sent forth to proclaim the Gospel, a presumption which has the support of all the earliest literature of the Church. If such a work as the supposed original Gospel did exist, it is questionable whether it must not have been quite too meagre to serve as a basis for the whole Gospel-literature which is referred to it ; whether some historical trace of its existence would not be likely to have remained if ever it existed at all ;† and whether if it was known to be of apostolic origin it is probable that it would have had such a fortune as the hypothesis assumes in the hands of copyists, interpolators, and the whole series of manipulators through whom it appears to have almost lost its identity.

Finally, the tenability of the hypothesis depends on its standing the test to which it is subjected when applied to the explanation of the synoptic phenomena. Eichhorn

---

* Holtzmann, Einleit. p. 359.
† Baur, Krit. Untersuch. über die kan. Evangelien, p. 28.

went so far as to affirm that by comparing the first three Gospels we are able even now to separate the original life of Jesus, or the original Gospel, from all subsequent additions, and collecting it out of those Gospels to restore it free from all traditions of later times.* He actually undertook to do this on the principle that "all those portions which are common to all three evangelists were originally contained in the common document," and he devoted to the task more than one hundred pages of the first volume of his Introduction. But he himself admits the difficulty of a satisfactory execution of this task when he says: "We are seldom able to determine as to the words how much originally belonged to the primitive text, since we are acquainted with it only through translations." When the supposed original Gospel has been thus separated from the three records, we have a certain number of passages parallel in the sense that they relate to the same events, but they present wide divergences in many respects. No one will pretend, says Norton, when the statement is brought distinctly to this point, that there may be found in each Gospel a series of words coincident in meaning with a similar series to be found in each of the other two, which may, therefore, be considered as representing the text of the original Gospel.†

As an Englishman, Bishop Marsh, had the honor of elucidating and modifying the hypothesis of Eichhorn, so a countryman of his, Edwin A. Abbott, has recently presented a new form of the same theory with important changes, and has attempted to show by a sort of harmony of the synoptics the contents of the original Gospel.‡

---

* Einleit. in das N. T. i. p. 145.

† Genuineness of the Gospels, i. Additional Notes, p. clix.

‡ The Common Tradition of the Synoptic Gospels, 1884. Also article on The Gospels in the Encyclop. Britannica, ninth edition.

But his "Common Tradition" is so fragmentary that it is difficult to think of it as having constituted a connected writing. Besides, the work is far from being a thorough treatise on the synoptic question, and leaves many of the most difficult problems connected with it unconsidered.

3.—THE HYPOTHESIS OF ORAL TRADITION.

Yet another attempt to solve the synoptic problem was made by Gieseler, who, after refuting the theory of Eichhorn, presented the hypothesis of a fixed oral tradition as the source of the three narratives, claiming that since it admitted of historical justification, and fully explained the origin of the Gospels in their existing relations to one another, it ought to have the preference over that.* His hypothesis has been called the counterpart of that of F. A. Wolf on the origin of the Homeric Poems. It proceeds from the historically-established statement, that in the early years of the apostolic age, the Gospel was not written down for purposes of instruction, but was orally propagated. The apostles, being men without culture, could only by necessity be moved to write, and no demands could have been made upon them which they were not able to meet by means of oral communication. In the direct application of his theory to the phenomena of the synoptic Gospels, Gieseler maintained that the circumstance that all three have sections that are common is explained by the supposition that the oral standard was not determined by a council, but arose, as of itself, among the apostles by means of frequent repetitions of the same narratives. As the evangelists afterwards wrote independently, there was naturally made by each a different

* Historisch-kritischer Versuch über die Entstehung und die frühesten Schicksale der schriftlichen Evangelien, 1818.

selection out of the existing abundant material, which was partly determined by the individuality of each writer, and partly by the needs of those for whom the writing was intended. The similar arrangement of the narrative creates the least difficulty. For if the events of the life of Jesus appeared to the evangelists to be of the greatest importance, a correct knowledge of their succession could not be lightly esteemed. The deviations are explained by the large liberty which the oral tradition must have allowed them. The fact that the language of all the evangelists, even that of Luke, who was a master of the pure Greek idiom, is that of a Hebraizing-Greek, is best explained by the assumption of an oral source sanctioned by constant usage; since it would otherwise be inexplicable that Luke, who wrote for Greeks, should not have elaborated the existing accounts in a language better suited to them. It is further argued that if such an oral type was the basis of our Gospels, there must arise an agreement in expression along with deviations in often unimportant synonyms, in peculiarities in adding single circumstances, and in the transposition or altered representation of the same thoughts, similar to the phenomena which these writings present.

It is supposed that among the apostles, the memory of each came to the assistance of that of the others, and that the men who were made fellow-laborers of the apostles were instructed by one of them in the presence of the rest, so that these memorabilia, or memoirs, assumed a tolerably fixed historical form which substantially appears in the similar parts of the synoptic Gospels. But since in the repetitions of the history considerable freedom of representation must be assumed, together with the admission into their discourses by the apostles of various circumstances and events drawn from the memory of each, the tradition must have been constantly changing internally and receiving additions. Hence the deviations from one another in our synoptic records. This originally Aramaic oral type of the Gospel-tradition was carefully translated into Greek, as considerable numbers of Hellenists were received into the Church. Finally, each of the evangelists adapted himself in the choice and use of the historical material of the tradition to the circle of readers for whom his work was primarily intended, so that Matthew wrote a purely Palestinian Gospel, Mark a modified Palestinian one, and Luke a Pauline work from the point of view of the great apostle's interpretation of Christianity.

Although this hypothesis sets out from a point of view which has much plausibility, and is, indeed, not without a considerable degree of justification, it is open to so many serious objections that it can hardly be regarded as a satisfactory solution of the problem in question. It has been received with favor by many Catholic and Protestant theologians probably in part for the reason that more than either of the other two theories it preserves the dignity of the evangelists as independent writers, and at the same time lends to their differences a relatively innocent appearance, so far as oral tradition in the nature of the case must offer more room for individual variations.*
Weiss attributes its popularity in some quarters to an apologetic interest which is zealous in denying the dependence of the evangelists on one another, or on written sources, in order not to be obliged through the establishment of either of these hypotheses too directly to acknowledge the human origin of our Gospels and the intentional variations of one writer from another. As the

* Holtzmann, Einleit. p. 357.

hypothesis of an original **Gospel when** developed as it was by its advocates explained the agreements of the several writers much better than their differences, while **the** assumed dependence on written sources allowed, perhaps, far too little play to their individuality, that **of an** oral original Gospel **has been** thought **to account for the** differences while **leaving the similarities unexplained.**

For how, asks Baur, can we make it intelligible to ourselves that the three evangelists, if they took the contents of their narratives from the common tradition, should agree as they do not only in the matter, but also literally in the expression? Still less is it explicable that this agreement is again only partial not with the three together, but only with two of them. If this verbal agreement of only two evangelists in certain cases has its ground in the tradition, then there must have been different branches of the tradition. But if the tradition was so divided as we find it in every such case, is not the conclusion to be drawn that it was, indeed, something so changeable and so variously modified that such a verbal agreement as exists with all the variations in a great part of the Gospel-history must be the greatest of riddles? It cannot, indeed, be denied that nothing is more natural and necessary than the assumption that the Gospel-history first propagated itself through oral tradition, which may have become at length a continuous source of evangelic narratives. Testimonies, such as that of Papias, show what importance was attached to it even in his time, when written Gospels were already in existence. But to refer all the antecedents of our Gospels to oral tradition alone is to disregard a very natural inference from the prologue to Luke's Gospel, in which written narratives (sources?) are expressly mentioned.* It has also been urged against

* Kritische Untersuch., etc. p. 33.

this hypothesis that there is no **historical evidence of the existence of such a** standing apostolical tradition **as it** assumes; that such a mechanism of memorizing as it requires is opposed to the entire **spirit and** activity of **the times;** that the want of agreement **in the synoptic narratives of the** most important events, the passion and resurrection of Christ, is irreconcilable with it; **and that** the chief mass of the synoptic historical material is of such a nature as to presuppose an antecedent literary form.* Mr. Norton has adopted this hypothesis, and given it an **elaborate** exposition. † He **has not,** however, removed **the objections which lie** against it. **Westcott has also advocated it, but with no better results.** ‡

4.—THE COURSE OF MORE RECENT CRITICISM.

The synoptic problem was apprehended by Schleiermacher from **a new point of view.** Rejecting the dilemma by which previous **inquiries had been limited, that there** must **have been** a dependence **of one of the** synoptists upon another **or an** original **source for** all, he sought **to explain the synoptic** phenomena by the assumption **of several sources, embracing only parts of the history, which were variously combined by the three writers of the Gospels. The oft-recurring appearance of parts of the history which are common to two or three, and** again of **parts which are peculiar to one or two, seemed to** this critic **to indicate several antecedent sources which the evangelists had partly in common, partly not, while the deviations in the order of the common narrative rendered** improbable **the assumption of an original writing** embracing **the entire history. The application of this** hypoth-

---

* Holtzmann, p. 358; Meyer, Commentar über das N. T. i. 1, p. 29.
† Gen. of the Gospels, i. Additional Notes, p. clxviii f.
‡ Introduction to the Study of the Gospels, etc. chap. iii.

esis, however, by its author to the Gospel of Luke,* which he broke up into numerous fragments, did not serve to commend it to the judgment of critics. Baur has characterized this criticism of the Gospels as arbitrary, ingenious, and, on the whole, resulting in dismemberment and dissolution.† Schleiermacher was, however, more successful in his famous treatise on the Testimony of Papias as to our first two Gospels, ‡ in which he argued that our first Gospel is founded on a collection of the sayings of Jesus made by Matthew, or the logia-collection of Papias, and a brief work by Mark.

De Wette, whose position has been characterized as one of "sceptical indecision," apprehended the synoptic problem substantially from Griesbach's point of view, holding that Mark's Gospel was an abridged combination of the other two. § He cast doubt upon the apostolic authorship of the first Gospel, held that of the second to be uncertain, and as to the third evangelist was sure only that he was a disciple of Paul. To John he accorded only a certain share in the fourth Gospel, the composition of which might have been the work of a disciple of that apostle.

The mythical view of the Gospel-history set forth by Strauss in his celebrated Life of Jesus ‖ was founded on the total untrustworthiness of the narratives of the New Testament, and resulted in giving a new impetus to scientific investigation into the origin of the Gospels. Among the writings which this work called forth that of Weisse is one of the most important not only for its intrinsic merits

---

* Kritischer Versuch über die Schriften des Lukas, 1817.
† Krit. Untersuch. p. 35.
‡ Werke zur Theologie, ii. p. 361 f.
§ Lehrbuch der hist.-krit. Einleit. in das N. T. 1826, 5th ed. 1848.
‖ Das Leben Jesu, 1st ed. 1835 ; 4th ed. 1840.

as a critical treatise on the Gospels, but also for the influence which it has exerted.* Without sympathy with Schleiermacher's predilection for the fourth Gospel, Weisse adopted in part the former's theory of the synoptics, and modified it to the effect that the writing by Mark, mentioned by Papias, was no other than essentially our canonical second Gospel; that our canonical first Gospel was composed from this and the logia-collection of Matthew, and that Luke is a freer revision of it. He is regarded as the real author of the so-called "conservative" † Mark-hypothesis.

This Mark-hypothesis was developed in a more radical way by Wilke,‡ who, while assuming a literary dependence of the synoptists on one another, called especial attention to the influence of the individual reflections of each as accounting for the differences in their narratives. His conclusion was that the Gospels "are formed on a literary plan, and are no compositions of legend or of oral tradition." This "literary plan" he traced to a written original Gospel, which was not with Eichhorn to be found outside the canon, but was, in fact, our canonical Mark, which Luke first revised, and finally, Matthew with the use of Luke's record. The little that Mark has which is not found in the other two records he regarded as later additions, whereby Hilgenfeld thinks, apparently without good reasons, that he gave the death-thrust to his hypothesis. §

The historical criticism of Baur marked an epoch in the study of the New Testament. Setting out from the study

---

* Die evangel. Gesch. kritisch und philosoph. bearbeitet, 1838.

† Hilgenfeld, Einleit. p. 191.

‡ Der Urevangelist, oder exegetisch-kritische Untersuch. der Verwandschafts-Verhältnisse der drei ersten Evangelien, 1838.

§ Kanon und Kritik, p. 163.

of the Epistles of Paul to the Romans and the Corinthians, in which he detected the strife of Jewish Christianity and Paulinism, he used this party-contest, which Semler had noted as a factor in the formation of the canon, as the key to the problems of Gospel-criticism. The Gospels, which Strauss had apprehended as the naïve productions of early Christian legend, and Wilke as works of literary reflection and intended oppositions, appeared to Baur as products of those partisan strifes and of their overcoming and adjustment in the catholic Church. For him the criticism which places the Gospels under the point of view of tendency-writings is rightly called historical, because it makes it its principal task to transport itself into the times out of which they proceeded. He began his criticism with the fourth Gospel, which he regarded as an ideal composition, a tendency-writing, which originated in the late transition-time from the oppositions of the Pauline and Jewish-Christian parties to their final accommodation in the catholic Church about the middle of the second century. The third Gospel was a purely Pauline writing in the original form in which Marcion had it, but in its revision by Luke in the canonical form it manifests the conciliatory tendency which appears in the Acts.* In regard to Mark, he accepted the theory of Griesbach, that it was a compilation or epitome made from the two other synoptics. It was a colorless writing, neutral with respect to the Pauline-Jewish controversy, and did not even possess independence. The first Gospel was the oldest, and in it appears the original Jewish-Christian view of Christianity. It received its present form about the year 130.† If

---

* Baur's opinions on Marcion's Gospel were somewhat modified at length by Volkmar's criticisms.

† Krit. Untersuch. über die kan. Evangel. 1847.

there is, said Baur, in the series of our canonical Gospels, one in which we have the substantial contents of the Gospel-history in an original, genuinely historical source, that can only be Matthew's Gospel. But he held that even in it the dogmatic point of view of the evangelist had influenced the representation of the facts. Absolute historical credibility could not, certainly, belong to a writing which was a later revision of Matthew's Hebrew Gospel with additions from tradition.

That Baur's criticism exceeded the right measure of moderation was conceded by some of the ablest of the adherents of his school. His position on the fourth Gospel has been ably contested by conservative scholars, and representatives of the critical tendency have found in the history of the canon attestation of a higher antiquity of the Gospels than he acknowledged. Hilgenfeld places Mark before Luke as a Petrine Gospel representing the transition from the Jewish Christianity of Matthew to the Paulinism of the third Gospel. The first Gospel, founded on a writing by Matthew (not, however, a mere collection of sayings of Jesus), which dates from the sixth decade of the first century, received, according to him, its present form through a free revision soon after the destruction of Jerusalem. The Jewish-Christian tendency of the original was counteracted in the revision in the interest of a freer interpretation of Christianity, and shows the influence of Pauline ideas. The third Gospel arose at about the end of the first century out of a Pauline revision of the first two and other Gospel-writings. Finally, on the basis of the preceding histories of Jesus in the heat of the Gnostic excitement from 120–140, the fourth Gospel was written by an unknown author.* The author of this theory claims

* Die Evangelien nach ihrer Entstehung und geschichtlichen Bedeutung, 1854; Einleit. in das N. T. 1875.

for it that it shows the process of the formation of the canonical Gospels to have begun in a genuinely historical basis in the circles and age of the original apostles, and to have passed through the principal phases of the primitive Christian consciousness.

While Schwegler * and Zeller † carried out the theories of the Tübingen school with considerable fidelity to the principles of its distinguished founder, Volkmar developed the tendency-idea to the most untenable extremes. According to him, all the Gospels, beginning with the supposed original Gospel of Mark, are purely tendency-writings composed in the interest of Paulinism, which was suppressed at first, at length victorious. Some real tradition from primitive apostolic times may be conceded to Mark, but the Gospel is not a writing of the interpreter of Peter, but a Pauline polemic against the Jewish-Christian tendencies of the Apocalypse. The third Gospel was called forth by Judaistic additions to the original Pauline Gospel, such as the genealogy of Jesus in Matthew, and the saying that Jesus came to fulfil the law, and was written between 100 and 105. But the harmonizing, Jewish-Christian-Pauline Gospel was that of Matthew, erroneously placed first in the canon, which combines the other two with an eye to both parties in the controversy. "The Gospel of the Logos," our fourth, he places at 155.‡

Ewald declared a war of extermination against all that bore the name of tendency-criticism. He was not, however, fortunate in his complicated scheme of Gospel-

---

* Das nachap. **Zeitalter,** 1846.

† Articles in Theol. Jahrbücher, 1842–1857. Die Apostelgeschichte nach ihrem Inhalt, etc. 1854. **Vorträge und Abhandlungen, etc. 1865.**

‡ Die Religion Jesu und ihre **erste Entwickelung, etc. 1857.** Der Ursprung unserer Evangelien, etc. 1866. Die Evangelien, **oder Marcus und die Synopsis der kan.** und ausserkan. Evang. 1870.

building, a combination of the conclusions of Eichhorn, Schleiermacher, and Weisse, along with a zealous defence of the apostolical origin of the fourth Gospel.* His scheme for the synoptics is the following: (1) The most ancient Hebrew Gospel probably by Philip, used by Paul; (2) the logia-collection by Matthew; (3) the first of the complete Gospels, that of Mark, not our canonical second Gospel, however, but an older writing mentioned by Papias; (4) the first book of the "higher history," a new edition of No. 1; (5) the existing Gospel of Matthew, founded on Mark and the logia; (6-8) "traces of a sixth, seventh, and eighth demonstrable book"; (9) Luke, which concludes the development of the Gospel-literature by using the preceding writings, with the exception of Matthew, and making a few additions, "so that this great work has still more than our present Matthew the character of a mere collection without much inner connection." This wonderful hypothesis on the origin of the synoptic Gospels has never secured the approval of critics, and could not, indeed, make its way with all its arbitrary assumptions and want for the most part of historical support.

Much simpler is the solution of Meyer, the eminent commentator on the New Testament. He reasons that since the testimony of Papias on the writing of Mark furnishes no reason for regarding this writing as different from our canonical second Gospel; since our Matthew is not identical with the logia which tradition ascribes to this apostle, but is an unapostolic historical work which gradually grew out of this original writing; since, finally, Luke, who presupposes an evangelic literature, and wrote

* Jahrbücher der biblischen Wissenschaft, 1849-61. Die drei ersten Evangelien, etc. 1850. Gesch. Christus, etc. 1855.

after the destruction of Jerusalem, must in any case be regarded as the last of the synoptists, therefore the Gospel of Mark (all theories of an original Mark being rejected as untenable) presents itself as the oldest Gospel and the determining standard of the other two in connection with oral tradition and other writings employed as sources. The author of Mark used the logia-collection of Matthew according to his peculiar purpose, which did not lead him to make a detailed report of discourses. As the original logia-collection gradually took the form of the Gospel according to the Hebrews, that of Mark must have influenced its formation in respect to contents and the course of the history. At length, when Matthew was finally edited as our Greek Gospel, Mark was doubtless used in such a way as to afford an explanation of the frequent similarity of expressions in the parts common to both. Later, again, Luke must have had Mark among his sources; and so the way in which the latter has been used has given rise to the appearance that it stood between the other two as dependent and a mere borrower. But in respect to this appearance great injustice has been done to Mark in the hypothesis of Griesbach, particularly as applied by De Wette, Baur, Köstlin, and Bleek. If, then, along with oral tradition, the logia of Matthew and our Mark must be regarded as the chief written sources of our first Gospel, to which latter it often holds the relation of omitting or making excerpts, there must also have been other Gospel-writings which were used in the composition of it. Certainly recognizable are such single writings in the genealogy and the prehistorical accounts, and less certainly determinable, yet not to be denied, are they in the further course of the history.*

* Krit.-exeget. Commentar über das N. T. 5te Aufl. 1864, i. 1, p. 35 f.

5.—CONCLUSIONS REGARDING THE SYNOPTIC PROBLEM.

In the foregoing historical survey of the course of critical inquiry into the composition and relation of the synoptic Gospels no attempt has been made at completeness, and the works of many distinguished scholars have not been mentioned. Its purpose has been accomplished if there have been shown certain well-defined and persistent tendencies, which may be regarded as prophetic and determinative of the conclusions which this inquiry has reached after a century's investigation and discussion. In the first place, it is evident that neither the hypothesis of the use of the work of one evangelist by another in any form whatever, nor that of an original Gospel, nor that of oral tradition, has been able to maintain itself as alone furnishing an adequate solution of the synoptic problem. In the second place, the course of criticism clearly indicates a tendency towards a combination of some of the features of the hypotheses of Griesbach, Eichhorn, and Gieseler. Finally, there is manifested in the course of criticism a persistent and indomitable tendency to hold to the priority of Mark, and to regard this Gospel, along with the original logia-collection of Matthew, as the chief source of the first Gospel in its present form and of Luke's record. Some attempts have, however, been made in recent times to revive the theory of Griesbach, for example by Bleek in general agreement with De Wette and by Delitzsch, Kahnis, and Nösgen in a dogmatic interest.

The most important critical investigations of the first three Gospels in recent times have been chiefly occupied with the further development of the hypothesis of Weisse,* which, as has been shown, assumes the dependence of our

---

* With a few notable exceptions, particularly Hilgenfeld.

canonical Matthew and Luke upon Mark regarded as an original source.* Weiss has attempted to supplement and correct this hypothesis by showing that the oldest written source, Matthew's logia, was not merely, as has been held by very many scholars since Schleiermacher, a collection of the sayings of Jesus, but contained also considerable narrative. He also holds that this writing was known to Mark and used by him in the composition of his Gospel. The solution of Holtzmann was somewhat different in his work on the synoptics published in 1863. He concluded that it was not our present Mark which lay at the basis of the synoptic narrative, but an original Mark, the work which he believed to have been referred to by Papias, and that our second Gospel was derived from it. This hypothesis found much favor, and was adopted by Schenkel in his life of Jesus, and by other critics of note.† But the distinguishing of our Mark from the supposed original Mark presented great difficulties, and Weiss claims to have detected repeatedly the untenableness of the various forms which the hypothesis

---

* This hypothesis has been supported in some of its various forms chiefly by Weisse, Die evangel. Gesch. 1838, Die Evangelienfrage, 1856; Wilke, Der Urevangelist, 1838; Reuss, Gesch. der heil. Schr. N. T. 6te Aufl. 1887; Ewald, Die drei ersten Evangel. 2te Aufl. 1871; Ritschl, in Theol. Jahrbücher, 1851; Réville, Études sur l'Évangile selon Matthieu, 1862; Renan, Vie de Jesus, 17me ed. 1882, Les Évangiles, 1877; Holtzmann, Die Synoptischen Evangelien, 1863, Einleit. 1887; Hausrath, Neutest. Zeitgesch. i. 1879; Scholten, Das älteste Evangel. 1869; Jacobsen, Untersuch., etc. 1883; Volkmar, Die Evangel. 1870; Pfleiderer, Das Urchristenthum, 1887, with the order Mark, Luke, Matthew; Weizsäcker, Untersuch., etc. 1864; Wendt, Die Lehre Jesu, 1886; Weiss, Einleit. 1886; Brückner, Die vier Evangel. 1887.

† Weisse and Wilke before him were obliged to assume that a form of Mark somewhat different from our present second Gospel lay before Matthew and Luke.

has taken in the hands of its advocates, Beyschlag, Scholten, Weizsäcker, and others. Holtzmann himself appears practically to have abandoned it at length,* and besides, to hold with Wendt, Jacobsen, Mangold, and others that Matthew was known to Luke, and used by him at least in a subsidiary way. †

It is conceded, however, that the first Gospel contains indications of great antiquity, since it has words ascribed to Jesus which clearly show an intention apparently held during a greater part of the Galilean period of his ministry to confine his work within the limits and to the law and customs of Judaism. The declaration that he is sent only to the lost sheep of the house of Israel, and the injunction to his disciples to go only to these, are found in no other Gospel. The same is true of the saying that he came not to destroy but to fulfil the law and the prophets. ‡ It is questioned whether these features are really historical which represent the mission of Jesus as a development of Judaism, or are to be charged to the acknowledged fact that this Gospel was intended for and adapted to the Jewish Christians. Their original character appears in most cases to be indicated by the fact that the other evangelists show traces of either intentionally omitting the passages or mitigating their force. Although these features of originality appear in the first Gospel, they are overbalanced by certain decisive marks of a later and derivative origin. For criticism finds the representation of the history to rest upon an arrangement of the material according to the subject-matter, which is carried out through most of the narrative, an artificial grouping of it which is dominated by a certain numerical symbolism of the genuine Jewish sort, as twice seven numbers of three

---

* Einleit. in das N. T. p. 357. † Weiss, Einleit. in das N. T. p. 485.
‡ Chap. xv. 24, x. 6, v. 17.

generations, three temptations in the desert and in Gethsemane, seven parables, seven woes, etc. A work showing throughout so systematic an arrangement, so much reflection and art in selection and composition, could hardly be the first record of the evangelic history.*

On the contrary, the priority of Mark is capable of being shown with great probability, not so much by a detailed comparison of parallel passages and in a mechanical way as by a study of his entire conception and plan of the history. It has been shown with tolerable clearness that in Mark the whole narrative is presented in its simplest, fundamental form. In fact, it is only in his Gospel that the great epochs of the Galilean ministry of Jesus can be shown with clearness. In this respect he alone represents the unity of the historical course of events which runs through the synoptical narratives, and has preserved their historical thread. If we take the succession of single narratives in Mark, and place on one side that in Matthew and on the other that in Luke, we can demonstrate step by step that each of the two others presupposes this as the original one.† With this theory that Mark is the oldest of the Gospels agree the distinguishing internal character of his record, the absence of all that is prehistorical, the immediate beginning of the history with the appearance of the Baptist, the undeveloped account of the temptation, the freedom from legendary interpolations in the history of the passion which are found in Matthew, the objectivity without theological intention and method, and especially the character of the immediate vivacity, picturesqueness, and clearness of the delineations and descriptions.‡

Of especial significance in favor of Mark's originality

---

* Holtzmann, Einleit. p. 366.   † Holtzmann, Einleit. p. 367.
‡ Meyer, Commentar, i. p. 36.

and priority is thought to be the consistent and steady progress in his narrative with reference to Jesus' proclamation of himself as the Messiah, in contrast with the confused and contradictory delineation of Matthew. In Mark it is neither John the Baptist nor the disciples who first recognize the Messiahship of Jesus, but the demoniacs.* An injunction of silence is laid upon them even after they have once proclaimed him before a multitude. A similar reserve is practised in the cure of the blind man at Bethsaida, and in two other cases which have parallels in Matthew. † In both cases Matthew omits the injunction of silence, apparently because in his narrative Jesus is openly proclaimed as Messiah from the beginning. In these omissions the dependence and secondary character of Matthew's record are thought to be indicated, and still more is this the case in places in which he appears to forget his part, as when Jesus having healed a leper in the presence of a great multitude, the injunction to tell no one is subjoined! But according to Mark the cure is privately performed in a house. ‡ Still more striking is it that just before the choice of the apostles Jesus heals many, according to Mark, and lays on the *demons* the injunction of silence, while Matthew abbreviates the account to the effect that many followed Jesus, and he healed them *all*, and enjoined them to tell no one! § Yet already his healing power had been represented as publicly known. ‖ Here Matthew appears to have retained a sentence of his original with an incorrect reference, so that his account becomes unintelligible. Again, only in Mark does Jesus'

---

* Chap. i. 24, 34, v. 7.
† Chap. viii. 22–26, v. 45, vii. 36 ; *cf.* Matt. ix. 26, 33.
‡ Matt. viii. 4 ; Mark i. 43, ἐξέβαλεν, sent him out [of the house].
§ Mark iii. 10–12 ; Matt. xii. 15, 16.
‖ Chap. iv. 23–25, ix. 26, 31, 33, 35.

saying to Peter when the latter proclaimed him have consistency, while in Matthew the apostles are represented as all along familiar with the idea of his Messiahship. In dealing with elements which constitute the kernel of the Gospel-history, there can hardly be any question whether priority and originality belong to the writer, who with consistency and unbroken purpose, carries out an idea, or to the one who represents the matter now in a self-contradictory way and now in opposition to the peculiarity of the other.*

A similar phenomenon is presented in the representations by the two evangelists of the ability of the disciples to understand Jesus. Mark carries out with great consistency the idea of their slowness of apprehension, while Matthew in many cases presents the opposite conception, and again, apparently influenced by Mark's narrative, falls into agreement with him. In respect to comprehending the parable of the sower, Matthew represents the disciples as those who have and to whom more shall be given, while in Mark they appear as not comprehending the parable at all and in peril of being deprived of what they have.† At the stilling of the tempest both evangelists, indeed, represent the disciples as having little faith, but in Matthew the words, "Who then is this that the winds and the sea obey him?" are put into the mouth of the people, while in Mark it is the disciples to whom they are attributed.‡ In like manner, in the account of the walking of Jesus on the water, Matthew makes the disciples confess that Jesus is the Son of God, while Mark represents them as without insight and hard of heart.§ The

---

* Ritschl, Theol. Jahrbücher, 1852, p. 515.
† Matt. xiii. 11, 12 ; Mark iv. 13, 25, 29.
‡ Matt. viii. 27 ; Mark iv. 41 ; Meyer, Commentar in loc.
§ Matt. xiv. 33 ; Mark vi. 51 f.

unfitting request of the sons of Zebedee is ascribed by Mark to these disciples themselves, but by Matthew to their mother, while the latter follows Mark in representing Christ's answer as addressed to the sons, wherein it would appear that he added the mother's part in the interest of his theory of the insight of the disciples, and in so doing confused the narrative.

The oldest source of the Gospel-history, the apostolical writing by Matthew in Aramaic referred to by Papias, was undoubtedly used along with Mark by the first evangelist, and there is a very strong probability that it was also used by Luke. Favorable to this latter theory is the fact that Matthew and Luke have many fragments of discourses in common which are not found in Mark. These are so similiar in details of expression as to indicate that they were taken from a common source.* The "great interpolation" in the midst of Luke's narrative, † by which his agreement with Mark, whom he follows to this point, is interrupted, and the common thread of the narrative broken, furnishes an illustration. It has been pointed out that the greater part of the discourses which Luke isolates in this section are found in Matthew in different relations so as not to form sections, but to be brought into an already existing connection which they fill out along with sentences from Mark. In the sermon on the mount in Matthew a collection of sayings, probably spoken at different times, is given the appearance of a single discourse of instructions to the disciples. Again, seven parables are grouped together according to the writer's favorite numerical symbolism.‡ If we compare the sermon on the mount in Matthew with Luke, chapter

---

* For example, the unusual word, $\dot{\epsilon}\pi\iota\omicron\acute{\upsilon}\sigma\iota\omicron\nu$, Matt. vi. 11 ; Luke xi. 3.
† Chap. ix. 51—xviii. 14.   ‡ Matt. xiii.

vi., it will appear that the former inserts some passages in the great discourse which Luke alone appears to have in their right connection, since in the latter they follow words which give occasion for them.* The series of sayings concerning anxiety and the laying up of treasures appears in Luke in connection with a logical motive, but in the sermon on the mount detached, without motive, and in a reversed order.† A large number of similar illustrations might be quoted. There is a difference of opinion on the question whether the apothegms and short discourses which Luke presents detached and scattered were by him torn out of the "architectonic structures" of Matthew, or appear in his record in their original relations. Which is the more probable, asks Holtzmann, that Luke wantonly shattered the great structures and scattered the fragments to the four winds, or that out of what lay before the former as heaps of stones Matthew constructed these walls? To this critic the true solution of the problem appears to be that Luke had the source from which Matthew constructed his compositions of the discourses, but that to the former does not belong in all cases the priority in the framing of the single discourses and sayings. The suggestion of Strauss appears to come of a clear insight: "The pithy sayings of Jesus could not, indeed, be dissolved by the flood of the oral tradition, but were, perhaps, not seldom torn from their natural connection, floated away from their original strata, and landed like fragments of rock in places where they did not really belong." The hypothesis accordingly appears reasonable that in the earliest tradition the sayings of Jesus were handed down only as isolated fragments, and not until

---

* Matt. vi. 7–13, vii. 7–11; Luke xi. 1–13.
† Luke xii. 22–34; Matt. vi. 19–21, 25–34.

later were inquiries raised as to the occasions which gave rise to them. In some cases these inquiries appear to have been fruitless, so that it remains unknown what were the circumstances to which are to be referred the woes pronounced upon Bethsaida and Chorazin, the allusion to the sacrificed Galileans and the tower of Siloam. Accordingly, Holtzmann is led to conjecture that in the source in question, the original logia, the fragments followed one another as do the aphorisms in Hippokrates, since on no other supposition can the discourses of Jesus, which have no fixed place in the Gospel-history, appear in Matthew at one point of their wandering and in Luke at another.

Notwithstanding the objections of Wendt, Weiss' position, previously referred to, that the logia-source was known to Mark appears to be well taken. Assuming the entire independence of this Gospel as to the first and third, it is difficult to explain its origin without supposing the use of a written source. The discourse on the Parousia* is far too extended to have been propagated by oral tradition, and shows to a critical analysis a series of insertions and additions which are so much opposed to an original form of it that it must have been known to the author in a written form. The fragments of the discourse of Jesus in his own defence against the charge that he was in league with Beelzebub, of that on the occasion of sending out his disciples, and of that regarding the strife for precedence on the part of two of the twelve, † may with more reason than in the preceding case be thought to rest upon oral tradition. But it has been pointed out that in spite of the greater freedom with which these are reproduced in comparison with the original tradition in the older source, their verbal expression shows so great a

* Chap. xiii. † Chap. iii. 23-39, vi. 7-11, x. 42-45.

similarity with that of the logia preserved in the first and third Gospels that they can hardly be regarded as constructed independently of that document. Nearly all the sayings preserved by Mark outside the immediate connection of his narrative may be traced to reminiscences of discourses and series of apothegms whose existence in the logia may be shown with great probability, and the same is true of the verbal expression in these cases. It is difficult to think of the parables preserved in Mark as independent of those contained in the logia-source. The parable of the mustard-seed is apparently a graphic transformation of the first parable of the pair from the logia in Luke.* Of the parable of the sower there is a far simpler and more original statement in the source, † and the simile of the kingdom of God drawn from the sower is a transformation of a parable in the first Gospel. ‡ The only other parable which Mark has, that of the laborers in the vineyard, must have been derived from the source in question, since the text in Matthew appears to be more original, § and the interpretation which is retained is in conflict with the application borrowed from Mark. ‖ In the source it may have been one of a pair of parables with that of the marriage-feast, which the first evangelist connects with it. ¶

It is perhaps needless to pursue into greater detail the discussion of the synoptic problem. Even if the logia-source be not established in the third Gospel, the dependence of the latter on Mark is hardly open to question;

* Chap. iv. 30 f. ; Luke xiii. 18-21.
† Chap. iv. 3-9 ; Luke viii. 5-8.
‡ Chap. iv. 26-29 ; Matt. xiii. 24-30.
§ Chap. xii. 1-9 ; Matt. xxi. 33-41.
‖ Matt. xxi. 43.
¶ Matt. xxii. 1-14 ; Weiss, Einleitung.

and if we leave undetermined the question whether or no its author used the first Gospel, it would appear that we have in the relations of writings and documents already set forth ample means for the explanation of the synoptic phenomena, so far as they are capable of explanation. The logia-source written by Matthew and understood according to Schleiermacher's interpretation of Papias and the priority of Mark which may be regarded as an incontestable conclusion of recent Gospel-criticism furnish the key to the solution of the problem of the relation of the synoptic Gospels. The agreements and similarities in the three records find an adequate explanation in the use by the first and third evangelists of these two sources. The differences in the records are to be explained by the dependence of the writers to some extent on oral tradition and uncanonical written sources and by the individuality and literary independence of each.

Those readers who shall have had the patience to study the foregoing review of the course of investigation of the synoptic question will not fail to see the importance of the discussion of it to Gospel-criticism and the connection of the problem with many inquiries with which this is concerned.

CHAPTER IV.

THE GOSPEL ACCORDING TO MARK.

THAT our second canonical Gospel originated with a certain John Mark is the unanimous testimony of tradition. While this testimony is too vague to afford precise information as to the nature and extent of his connection with the composition of the writing, it particularizes the circumstance that he was intimately associated with the Apostle Peter.* Through Barnabas, to whom he appears to have been related by blood, he came into connection with Paul, and was the occasion of a dispute and separation between these two missionaries.† The tradition of his connection with Peter runs back to Papias, who depended, it appears, on a certain presbyter John for his information, according to whom Mark wrote down, so far as he remembered them and without order, the sayings and doings of Jesus as he had heard them from Peter. This tradition is largely dependent, as to its historical worth, upon the degree in which it is confirmed by a critical analysis of the Gospel. In some respects the account of Papias corresponds very well with the phe-

---

* Pupil, companion, and interpreter. Whether by this last term we are to understand, according to some critics, a linguistic assistant, or, according to others, a clerk, is not important. See Acts xii. 12; I. Peter v. 13. There appears to be no good reason for the conjecture of Grotius, Schleiermacher, and others that two persons of the name of Mark are to be distinguished in the New Testament.

† Acts xii. 25, xv. 37 ff.

nomena which the record presents. For this Gospel is distinguished in some parts among the synoptics for a vivid and life-like delineation which suggests the eye-witness. Among its peculiarities have been noticed a predilection for the story and the inner life of the disciples and a proportionally large number of narratives in which they are immediately concerned, particularly the three confidential friends of Jesus. The entire first part of the Gospel concerns affairs of which the first visit of Jesus at Peter's house forms the centre, and the climax is reached in the graphic scene of the Messianic confession of this apostle, who finally is especially mentioned at the close of the record, as one to whom the risen Christ would show himself.

To the objection that the testimony of the presbyter John does not apply to our canonical Mark, since this does not show the want of order ($\tau\acute{\alpha}\xi\iota\varsigma$) which he remarked in the writing of which Papias speaks on his authority in Eusebius' account,[*] it should be said that his judgment in the matter must be considered from his own point of view. If he judged it in this regard from a comparison of it with an arrangement of the discourses of Jesus in another work known to him, and that writing were the logia-collection of Matthew, it can only be concluded that in his opinion the order of the latter was the more original, as indeed it may have been if it contained, as some scholars suppose, along with the discourses of Jesus some slight connecting and explanatory narrative. Such a work, written by an eye-witness, might, even though it were very brief, have better answered than Mark's record to the presbyter's conception of the true order of the course of events. The worth of his judgment must also be deter-

[*] Hist. Eccl. iii. 39.

mined to some extent by the consideration that he could have had no very accurate knowledge of the actual order of the events of the life of Jesus. Davidson, whose advocacy of the Griesbach-hypothesis necessitates the placing of the composition of Mark after that of the two other synoptics, denies the applicability of the presbyter's testimony to our canonical second Gospel, because it is as much an orderly narrative as either of the others, as if the presbyter had given any intimation of a knowledge of these, or could, indeed, have had any acquaintance with them!*

While a critical analysis of the Gospel shows that the judgment of the presbyter and Papias as to the arrangement of the events of the life of Jesus is correct, since such an analysis results in finding that the evangelist in setting down from memory the teachings of Peter has rather followed an order determined by the subject-matter than attempted a strictly chronological account, there is no reason for regarding the tradition as an exhaustive and conclusive statement of the origin of the record in question.† The entire literary character of the Gospel is incompatible with the theory that its author was a mere clerk, who slavishly followed the preaching of Peter. If we may judge of the character of the preaching of this apostle from the record of it in the Acts, this Gos-

---

* Introduction to the Study of the New Testament, ii. p. 80.

† The tradition has internal and external evidences of trustworthiness. But a knowledge of the natural history of traditions warns us not to receive them uncritically. One form of this tradition, for example, represents Mark as having written after the death of Peter, and from another we learn that Peter was alive when the evangelist composed his record, and that he appeared quite indifferent to the work, neither hindering nor encouraging it. Again, the latter tradition has no support in the evident relation of the synoptics, since it places first the composition of the Gospels containing the genealogies, thus putting the writing of Mark's record after that of Luke's.

pel is far from being a reproduction of it. The extended discourse on the Parousia and several series of sayings besides can hardly have been carried in the memory either of Peter or his interpreter, and are probably free compositions. There are some sections which find their most probable explanation by the hypothesis that pithy sayings of Jesus which were well adapted to be remembered were set down without regard in all cases to the circumstances which called them forth. The tradition is doubtless accounted for and satisfied by the supposition that the teaching of Peter as Mark remembered its salient features was one of the sources of the Gospel, while there is nothing irreconcilable with it in the assumption that other sources which may have been available were also used. If we waive the claim of those critics who find that the author made extracts from Matthew's logia, there remain the abundant oral tradition from which he may have drawn and, perhaps, his own knowledge as an eyewitness of the closing scenes of the life of Jesus.

There is great probability that the fragments which form the series of narratives which Mark may have elaborated from suggestions received in listening to the instructions of Peter were not only connected by passages supplied by himself, but even enlarged by additions from other sources. A critical study of the discourse on the Parousia in the thirteenth chapter previously referred to and a comparison of it with the parallels in the first and third Gospels have convinced many critics of the first rank that it contains two different and independent sections, one of which is probably a fragment of a current Jewish apocalyptic composition.* In connection with the

* Chap. xiii. 1-6, 9 b-13, 21-23, 28, 29, 32-37. See Colani, Jésus Christ et les Croyances, etc., 1864; Weizsäcker, Untersuchungen, etc. 1864;

words of Jesus regarding **divorce is** inserted the statement peculiar to **Mark** that "**if she [the wife] put away her husband and marry another she committeth adultery.**" This passage is of **questionable** originality, **and appears to put into** the mouth of Jesus a reference **to a custom among the** Greeks and Romans regarding divorce.* **A Jewish woman** could not divorce **her husband. The account of the widow's mite has been thought by some critics to present a difficulty if regarded as history, since Jesus could hardly have known that the amount which she put into the treasury constituted her whole living. But as Jesus elsewhere** relates parables as if they **were historical** narratives,† it is probable that **this** was originally **a** parable which Mark, because it was not designated as parabolical, took for history, and so represented it.

The relation of this **Gospel to the first is a much contested question, and has already been considered briefly in the chapter on the synoptic problem. A few considerations should, however, be added here. Some sayings of** Jesus in the second Gospel appear **to show a dependence on their** parallels in the first, **and cannot, indeed, be regarded as framed without reference to them.** Notwithstanding the great freedom **with** which **they are given, and the appearance** which **they** present of **resting on an independent oral tradition, a** critical comparison of their phraseology **with that of the parallels indicates a contact**

Pfleiderer, Jahrb. für deutsche Theol., **1868**; Weiffenbach, **Der Wiederkunftsgedanke Jesu, 1873**; Wendt, Die **Lehre Jesu**, i. **1886. See Chapter VIII. of this work.**

* Wendt, Die Lehre Jesu, i. p. 40; Meyer, Commentar. i. 2, p. 140. **Baur regards** the passage as a **reflection of** Mark regarding the equality of **the sexes, but it** is more probably **referable to his acquaintance** with the **Roman custom.**

† Chap. iv. 3, xii. 1.

of the author with the latter, even though only through memory.* The saying of Jesus given in chapter ix. 35, and again in x. 43, shows on comparing it with its parallel that it is given once with a certain independence and again as if a recollection of the phraseology of the parallel had influenced the form of statement. So in chapter x. 46–52, although there is an appearance of independence, a trace is observed of a recollection of the phraseology of Matt. ix. 27–31. The mere reference to the temptation of Jesus is generally regarded as presupposing an acquaintance with an account of it more in detail. The undeniably secondary character of some passages in Mark is, then, opposed to the hypothesis of its priority. This fact led Wilke to assume later additions to Mark, Weisse to the hypothesis that certain passages which the other two Gospels contain over Mark originally stood in the latter, and Holtzmann to his former theory of an original Mark. The hypothesis, however, that Mark was acquainted with and indirectly at least used the logia-source of the first Gospel explains the secondary character of many of his passages, and solves some of the principal difficulties of the problem. At all events, no solution is practicable which attempts to explain the phenomena in question by the mere dependence of one of the synoptists upon one or both of the others. Mark's record, then, appears to be the oldest Gospel, though not the oldest writing dealing with the Gospel-history.

Some of the more extended historical passages may very likely have been derived from oral tradition. The detail with which some of these are presented is foreign to the later tradition as it appears in the first and third Gospels, and has been thought to denote the antiquity of

* Weiss, Das Marcusevangelium, 1872, p. 11.

that which is here preserved. The account of the ministry of the Baptist; of the baptism and temptation of Jesus; of the storm on the lake; of the raising of the daughter of Jairus; of the first feeding of the multitude; of the transfiguration, and the healing of the demoniac which immediately follows it, present now in brevity, now in vivid detail, the appearance of originality. In the second account of the feeding of the multitude the similarity of the circumstances with those of the former leads to the belief that it is a duplicate narrative of the same event, and that its repetition is due to the fact that the writer had two traditions before him with different statements of the numbers of the multitude. The tendency to such a change of numbers in the current tradition is illustrated in the accounts of the feeding of the multitude in the first Gospel, where for the "five thousand men" of Mark's narrative, in the one case, and the "about four thousand" in the other, we have "about five thousand men besides women and children" and "about four thousand men besides children and women"* respectively, thus at least doubling the numbers. An indication of a tendency to think parabolic sayings into parabolic acts appears in the narrative of the barren fig-tree through the connection in which Mark places the event with the words of Jesus in regard to the faith which might remove a mountain,† and through the symbolic reference to the judgment on the unfruitful Jewish people which is implied in the position given to the act. For in Luke's Gospel the tradition of the saying about the power of faith appears with the example of a sycamine-tree instead of a mountain, and a parable is related touching the judgment

---

* Chap. vi. 44, viii. 9; Matt. xiv. 21, xv. 38.
† Chap. xi. 12-14, 20-23.

upon the Jews in which a fig-tree is taken as the figure.*
In fact, the third evangelist appears to have exercised a
critical discrimination when, in his reproduction of Mark's
narrative, he has passed over the second account of the
feeding of the multitude, as well as the story of the
blasted fig-tree. There is, perhaps, a legendary expansion
of history in the general delineation of healings in the
sixth chapter, particularly in the closing remark,† for the
manner of healing here described is not in harmony with
Jesus' work elsewhere described by Mark, while it accords
very well with the conception of the unlimited wonder-
working of Jesus which the later tradition presents.‡

The most salient and striking literary peculiarity of this
Gospel is its vivid, graphic delineation. The writer is not
fettered by the requirements of a chronological order nor
encumbered with a dogmatic pragmatism. Those critics
who, like Volkmar and, in a less degree, Pfleiderer,§ find
in this record a marked Pauline "tendency" have greatly
mistaken its scope and purpose. Striving only to be
natural and direct, Mark has unconsciously produced a
picture. The reader sees Jesus surrounded by crowds of
people to whom he dispenses teaching and healing, his
vain attempts to withdraw into seclusion, and his miracles
made the theme of public talk in spite of his endeavors to
the contrary.‖ The places where events occur are sketched
with accuracy, and the situation is given in detail, even to

---

* Luke xiii. 6–9. † Verses 54–56.

‡ For example, instead of the "many" who, according to Mark i. 34, iii. 10, were healed by Jesus, Matthew and Luke report that "all" were cured. Matt. viii. 16, xii. 15; Luke iv. 40, vi. 19. Wendt, Die Lehre Jesu, i. p. 41 f.

§ Volkmar, Die Religion Jesu, p. 263 f; Pfleiderer, Das Urchristenthum, p. 359 f.

‖ Chap. i. 32 f, 36 f, 45 f, ii. 13, iii. 7 f, iv. 1 f, etc.

the vivid representation of the method of effecting a cure, the circumstances, gestures, emotions which accompany the act, and the effects which it produces.* The demoniacs are placed before us with their piteous and strange words and their terrible violence. **We see in the Gospel,** as in a panorama, how the ministry **of Jesus, beginning in** the vicinity of **the** Sea **of** Galilee and **taking** Capernaum **as its centre, extends in ever wider circles, and** how **the fame of the teacher spreads in all directions, and attracts increasing multitudes.** Over against the enthusiastic **crowds of** the common **people** appear **on the scene** the ominous forms of the scribes and Pharisees, whose opposition, rapidly rising to mortal enmity, is brought to view by a series of narratives expressly chosen for this purpose.† At the close of his ministry he is placed in Jerusalem in the midst of these **hostile forces** and tendencies, **the high-priests, the pharisees, the sadducees, the** scribes, and **even** the **party of the Herodians repeatedly mentioned by Mark.**‡ Again, we see how, out of the crowds of people who press about Jesus **for the sake of his** healing **powers or** from curiosity, who **first hail him as** Messiah, and finally **clamor** for his death, there gradually detaches itself a little **company of hearers** eager to learn of him;§ we learn of his relations to his kindred;∥ we hear of the women who **remain true** to him even at the cross and the tomb; of the **unknown man who** furnished the **colt, and put at his disposal** the room for **the passover-supper; of the youth who** followed him **to Gethsemane; of Simon** the Cyrenæan, who bore **his cross;** and of Joseph of Arimathæa, who provided a burial-place. **We see how he stands related to**

---

* See the healings, chap. vii. 31, **viii. 22-26.**
† Chap. ii. 1–iii. 6. § Chap. iii. 34, iv. 10.
‡ Chap. xi. 27–xii. 40, iii. 6, xii. 13. ∥ Chap. iii. 26, 31 f.

his disciples, and how the weakness of **their faith and their slowness of heart are again and again set forth, until finally he devotes himself almost** wholly **to their culture.** Out of the circle of the twelve, however, detaches itself a smaller group of his confidential friends, **among whom Peter is the foremost, whose great confession constitutes the climax of** the narrative. It is incorrect to say that **the Gospel is** occupied solely with the acts of Jesus. It is true that, apart from the discourse on the Parousia, no discourses are given **for the** sake of their doctrinal contents alone. What he taught **in the synagogue is not** communicated, but the **impression of his manner of teaching is** graphically delineated.* **The Gospel abounds in life-like conversations which show vividly the striking manner in which Jesus could answer questions and repel attacks. For the reason that it so immediately and** graphically represents **the event,** the writer **has a** predilection for the dialogue **and** the direct discourse, and even preserves some **Aramaic** words of Jesus.†

The linguistic usage of the writer is well **adapted to be** the expression of **the** literary character of the **work.** A critical examination of his style has shown **a** predilection **for the graphic imperfect tense and the vivid** historical **present ; for making** conspicuous the beginning of an act ;‡ **for plastic, marked,** highly-colored expressions, and especially **for** diminutives ; for formulas of comparison of **all sorts ;§ for a doubling** of the expression for the same thing, in particular **the negation ;** the connecting **of the positive and negative expressions ;** and for the **ever-recurring** εὐθύς,

---

* Chap. i. 21 f, vi. 2.
† Weiss, Einleit. p. 501. Das Marcusevangelium, p. 26.
‡ ἤρξατο twenty-six times.
§ πολύς forty-three times, πολλά fifteen times.

which is used forty times.* The narrative is also marked by an emphatic circumstantiality of expression; the repetition of the same or related words; the name instead of the pronoun; the frequent abundance of pronominal and adverbial terms; the paraphrase of the finite verb by εἶναι with a participle. The language is strongly Hebraistic, as is shown especially by the long-drawn-out constructions with καί and δέ. Participial constructions are comparatively rare, but when they do appear are sometimes clumsily heaped up.

The tradition concerning the composition of the Gospel favors Rome as the place where it was written. The internal evidences tend to confirm this tradition, the explanation of Aramaic words and Jewish customs † indicating that the Gospel was written for gentile readers. In favor of its Roman origin are the reference to the Roman custom in regard to divorce; the reduction of a coin to the Roman quadrans; ‡ the presupposition of the reader's acquaintance with Pilate; § and the mention of Alexander and Rufus, sons of Simon, as if they were well-known Christians in Rome, one of whom, Rufus, may be referred to by Paul in the Epistle to the Romans. ‖ The apparent object with which the Gospel was written furnishes the only indication attainable of the time of its composition. This object was not so much to present a chronological history of the life of Jesus as to encourage the believers in him by showing, in the first place, evidences

---

* Peculiar is the pregnant use of εἰς, of the ὅτι recitative, and of many Latin words, (κεντυρίων, κράβατος, ξέστης, πραιτώριον, κοδράντης, σπεκουλάτωρ, φραγελλοῦν), and phrases, chapter ii. 23, perhaps, and xv. 15.

† Chap. vii. 3 f, xiv. 12, xv. 6, 42. Davidson, ii. p. 119 f. Weiss, Einleit. p. 502.

‡ Chap. xii. 42. § Chap. xv. 1. ‖ Rom. xvi. 23; Mark xv. 21.

that he had adequately confirmed his Messianic character by his life and teachings, and, in the second place, by setting forth the promise of his early return in glory. The Gospel appears from the thirteenth chapter to have been written under the shadow of the impending overthrow of Jerusalem, at a time when the hope of the Christians in the Parousia was flagging. It is thought by some critics to represent a loosening of the immediate connection between the destruction of Jerusalem and the second coming of Christ. There is also wanting in it all reference to the overthrow of the city as an event already consummated even in the prophetic words in the second verse of the thirteenth chapter.* The most probable conjecture appears to be that which places its composition in the last years of the sixties, at which time Matthew's logia may very likely have existed in a Greek translation in Rome.† The record ends at chap. xvi. 8, and contains no account of an appearance of Jesus after his death.

* Those critics who regard these words as a vaticinium post eventum place the composition of the Gospel after the destruction of Jerusalem. Pfleiderer appears to incline to this view, although he thinks it "not impossible" that they may be a genuine tradition of words of Jesus. (Das Urchristenthum, p. 416.) Those who think Mark used Luke and Matthew, according to the Griesbach hypothesis, must, of course, date the Gospel much later. Keim supposes its date to have been about 100 (Gesch. Jesu von Nazara, i. p. 54) and Davidson about 120 (Introduction, ii. p. 111).

† Weiss, Einleit. p. 518.

CHAPTER V.

THE GOSPEL ACCORDING TO MATTHEW.

ACCORDING to an ancient Christian tradition the first attempt in evangelic literature was made by Matthew, whom the first Gospel designates as the publican.* The earliest form in which the tradition appears is preserved by Eusebius in the section of his history devoted to Papias, who wrote in the first half of the second century an explanation of the oracles, or sayings, of Christ.† Papias appears to have been a disciple of persons who had seen or heard Jesus and a man of influence who devoted himself to the collection of oral traditions regarding the earliest history of Christianity. His testimony, then, deserves to be heard and weighed. His statement regarding Matthew's writing is that the latter composed "The Oracles"‡ in the Hebrew dialect, and that every one translated them as he was able. Since the term "oracles," or logia, stands in the passage without qualification, its meaning is obscure, and has given rise to no little discussion. As has been shown in the chapter on the synop-

---

* Chap. ix. 9. Mark and Luke in passages undoubtedly parallel with this name the publican Levi, the former further designating him as the son of Alpheus, but Luke in the list of the apostles does not call him the son of Alpheus, while he mentions as such a James whose brother was Judas. Matthew's identity with Levi is accordingly doubtful, and the latter may not have been called as an apostle. Mark ii. 14., iii. 17 f ; Luke v. 27, vi. 14 f ; Matt. x. 2 f.

† Hist. Eccl. iii. 39.   ‡ τὰ λόγια.

tic problem, the conflicting solutions of that question and the most opposite theories as to the origin of the first three Gospels take their departure from this point. There can be no doubt, however, that the term "logia" describes a composition in the Aramaic dialect containing some account of the teachings and possibly of the life of Jesus. The remark concerning the translation of this writing by every one as he was able, very likely refers to the use of it in the public assemblies of the Christians or by private readers, rather than to any general circulation of copies of it or to written translations in considerable numbers. No inference can be drawn from the words of Papias to the existence of the original Aramaic writing in his time. Rather the reference to the original work and to the necessity of translations is to facts already passed.

Since Papias does not accurately report on the nature and contents of this writing by Matthew, the important question whether it was essentially our first canonical Gospel in Aramaic or a work of a different sort can be determined, so far as his testimony is concerned, only by a study of the single word with which he describes it. The reference of the passage to Christ being unquestionable, we have, then, first to determine what Papias meant by the logia of Christ. It appears arbitrary to divide the question as Holtzmann does on the supposition that Papias may have been thinking in making his report of a different work from that known and testified to by his supposed informant, the presbyter John, that is, of an Aramaic Gospel used by a heretical sect of Jewish Christians and given out by them as the original of Matthew's Gospel.* To assume that the witness, on whose testimony the whole question rests, did not understand his

* Einleit. p. 387.

informant, and was ignorant in regard to a vital part of the matter, is needlessly to cast discredit upon him. On this hypothesis it is inexplicable that Papias should have used the term "logia" to designate the work in question instead of the usual εὐαγγέλιον to denote Gospel. Now the Greek word λόγιον (plural λόγια) is a diminutive of λόγος, and means "a little word," "a brief utterance," "an oracle," but "chiefly any utterance of God, whether precept or promise." * It is applied to oracles which commonly take a sententious or gnomic form. † Accordingly, in Romans,‡ Paul writes of the Jews as having been "entrusted with the oracles of God," apropos of the law of which each precept was regarded as an *effatum Dei*. In Christian literature the word is applied to passages in the Bible taken separately and regarded as an expression of a will or a truth divinely revealed.§ The λόγιον is, then, essentially something of a didactic character, and is not necessarily connected with the narration of events. The fact that it is sometimes applied to the Bible as a revelation does not affect the conclusion respecting the use of it by Papias, for in his time nothing was known

---

* Grimm's Wilke's Clavis N. T. *sub voce*.

† According to Suidas, λόγια are τὰ παρὰ θεοῦ λεγόμενα καταλογάδην, "the things said in prose from God," distinguished from χρησμοί, oracles in verse. Réville, Matthieu.

‡ Chap. iii. 2, *cf.* Acts vii. 38.

§ Eusebius frequently employs the word in the senses referred to. He calls the ten commandments treated of in a work by Philo τὰ δέκα λόγια, Hist. Eccl. ii. 18. Ephraim, the Syrian, also designates the N. T. in reference to its containing proof-texts for the Trinity as λόγια κυριακὰ καὶ ἀποστολικὰ κηρύγματα, whereby he does not mean the Gospels and Epistles as such, but the sayings of Jesus and the apostles as alone furnishing the proofs in question. Schleiermacher, Ueber das Zeugniss des Papias, Werke zur Theol. ii. p. 367. Compare the Epistle of Polycarp, vii., καὶ ὃς ἂν μεθοδεύῃ τὰ λόγια τοῦ κυρίου πρὸς τὰς ἰδίας ἐπιθυμίας, κ.τ.λ.

of inspired Christian writings, as has been shown in the discussion of the canon. He, then, could not have used it in reference to a canonical writing supposed to possess divine authority, but, as in the title of his own work, only of discourses of Christ with the difference that his writing as an ἐξήγησις, or explanation, may very likely have contained considerable matter explanatory of the λόγια κυριακά, or oracles of the Lord (Christ).

The evident intention of Papias to mark a distinction between the writings of Matthew and Mark which were known to him leads to the conclusion regarding the former which has already been indicated. Mark's work he describes as an account of the words and deeds of Christ,* and immediately after mentioning it he proceeds to give an account of the tradition concerning the writing by Matthew, which he characterizes simply as the logia, the oracles, the *effata* of Christ. It is true that, continuing, he says of Mark that, not having been a hearer or a follower of Christ, but only of Peter, he received no instruction which could qualify him to give an orderly narrative of the *discourses* of Jesus. The conclusion has been drawn from this remark that Papias puts the writings of Matthew and Mark on the same footing, since, after referring to the former as the logia, he mentions the latter as an account of the *discourses* of Christ.† But that he intends to draw a clear distinction between the two writings is evident from the manner in which he speaks of the one as simply the logia and of the other as the things said and done by Jesus. The difference between λόγια, oracles, and σύνταξις τῶν λόγων, ‡ a narrative of the discourses,

---

* τὰ ὑπὸ τοῦ χριστοῦ ἢ λεχθέντα ἢ πραχθέντα.

† Davidson, Introduction, i. p. 467.

‡ λόγων is the reading of Val. B. C. D. F. H.

is too manifest to require illustration, even if the sense of the latter term had not previously been fixed by the words, "things said and done." Even Weiss, who holds, on grounds of Gospel-criticism, that the logia contained some connecting narrative, remarks that it is quite untenable to argue from the misunderstood testimony of Papias in regard to Mark that he meant by the term logia the things said or done, or used the former term in the sense of the later usage of the Church, according to which λόγια κυριακά designated the Gospels on account of their really canonical contents, and τα λόγια (θεοῦ) the divine revelation of the Scriptures, as if there were any import in which it could be said (from the point of view of the history of the canon, of course) that Matthew collected the λόγια in such a sense.*

The state of the case is quite different when we come to the later testimonies regarding Matthew's writing, so that some scholars have been led to the conclusion that there existed an original Hebrew Gospel according to Matthew, of which our canonical first Gospel is a Greek translation. Some of the advocates of this view, however, maintain that Matthew's part in the composition of this work was confined to the writing of the logia.† The testimony of Irenæus is that "Matthew among the Hebrews published a Gospel in writing in their own dialect.‡ Pantænus, who lived in the latter part of the second century, is said by Eusebius to have found in India (southern Arabia?) a Gospel of Matthew in Hebrew which had been left there by Bartholomew.§ Jerome makes a similar statement.‖ Elsewhere he says that Matthew wrote a Gospel in Hebrew

---

* Einleit. p. 493.
† Meyer, Commentar, i. 1, p. 14.
‡ Adv. Haeres. iii. 1.
§ Hist. Eccl. v. 10.
‖ De Viris illust. c. 36.

for the benefit of those of the circumcision who believed, and that it was uncertain who translated it into Greek. He further says that the Nazarenes, who had a copy of it in Pamphilius' library at Cæsarea, allowed him to make a transcription of it. Again, he says that he translated the Gospel according to the Hebrews, *which the Nazarenes and Ebionites used*, into Greek and Latin.* Yet Epiphanius is positive that the Gospel used by the Nazarenes and Ebionites was the Hebrew Matthew,† although it was known as that according to the Hebrews. But again, Clement and Origen distinguished it from Matthew's Gospel as independent and different. There can be little doubt that the two writings were different, since citations are preserved from the former of passages which are not in our first Gospel. Now there is no little uncertainty in all this testimony. The story of Bartholomew is legendary, and there is no evidence that Pantænus made an examination of the Gospel which he found in Arabia, so as to be qualified to affirm that it was an original writing by Matthew. It might, in fact, have been a translation of the Greek first Gospel into Aramaic. It appears that Jerome confounded the Gospel according to the Hebrews with a supposed Aramaic Matthew, and afterwards wavered, and said that it was simply thought by most people to be identical with the latter. ‡ His commentary on the Gospel of Matthew shows no acquaintance with a Hebrew original. § If we accord to Hilgenfeld that Papias knew of various Gospels which were modifications of an original work by Matthew, this critic's conclusion by no means follows that Papias meant by the λόγια a complete

---

* *Ib.* c. 2 and 3. † Haeres. xxix. 9.
‡ Ut pleri autumant secundum Matthæum. Comm. supra Matt. xii. 12.
§ Weiss, Einleit. p. 496.

Aramaic Gospel.* For the demonstrable differences between our Matthew and the Gospel according to the Hebrews in its varied forms indicate nothing so much as that the former was an independent elaboration from traditional and legendary sources of the original logia-collection itself. The statements of Eusebius, Origen, and others as to a complete Aramaic Gospel by Matthew were probably echoes of an early tradition which grew out of the testimony of Papias. This testimony as to the logia stands unimpaired in spite of the attempt to show on the one hand that it is to be referred to an Aramaic translation of a work written by Matthew in Greek, and on the other to a complete Aramaic Gospel. The conclusion of Weiss is probably in accordance with the general tendency of criticism at the present time, viz., that of this original writing by Matthew, which had already gone out of use in the time of Papias, and was known to none of the later fathers, we have no other knowledge than that given by him.

With the early existence of a complete Gospel by Matthew are irreconcilable the phenomena presented by the Gospel of Luke, who in his prologue indicates an acquaintance with many written accounts of the life of Jesus. It is hardly supposable that if such a writing by the hand of an apostle had existed when he wrote he would not have known and consulted it. But knowing such a work he could not have departed so widely from it in so many particulars. Had he believed in the apostolic origin of the story of the flight into Egypt, of the infancy, and of the appearance of Jesus after his resurrection to his disciples in Galilee, it is incredible that he should have written about these matters in a manner wholly irreconcilable

---

* Die Evangelien, etc. p. 119.

with these accounts.* Likewise, if Papias had known a complete Matthew, it is not likely that he would have been ignorant of the account of the death of Judas as reported in that Gospel, and would have published the entirely different story which has been preserved, especially since he declares, in the fragment in Eusebius, that he was careful to inquire what Matthew had reported, as well as what was said by certain others. Either Papias was false to his own principle, an assumption for which there is no ground, or his Matthew was not our first Gospel.† Again, if our actual first Gospel had appeared during the life of the apostle Matthew, and been stamped with his apostolic seal, an ancient Bishop, very curious to know just what the apostles had said, would not, towards the middle of the second century, have regarded tradition as the best means of learning what Matthew had said. ‡

That our canonical first Gospel is an independent composition in the Greek language and not a translation from an Aramaic original is capable of demonstration from internal evidences, and may be regarded as an established result of modern criticism. § The decision of the question turns largely on the writer's way of quoting passages from the Old Testament. As to these citations Credner remarks that few subjects have had so much investigation as this without a satisfactory result. Proofs have been found in them both for and against an Aramaic original, and, indeed, if single passages are considered alone, they will furnish evidence for either hypothesis. Credner's

---

* Compare Matt. iii. 13-23, xxvii. 16-20 with Luke ii. 39, 40, xxiv. 13-53.
† Credner, Einleit. in das N. T. p. 91.
‡ Réville, Études sur Matthieu, p. 6 ; *cf.* Eusebius, Hist. Eccl. iii. 39.
§ Holtzmann regards this conclusion as unquestionable. Baur, Hilgenfeld, Meyer, Davidson, and others understand by translation a more or less free transformation of an Aramaic original.

most **searching and learned** investigation of the subject is one of the most valuable contributions to Gospel-criticism.*
His conclusions are that the author of the first Gospel quotes freely from, and holds throughout in **his citation of passages from the Old Testament to, the Greek translation (the Septuagint), but in the Messianic passages, and** in these alone, makes comparisons and alterations according to **the Hebrew text, or, as Gesenius** supposes, according to **an ancient Targum.** From the Pentateuch are quoted several passages, some **twice, none of which have a Messianic** reference. All **show a Greek** origin, that is, dependence on the Greek translation of the Old Testament.† From the Psalms eight passages deserve attention, the most of which are freely interwoven according **to the Septuagint, and** others verbally **reproduced. There are no strictly Messianic passages among these.** ‡ Sixteen important quotations are **made from the prophetical writings, being eight from Isaiah, one from Jeremiah, and** seven from the minor **prophets. These are the really** Messianic proof-texts, and in **them is apparent the strongest inclination to the Hebrew text; yet** this inclination is of such **a nature** that the Greek **basis remains** unmistakable.§ The writer of Matthew sometimes makes his quotations from the Septuagint when that version, often incorrect, is more suitable to his dogmatic purpose than

---

* Beiträge zur Einleit. in die bibl. Schriften, Bd. ii.
† Chap. ii. 20, iv. 4, 7, 10, v. 38, xv. 4, xvii. 16, xix. 5, 18, xxii. 37.
‡ Chap. xxi. 9, 16, 42, iv. 6, vii. 23, xiii. 35, xxii. 44, xxvii. 46.
§ Chap. i. 23, *cf.* Is. vii. 14; iv. 15, *cf.* Is. viii. 23; xii. 18-21, *cf.* Is. xlii. 1 f; viii. 17, *cf.* Is. liii. 4; all purely Messianic passages. *Cf.* iii. 3, xiii. 14 f, xv. 8 f, xxi. 13. From Jeremiah, xxxi. 15, Matt. ii. 18, deviating somewhat from the Septuagint. From the minor prophets, Hos. xi. 1, Matt. ii. 15; Micah v. 2, Matt. ii. 6; Zech. ix. 9, Matt. xxi. 5. Inclining more to the Septuagint are chaps. ix. 13, xi. 10, xii. 7.

the original **Hebrew text. The quotation, i. 23, from Isaiah vii. 14, furnishes an illustration. The historic sense of the prophecy is that a young woman, perhaps the wife of** the prophet,* **is with** child, **and will bring** forth a son whose birth will be the sign of **the judgments of** Jahveh upon Israel. By following the Septuagint **in the translation of the** Hebrew word for marriageable young woman by **the** Greek word for virgin,† the writer of Matthew makes the prophetic text serve as a proof of the doctrine **of** the miraculous conception of Mary, a **proof, of course, from** his exegetical point of view.

On the other hand, the evangelist sometimes departs from the Septuagint-version when it suits the purpose for which a quotation is made. In viii. 17 he finds the cures performed by Jesus predicted in Isaiah liii. 4, where the original reads: "**He hath** borne our griefs [sickness], and carried our sorrows." **The Septuagint translates the passage**: "**He** bears **our sins, and is distressed on our account,**" and this **expiatory idea is expressed in I.** Peter, ii. **24. This** rendering did not **suit** the connection in which **the evangelist** wished **to use the quotation,** and he **accordingly departs from the Septuagint, and adheres** pretty **closely to the Hebrew text, rendering it:** "Himself took **our infirmities, and bore our sicknesses."** Again, a knowledge of Hebrew is indicated in ii. 23; "And he shall be called a Nazarene," a saying which is referred to "the

---

* Gesenius, Comm. über den Jesaia; Knobel, Der Prophet Jesaia, etc.

† The Hebrew word, עַלְמָה, used in this passage, means "a marriageable young woman," *i.e.*, one of the age to marry, and not "a virgin." The Hebrew word for the latter is בְּתוּלָה. Other Jewish translators of the Old Testament were more correct in rendering the former in Greek by νεᾶνις than the seventy, whom the first evangelist followed, by παρθένος. Justin, ignorant of Hebrew, reproaches the Jews for translating it by νεᾶνις. Dial. cum Trypho, 71.

prophets." The idea was evidently derived from two passages in Isaiah xi. 1, and lx. 21, in one of which there is a prophecy of a royal descendant of the line of David who is designated as "the Branch," the Hebrew for which word is similar to the first two syllables of Nazarene.* The strange idea of the evangelist could not have come from the Greek version,† and can only be explained by supposing that he had studied the Hebrew text. These are only a few of the examples which might be cited to show that the first evangelist used both the Septuagint and the Hebrew text of the Old Testament in his quotations from that book, but that in the great majority of cases he depended on the former. The conclusion is that the first Gospel was composed in Greek, and that the author was a Jew versed in the Old-Testament Scriptures.‡

The acceptance of the testimony of Papias to the composition of the logia by Matthew in Aramaic and of the evidence already adduced for the writing of the Gospel in Greek in its present form, leads to the inquiry as to its author. The external evidence carries us no farther than Matthew's authorship of the work mentioned by Papias. An examination of the Gospel furnishes strong support on internal grounds for the opinion that it is not the work of an apostle or of an eye-witness. Not to emphasize the fact that a contemporary would not be likely to employ the expression, "until this day,"§ the legendary portions of the narrative are conclusive against its apostolical authorship. Such are probably the accounts of the birth

---

* נֵצֶר, Nezer. It is, however, nowhere said by a prophet, much less by "prophets," that the person in question should "be called a Nazarene."

† The Septuagint translates the word by φύτευμα.

‡ Weiss, Einleit. p. 527 ; Réville, Études sur Matthieu, p. 31.

§ ἕως, or μέχρι τῆς σήμερον. Chap. xxvii. 8 ; xxviii. 15.

and infancy of Jesus; the details of the temptation in the desert; the episode of Peter's walking on the water; the story of the piece of money to be found in the mouth of a fish; the rending of the veil of the temple; the resurrection of the saints at the time of the crucifixion; and the corruption of the guard placed at the tomb.* To any one who may repudiate these objections on the ground that they are subjective, it may be replied that they are not urged from a prejudice against the supernatural as such, but partly because they offend the historical and critical judgment which, when unbiassed, cannot but pronounce some of them to be of the nature of legendary stories, which in apocryphal Christian writings would be unhesitatingly set aside as such, and partly because of internal difficulties. The apostolic origin of the story of the infancy is, as has already been remarked, irreconcilable with Luke's narrative. The detailed account of the temptation furnishes in itself no grounds of historical verification, and has rather the appearance of an expansion of symbolic ideas into a narrative than an account of actual occurrences. The symbolism of the abolition of the Jewish cultus, which lay in the rending of the veil of the temple, and of the resurrection of believers to be effected through the death of Christ, in the opening of the graves, may have received a similar historical expansion in the related legends. The account of the guard of soldiers at the grave of Jesus and of their corruption by the Jewish authorities is beset with insuperable difficulties, and is correctly characterized by Meyer as belonging to "unhistorical legends." Réville, in a work crowned by the "Society of The Hague for the Defence of the Christian Religion," remarks in regard to the foregoing accounts:

---

* i. ii. iv. 1-11, xiv. 28-31, xvii. 27, xxvii. 51, 52, 53. Compare, Meyer, Commentar, i. 1, p. 601.

"Now we regard it as evident that an author contemporary with Jesus, witness of his life, his death, and his resurrection, would not give place in his evangelic narratives to these impressions more or less accentuated by legend pious or mythic. In order to conceive of their possibility, it is necessary to allow between the primitive fact and its recital a sufficient lapse of time for the nimbus produced by distance, to permit the imagination thus to color the objects without prejudice to the naïveté and the perfect sincerity of intention which lend so much charm to our sacred books." *

There are, moreover, apart from all objections which may appear to be tainted with subjectivity, several considerations of weight against the apostolical authorship of the Gospel. There are no intimations in the book that it was written by Matthew. An eye-witness would hardly have passed over in silence the ministry of Jesus in Judea, which is in itself probable, and is presupposed by the evangelist himself.† The order of time appears to be in part arbitrary and in part to have been determined by an arrangement of events according to an order of the subject-matter. There is wanting throughout the vividness of narration which denotes the eye-witness, especially in the account of the crucifixion. In this respect the Gospel is admitted to be inferior to Mark's. The discourses of Jesus are artificially constructed by a combination of elements which, though sometimes related, evidently belong to different occasions. Two accounts are repeated with slight variations.‡ Two animals are

---

* Études sur Matthieu, p. 33.
† Chap. xxiii. 37.
‡ Chap. xiv. 16–21, cf. xv. 32–38; chap. ix. 32–34, cf. xii. 22–20. Other doublets, v. 29, 30, cf. xviii. 8, 9; v. 32, and x. 22, cf. xix. 9 and xxiv. 9, 13.

mentioned on the occasion of the entry into Jerusalem in triumph in order that there may appear to have been a fulfilment of a prophecy which the evangelist evidently misunderstood. The scene in the synagogue at Nazareth is misplaced, and Matthew's call has an improbable relation of time in the narrative. From these considerations and many others which it is not necessary to urge, it must be concluded that, as a whole, the Gospel is not of apostolic origin, and cannot be the work of an eye-witness. Its immediate composition by an apostle is accordingly denied at the present time, not only by representatives of the strictly critical school, but by all those who in reference to the synoptical question hold to the theory of two sources, the logia and Mark, or in regard to the Johannean question favor the apostolicity and historical credibility of the fourth Gospel ; for on account of the differences between the narratives of Matthew and John, one of these records at least must be struck out of the number of primitive historical sources.*

The editor of our first Gospel doubtless used as the sources of his narrative the logia of Matthew, the Gospel of Mark, and oral tradition. The entire material of Mark's Gospel, with trifling exceptions, has been incorporated into this record, and generally in the same arrangement in which it stands in the former. The order, however, appears to be frequently determined according to the subject-matter rather than by regard for chronology. The secondary character of the Gospel as compared with that of Mark appears in various deviations from the latter, often determined by literary motives. Places and persons are more definitely determined.† Additions are made by

---

* Holtzmann, Einleit. p. 387.
† Chap. iii. 1, "of Judæa" added, cf. Mark i. 4 ; the going to Capernaum

way of explanation, enlargement, and coloring.* Entirely new features are inserted in several places.† Words which in Mark are only intimated receive a more pronounced and formulated statement; questions introducing a saying of Jesus are shaped according **to the answer, and the** whole narrative appears intended **to smooth and** alleviate **what is rough and harsh in the other.** ‡ There are several passages which are evidently insertions into the text of Mark.§ The revision of Mark's text by the first evangelist nowhere appears more **evident than in the** history of the passion which the former has reported in a quite original way. The beginning of this history is plainly a transformation of Mark's opening sentence. The demand of money by Judas and his payment with the thirty pieces; his direct unmasking; the climax of the three acts of **prayer** in Gethsemane **and of the three denials;**

---

is determined by a prophecy, iv. **13,** *cf.* **Mark i. 14–21** ; **John** is designated as " the Baptist " **on** his first appearance, iii. **1 ; Simon is mentioned** at once with his cognomen of Peter, **iv. 18,** and **many** similar **cases, xiv. 1,** xix. 20, xxvi. 3, xxvii. 56, etc.

* " By a word," added to describe method of healing, viii. 16 ; the reason added for plucking the ears of corn, xii. 1, and for Peter's following of Christ, **xxvi. 58 ;** the manner of Christ's death, xx. 19, and the object of the shedding **of his blood, xxvi.** 28, *cf.* Mark x. 34, xiv. 24.

† Chap. xvi. 1, Sadducees added ; xix. 19, the commandment of love to neighbor added to the decalogue ; xxvii. 29, the reed placed in the right hand as a sceptre.

‡ Formulas made more precise or enlarged, iii. 2, *cf.* Mark i. 1, **2 ; xvi. 22,** *cf.* Mark viii. 32 ; xxvi. 27, 50, 52, 54, *cf.* Mark xiv. 22 f., 45, 47, **49 ;** questions modified, etc., xvii. 19, *cf.* Mark ix. 19 ; xviii. 1, *cf.* Mark ix. **34 ;** xix. 3, *cf.* Mark x. 2 ; xix. 27, *cf.* Mark x. 28 ; xxiv. 3, *cf.* Mark xiii. 4 ; difficulties removed, etc., xiii. 10–13, *cf.* Mark iv. 10–13 ; xv. 16–20, *cf.* Mark viii. 18–23 ; xvii. 10–13, *cf.* Mark ix. 12, 13 ; **xiv.** 34–36, *cf.* Mark vii. 54–56.

§ **Chap. xiv.** 28–31, xvii. 24–27, **xxvii. 3–10,** 19, 24 f, 52 f, 62–66, xxviii. **2–4.**

the proposal of a choice between Barabbas and Jesus by Pilate, are evidently secondary features.* Again, the fact that much of Mark's peculiar use of words has passed over into the first Gospel shows it to be a revision of the former.

The evident dependence of our first Gospel upon the second does not, however, account for an important portion of its contents, consisting principally of material not contained in Mark and apparently inserted in the framework of the latter. This portion is composed chiefly of discourses and sayings (logia) of Jesus, partly grouped in great masses and partly dispersed. Its extent is so great that it cannot have come to the writer through oral tradition. The logia reported to have been written by Matthew are probably its source. That the evangelist found this material in a written form is capable of proof by tracing the logia back through Luke's revision of the discourses to their original form, from which they were combined by the first evangelist into larger masses, and by distinguishing the original sense of some portions of them from that which they have received in the connection given them by the latter.† Another evidence that the first evangelist borrowed these sayings of Jesus from a written document is found in the duplicates of expressions which he gives once in the connection of Mark and in dependence on his setting, and again in a quite different connection and a modified setting. This phenomenon can only be explained by the hypothesis that he regarded

---

* Chap. xxvi. 1–4, xxvi. 15, 25, 42, 44, 72, 74, xxvii. 17, 21. Weiss, Einleit. p. 520. That the text of the first Gospel is in the most peculiar narrative portions a literary revision of that of Mark, so far as the latter is wholly original, has been shown by Weiss in a thorough parallel exegesis in his Marcusevangelium.

† Weiss, Einleit. p. 521.

the sayings which he found in different literary settings as different expressions.*

There are good reasons for thinking that the first evangelist regarded the logia, an apostolical writing, as his principal source, and accordingly gave it the preference over all others at his disposal, whenever a question arose as to the form of expression or actual contents. This view is confirmed by the fact that in many cases, although having the text of Mark before him, he has preferred the older source, and so, in spite of his dependence on the former, has in these passages preserved the original form.† While many of the critical conclusions regarding the relation of the evangelist to his sources must be conceded to rest on a somewhat fragile support of conjecture, a most careful and patient examination of the subject, conducted with freedom from bias and carried into great detail, appears to have shown, in the way in which he uses the logia and Mark, the fundamental thought of his composition. This was not, then, merely to enlarge the Gospel of Mark by the insertion of new material from another source, however probable this purpose may appear on a superficial glance at the distribution which he makes of that source in his Gospel, but to expand into a biography of Jesus the old apostolic document so as to adapt it to the needs of

---

* The saying about the offending hand, etc., v. 29 f, occurs again, modified according to Mark, in xviii. 8; that on divorce, v. 32, again in xix. 9; that as to bearing the cross, x. 38, again in xvi. 24; that of the sign of Jonah, xii. 39, again in xvi. 4; that of wonder-working faith, xvii. 20, again in xxi. 21; and *vice versa*, that according to Mark xiii. 12, again according to the logia, xxv. 29; xix. 30, again in xx. 16; xx. 26, again in xxiii. 11; xxiv. 42, again in xxv. 13. But the most striking duplicate of the sort is the series of sayings, x. 17-22, which, because Mark has received them into the discourse on the Parousia, xiii. 9-13, are repeated, slightly changed, in xxiv. 9-13.

† *Cf.* Matt. xiii. 24-30, with Mark iv. 26-29.

his time and of the Jewish Christians, which, in its existing form, it no longer satisfied. As a means to this end there offered itself to him the historical frame-work of Mark's Gospel, which he did not essentially modify except in the earlier portions. But in order to provide for the abundant materials of his chief source in this, it appears to have suited his purpose and the plan of his work to mass the dispersed groups of sayings and parables which he found in the former into larger and more compact discourses. If the hypothesis is correct which assumes the logia to have been one of Luke's sources, it would appear from the parables and sayings which his record has that are not in the first that the author of the latter did not succeed in utilizing all the material of the common source, but it is believed that he has preserved it in the greatest abundance and with the utmost fidelity, and accordingly in his work has been rightly recognized the old Gospel of Matthew, although it is an enlarged and greatly modified edition of that writing.*

The first evangelist and Luke being supposed to have used the logia-source, the complete reconstruction of it is made from these two Gospels, with results varying according to the critical point of view. Since the former followed Mark's record with considerable dependence, it is evident that one cannot pretend to entire accuracy in the process of separating between the two sources, especially when discourses and parts of them are in question. The reconstructions by Weiss and Wendt leave little to be expected from further critical research, however much they may leave to be desired.† It is believed that both

* This is substantially the conclusion of recent criticism in the interest of the " conservative" Mark-hypothesis.

† Weiss, Das Matthäusevangelium, p. 18 f; Wendt, Die Lehre Jesu, i. p. 44 f. *Cf.* Weizsäcker, Untersuchungen, etc.; Réville, Études sur Matthieu; and Holtzmann, Einleit.

the first and the third evangelists had an independent knowledge of the logia, since now the one and now the other gives the source in the greater completeness, in the more correct connection, or with the more original details. It is hardly to be assumed, however, that they had before them written copies of this source, or if they had them felt constrained to follow their order and arrangement, since their reproductions show many displacements of the single sayings. On the other hand, it must be concluded from the frequent and often surprising agreement of the two in the Greek wording of the logia-fragments that the source used by them was Greek, and accordingly that if it was identical with the writing mentioned by Papias, it was not known to them in its original Aramaic form, but in a Greek translation. This conclusion is, indeed, not unquestionable, because we can see from certain indications that Luke was probably acquainted with our first Gospel as well as with that of Mark and the logia. It is hence possible that his agreement with the first Gospel in the wording of the logia-fragments may be explicable by a reminiscence of that record, just as his agreement with its many slight modifications in the reproduction of the record of Mark is explicable on the same ground. Further, it has been concluded that the manner in which the writer of the first Gospel and Luke have connected the contents of the logia and Mark's record is so far essentially different, as the former has united those portions which are similar in subject-matter, while the latter has inserted the principal contents of the logia into Mark's account in two great connected parts.* By this procedure Luke has not only preserved single fragments of the logia which the first evangelist has omitted because, perhaps, he found in Mark's narrative no opportunity of joining

* Luke vi. 20–viii. 3, and ix. 51–xviii. 14. Weiss, *ut supra*.

them with it, but has also in general correctly reproduced the original succession of these fragments.

Our first Gospel does not, however, find its complete explanation in the two sources, the logia and Mark, but contains portions which must be assigned in all probability to the abundant oral tradition, the existence of which is not only known through Papias, but also through the early literature of the Church. The absence in Mark of certain apparently legendary narratives is one of the evidences commonly adduced for its greater antiquity, or at least its more intimate relation to an apostolical source. But the first evangelist appears to have thought that an account of the birth and infancy of Jesus and of his appearance after his resurrection was necessary to a complete biography of him. It is not necessary to suppose that written sources were employed in the writing of chapters i. ii. and xxviii. The genealogy bears so plainly the stamp of the writer's doctrinal point of view that there can be little doubt of its origin with him in its essential features. It is Jewish in its character, and aims to establish the descent of Jesus from Abraham and David. The entire account of the infancy has unmistakable marks of popular tradition—naïveté, vagueness in regard to persons and things, and pious confidence in the incessant intervention of the finger of God to make the good cause triumph.*
The theory of the construction of the Gospel from sources requires the reference to tradition of some passages which have already been assigned a legendary origin on other grounds.† The explanation of the parable of the tares

* Réville, Études, etc. p. 185.

† In particular the stories in which Peter is especially concerned, chaps. xiv. 28 f, xvii. 24 f; the end of Judas; the dream of Pilate's wife, and Pilate's washing of his hands; the signs at the crucifixion, and the mention of the corruption of the guards at the tomb, chap. xxvii. Some sayings of

and of that of the draught of fishes,* the remarks on the **fulfilment of** prophecy in the life of Jesus, and all other portions of the record which the evangelist **has** added himself, are distinguished by **a peculiar use of words** found only in his revision and **clearly** revealing his hand. On the other hand, **his** dependence on documents **shows** itself when sayings **once** given from memory are **re-inserted where they appear to have** been **found in the connection of one of his sources.** †

In the absence of historical information **as to the** place and time of the composition of this Gospel there **is no** recourse except to indications given here and there in the narrative. Weiss' judgment that the author did not write in Palestine, but was a Jew of the dispersion, is supported by very good reasons. **A** Palestinian would not speak of his country as " that country." ‡ He appears, indeed, as has been remarked, to have been **a Jew learned in the Old** Testament and able **to read it in the** original, **and he** speaks of Jerusalem **as the holy** city,§ but there **are** indications that he was not familiar with the geography of the country so as to speak of the places after the manner of a resident writing for residents. ‖ Besides, it has been ques-

Jesus, whose connection we are not able to show in **the logia, may also have come** to the evangelist through oral tradition. See chaps. v. 7 f, **14,** vii. 6, x. 16, xv. **13,** xviii. **10,** xix. 10 f, xxi. **14** f, xxvi. **52 f.**

* Chap. xiii. **36–43, 49 f.**

† Compare ix. **13** with xii. **7** ; xvi. 19 with xviii. **18** ; x. **15** with xi. 24, or *vice versa* ; iii. **7** with xxiii. **33** ; iii. **10** with vii. **19.**

‡ Chap. ix. **26, 31,** ἡ γῆ ἐκείνη.

§ Chap. iv. 5, xxvii. 53.

‖ " The wilderness " **of** Mark is mentioned **as** " the wilderness *of Judæa,"* **and** the writer apparently takes the city **on** the east coast **of** the Jordan mentioned in his source for Gadara, chap. iii. 1, 6, viii. 28, **33.** That the **Gospel** was intended for Jews of the dispersion appears from the fact that **the** writer translates for them the words Immanuel, Golgotha, and those **from the** Psalms in the prayer on the cross.

tioned, with very good reasons, whether a Palestinian who wished to enlarge the oldest apostolical source would, in Palestine where numerous eye-witnesses must still have been living, have depended almost entirely on the writing of Mark, who was not an eye-witness, and would have added from an independent source nothing but a small number of traditions which bear evident marks of being second-hand. The manner in which he writes of the settlement of the parents of Jesus in Nazareth after their return with the child from Egypt indicates an ignorance of their original place of residence.* It has been maintained that certain passages in the Gospel are directed against a prevailing gentile-Christian libertinism, and that the evangelist put these denunciations into the mouth of Jesus with regard to the fact that the Jewish-Christian readers for whom the Gospel was intended lived in the midst of circumstances to which they would apply.† These intimations are supposed to refer to Asia Minor, where, according to certain Epistles of the New Testament, this libertinism appeared in a threatening form in the latter part of the apostolic age. From this point of view the question as to the original language of the Gospel cannot remain in dispute, since it must have been, as a matter of course, the Greek in current use by the evangelist and his readers.‡

The Jewish point of view and interest of the evangelist are plainly indicated in the Gospel. An internal conflict there is, indeed, in it between the Jewish-Christian and Pauline tendencies; and however this phenomenon may be explained, whether by the hypothesis of a later revision

---

* Chap. ii. 22 f, cf. Luke ii. 39.
† Chap. vii. 22 f, xiii. 41, xxiv. 12.
‡ Weiss, Einleit. p. 535.

of a Pauline writer, or by assuming that the passages which indicate the universal destination of Christianity belonged to the original tradition of Jesus, the ancient opinion that the Gospel was written " for those of the circumcision " must be the conclusion of criticism. To the historic sense there is revealed in it the influence of that early strife over the Messiahship of Jesus in which the disciples must have been engaged with their Jewish opponents in Solomon's porch, when, for publishing " the glad tidings concerning Jesus the Christ," the rude hand of authority was laid upon them. Historical criticism cannot regard the book as written without a purpose, or a " tendency," to employ a much-abused and much-contested word, yet a word which will never disappear from the terminology of this science.* The purpose, or "tendency," then, of the first Gospel is to convince the Jews of the doctrine and to confirm the Jewish Christians in it that Jesus was Israel's true Messiah. Along with this is also discernible a polemical purpose, for the Jews are scourged in it for their unsusceptibility and obduracy towards the Messianic message as in no other Gospel, and the discourses of Jesus to this end are reported with great fulness and detail.† To the writer as to Justin Martyr the whole life of Jesus is determined by prophecies of the Old Testament, and everything, even the episodes of the passion, takes place in order that these may be fulfilled. Jewish, too, is the prominence given to legalism and to the conception of Jesus as sent only to the chosen people, as well as the oriental numerical symbolism already referred to which characterizes the literary method of the writer.

* See chapter ix. of this work.
† Hausrath, Neutestamentliche Zeitgeschichte, 1873. iii. p. 319 ; Keim, Geschichte Jesu von Nazara, 1867, i. p. 52 ; Holtzmann, Die synoptischen Evangelien, 1863, p. 381.

The date of the composition of the Gospel in its present form is altogether a matter of conjecture so far as any precise determination of it is concerned, and some modern critics express more positive opinions regarding it than the data warrant. It is generally conceded by Protestant scholars that the final editing did not take place before the year 70 and that the date of the logia must be placed several years earlier. The Gospel undoubtedly contains passages which presuppose the existence of the Jewish state and the worship in the temple. But sayings retained unchanged from the original source furnish no evidence as to the time of the final revision of the work. The passage in which it is declared that the second coming, or the Parousia, will take place "immediately after"* the destruction of Jerusalem does not prove that the Gospel was completed before the latter event, since the coming of Christ might have been expected immediately after it, though the word should not be subjected to too great a pressure. Such passages as that which mentions the detruction of a city and its inhabitants for unbelief,† that containing the threefold formula of baptism,‡ a formula which is certainly of late origin, and that indicating the delay of the Parousia,§ have decided the judgments of some critics in favor of a date later than the year 70, and have determined significant changes of opinion. ‖ The reasons of Hilgenfeld, Köstlin, and Réville for placing the composition of the Gospel about ten years after the overthrow of Jerusalem are cogent, but hardly conclusive. Baur, who brings the composition down to about 130, and finds in chapter xxiv. an allusion to the time of Hadrian, has not convinced many.

* εὐθέως, chap. xxiv. 29. † Chap. xxii. 7.
‡ Chap. xxviii. 19, *cf.* Acts ii. 38, viii. 16, x. 48, xix. 5 ; I. Cor. i. 13, vi. 11 ; Gal. iii. 27 ; Rom. vi. 3.   § χρονίζειν, chap. xxiv. 48, xxv. 5.
‖ Notably in Keim and Holtzmann.

CHAPTER VI.

THE GOSPEL ACCORDING TO LUKE.

SINCE Irenæus' time* tradition has ascribed our third Gospel to Luke, who, according to the Epistle to the Colossians,† was a physician, and a friend and fellow-laborer of Paul, and was with him in Caesaræ and Rome. Little is known of his biography, but it would appear from the way in which he is mentioned in Colossians that he was not "of the circumcision." His birth is rather conjectured than known, but that he was probably a Greek is indicated by the pure style of his prologue which is in strong contrast with the Hebraizing-Greek of his sources in the rest of the Gospel. The supposition that he was one of the seventy disciples is in contradiction to the acknowledgment which he makes in his prologue as to the sources of his information ‡ in which he distinguishes himself and those of his time from the "eye-witnesses." The study of his Gospel naturally begins with the consideration of this prologue by which it is distinguished from the other three records in our canon. We here learn from him something of his qualifications for his task and of the manner in which he proceeded to accomplish it. He expressly compares his work with that of many others

---

* Adv. Haeres. iii. 1, 1.

† Chap. iv. 4, cf. Phil. 24, II. Tim. iv. 11, Epiph. Haeres. li. 12.

‡ This legend arose, perhaps, from the fact that Luke alone gives the account of the seventy, cf. Meyer, Commentar. i. 2, p. 224.

who before him had undertaken from the traditions of eye-witnesses to write accounts of the life of Jesus, and evidently implies that he thinks himself able to improve upon their work, since he had "accurately traced up all things from the first." He proposes also to write a narrative which shall be in order,* that is, shall have a proper chronological arrangement, whereby it is perhaps implied that the "many" who had undertaken to write Gospels had not satisfied him in this respect. The mention of many attempts to write similar accounts does not, however, necessarily imply Luke's acquaintance with nor his use of all of them. Much less is there sufficient reason for believing that he combined them into a mosaic-work according to Schleiermacher's theory of the composition of the Gospel, with which the author's claim to have "accurately traced up all things from the first" is hardly reconcilable. On the contrary the work has throughout a uniform linguistic character, and shows frequent traces of recasting and critical revision. He did not, however, compose the Gospel in the classic Greek of which we may infer from his fine prologue that he was a master, but adopted the Hebraistic style of his predecessors in this kind of writing, thus yielding to the influence of his sources and his environment.

It appears from the prologue that the Gospel was written with no general purpose of instructing mankind nor with a consciousness of composing sacred Scripture for future generations, but especially for the benefit of a friend whom the writer names as Theophilus. Nothing is known of this person, and his place of residence is a matter of conjecture. The opinion has been favorably received that he lived in Rome. The Gospel was evidently written for

* καθεξῆς.

a gentile reader or for readers not familiar with Jewish localities and customs. This is apparent from the explanations which the writer seems to find it necessary to make of the feast of unleavened bread,* of Nazareth, of Capernaum, of Arimathea, of the country of the Gadarenes, of Emmaus, and of the Mount of Olives.†

With regard to the sources of Luke's Gospel it is capable of being shown with great probability that apart from a few omissions the entire Gospel of Mark has been incorporated into it even more completely than into the first Gospel. Even in the rare cases in which a fragment of Mark's narrative has been replaced from another source, as in the scene in the synagogue at Nazareth and in Peter's draught of fishes, criticism discerns features of Mark's representation interwoven.‡ A departure from the order of Mark is made in the position given to this scene in the synagogue at Nazareth which is placed immediately after the temptation. § The whole account appears to have been taken from another source than Mark, like that of the calling of the disciples, which is also transposed. The awkward attachment of the narrative to that of Mark appears in the twenty-third verse where acts done in Capernaum are presupposed, while not until the thirty-first verse is reached is the removal to Capernaum mentioned. But apart from this episode the order of the second evangelist is almost exclusively followed, although there are evidences in many places of an attempt to revise his narrative in the matter of style, in enlarging, and in explanation.‖ So familiar is Mark's narrative to

---

* Chap. xxii. 1. ‡ Chap. iv. 22, 24, v. 10 f.
† Chap. i. 26, iv. 31, xxiii. 51, viii. 26, xxiv. 13, xxi. 37.
§ Chap. iv. 16–30.
‖ Revision in style, chap. iv. 32, 36, 37, compared with Mark i. 22, 27, 28; the explanatory πόλις τ. Γαλ., iv. 31; ἔχων πν. δαιμ. ἀκαθ., iv. 33;

Luke that he frequently applies traits of it in narratives derived from other sources, and the influence of the former's diction is evident in many places in Luke's record.*

Luke was not, however, confined to Mark, but among his "many" sources it is possible to trace another already known to us in the first Gospel, and probably also in the second. The recurrence in another connection of sayings apparently derived from Mark is most naturally explained by the hypothesis that the author must have found them in that connection in a written form.† The most striking example of such doublets is the discourse on the occasion of sending out the apostles

ἐν ἐξουσ. καὶ δυναμ., iv. 36; συνεχομ. πυρ. μεγάλῳ, iv. 38; γενομένης ἡμέρας, iv. 42; the paraphrase of the κηρύξω, iv. 43; the more accurate description ῥῖψαν αὐτ. εἰς τὸ μέσον, iv. 36; ἀναστὰς ἀπὸ τ. συναγ., iv. 38; ἠρώτησαν αὐτ. instead of λεγ. αὐτ., ib; the reflective remark, μηδὲν βλάψαν αὐτ., iv. 35. In chap. v. 17 the presence of the Pharisees and teachers of the law is anticipated; in viii. 23 Jesus' falling asleep is mentioned; in viii. 27, the nakedness of the demoniac; in viii. 42, the age of the maiden; in viii. 51, the presence of the parents. Weiss, Marcusevang., Einleit., etc.

* For Mark's frequent εὐθύς Luke has παραχρῆμα except in chap. v. 13, and ὑπάγειν, elsewhere avoided, is used in xix. 30, εἰς τὸ πέραν in viii. 22, and Ναζαρηνός for Ναζωραῖος in iv. 34. Expressions frequent in Mark occur only rarely in the parallels in Luke, as καθεύδειν, ξηραίνειν, δαιμονίζεσθαι, διδαχή, σίνδων, στάχυς. Other favorite expressions of Mark are borrowed, as κρατεῖν, συζητεῖν, etc. Davidson has collected many peculiarities of the style of Luke, Int. ii. p. 56 f. The subject is fully treated by Holtzmann, Die synopt. Evangel. p. 302 f.

† The separate elements of the series of sayings in chap. viii. 16–18 (Mark iv. 21–25) recur in chap. xi. 33, xii. 2, xix. 26; chap. ix. 23–26 (Mark viii. 34–38), in chap. xiv. 27, xvii. 33, xii. 9. On the other hand, chap. xx. 46 (Mark xii. 38) was already in chap. xi. 43, and chap. xi. 14, in a more original form in xii. 11. Luke also interweaves sayings independently which he adopts in another place from a connection probably existing in a written form. Compare chap. xvii. 31 with xxi. 22, and chap. xviii. 14 with xiv. 11.

which is given once from Mark, and again soon after
under a different title.* That the discourse in the latter
form was addressed to the twelve in Luke's source is
apparent from an allusion which it contains appropriate
only to them.† Again, series of sayings and parables
are often transplanted by Luke into a connection with
which they do not accord, and may accordingly have
been borrowed from a writing in which they had a different connection.‡ The fact that the principal part of the
sayings of Jesus which Luke has, and Mark has not, is
found in the first Gospel, and, indeed, in those elements
of it which are assigned to the apostolic source, leads to
the conclusion that the same source was used by Luke.
Davidson's objection to this hypothesis, that Luke would
not be likely to use the logia-document, since the first
Gospel was in existence when he wrote, and had sup-
planted the former,§ is entirely *à priori*, and rather suggests stronger probabilities for the opposite view. For
the logia-source, being apostolical, would naturally commend itself to an historian like Luke, while our Greek
Matthew would be regarded by him as a work of the

---

* Chapters ix. and x.

† Chap. x. 4, xxii. 35.

‡ The meaning of chap. xii. 2 is obscured by its connection with the saying about the leaven, xii. 1. The same words occur in chap. viii. 17 in a
better connection. See also Mark iv. 22. The sense of the saying regarding the blasphemy against the Holy Spirit in chap. xii. 10 in its connection
with xii. 11 can hardly be the original one, and just as little that of chap.
xiii. 30 in connection with xiii. 28 f. The saying in chap. xiii. 34 is unintelligible in its connection. The parables in chap. xiv. 16-24, xv. 4-10,
xviii. 2-8, and xix. 12-27 betray meanings which do not accord well with
their introductions, and those in chap. xiv. 8-14 lose, by their introductions,
xiv. 7, 12, their parabolic sense, which is definitely established by chap.
xiv. 11. Weiss, Einleit., and Marcusevangel.

§ Introduction, ii. p. 5.

same rank as his own, and perhaps as most of the sources accessible to him. It is not, indeed, improbable, but rather the contrary, that he knew and consulted our first Gospel, but, as Davidson acknowledges, the evidences of his use of it are few.* On the other hand, the indications are very clear that he made a liberal use of the document on which the first evangelist largely depended for the materials of the discourses and the "oracles" of Christ, adopting from it the discourse of the Baptist, that against those who asked for a sign, that announcing woes, the second on the Parousia, and many lesser series of sayings and parables.

The question whether Luke took these discourses from the first Gospel or from the logia-document finds its solution in favor of the latter alternative, for the reason that he has not in his use of the material followed the arrangement of the first evangelist, who has massed the sayings of Jesus into great discourses, but has presented them rather in their original separation, with a statement of the occasion which gave rise to them,† or in their evidently original connection.‡ Sometimes, however, he gives them without occasion,§ or with an incorrect one,‖ or, again, in a separation from the fine connection of the first Gospel,¶ a procedure which it is difficult to account for on the hypothesis of his use of the latter. The form of the parables of the sower and of the grain of mustard **

---

* Davidson quotes only two passages, but Simons has written a volume on the subject.

† Chap. xi. 1–13, xii. 13–34, 54–59, xiv. 25–35, xvii. 22–37.

‡ Chap. xi. 33 f., xiii. 24–29, xxii. 25–30.

§ Chap. xii. 51 f., xiii. 18–21, xvii. 1–4.

‖ Chap. xii. 2 f.

¶ Chap. vi. 40, cf., Matt. x. 24.

** Chap. viii. 4–8 ; xiii. 18.

is probably the most original in Luke. Matthew appears to have adopted them from Mark in an altered form. In the discourse on the Parousia, the second of the insertions which the first evangelist makes from Mark is omitted,* and the first one is subjected to a very free treatment,† which appears to indicate that it did not belong to the original four, and was taken, not from the first Gospel, where it appears in an entirely different connection, but from the logia-document. Luke's revision of this document is regarded as much freer than that of the first evangelist, so that the form in which he has preserved it is on the whole not very original. In both there frequently appear, however, independent and different revisions of the source.‡

Both the third and the first evangelists proceed with independence and freedom in their use of Mark. They are not bound by his arrangement, and occasionally break through it in different ways. How both take the liberty to correct in different senses a text that is obscure may be seen by consulting the parallels to Mark ii. 15-18, especially Matt. ix. 10, Mark ii. 15, and Luke v. 29. How each in his own way explains a figure appears in the case of the warning as to the leaven of the Pharisees,§ and how an obscure connection is variously cleared

---

* See Matt. xxiv. 23 f.

† Compare Luke xxi. 12-19 with Matt. x. 17-22.

‡ The sermon on the mount can hardly be original either in the form in which the third or the first evangelist gives it. The former abridges, the latter enlarges it. Transformation hence became necessary. The first evangelist gives seven beatitudes in the place of the four of the third, and the latter reinforces them by a series of woes. The parables of the talents and the supper are presented by both allegorically, but in different ways. How now in one, now in the other, the original is retained is shown by Weiss, Matthäusevangel. See Einleit. p. 540 f.

§ Mark viii., 15; Matt. xvi. 12, Luke xii. 1 f.

up may be seen in the parallels to Mark ix. 33–37. Luke's ignorance or disregard of the record of the first evangelist is apparent from the fact that he seems to know nothing of the latter's characteristic additions to the text of Mark, and all the peculiarities of the passion and the resurrection in his account. The prehistorical portions of the two Gospels* and their accounts of the appearances of Jesus after the resurrection are, as has been already pointed out, directly exclusive of each other.† Of the peculiarities of language which characterize the first evangelist there is scarcely a trace in Luke. Weiss accordingly concludes that it is one of the most incontestable results of Gospel-criticism that Luke used the apostolic source of the first Gospel, but was unacquainted with that record itself.‡

The third Gospel doubtless contains considerable material which was not derived from the logia-document and Mark. It is, of course, impossible precisely to determine what this is, as also to decide exactly what parts of it came from written and what from oral sources. But the striking contrast of the narrative of the birth and infancy of Jesus, beginning at chapter i. 5, in its Hebrew-Greek with the classic Greek of the prologue indicates the use here of a written source. Weiss thinks it highly probable

* It is doubtful whether a writer acquainted with the second chapter of Matthew could have written Luke ii. 39 if he attached any importance to the former; and if he knew of the genealogy of the first Gospel which shows Jesus to have been a descendant of David in the royal line he would hardly have traced his descent on an obscure parallel line.

† Luke must either have been ignorant of the first evangelist's account of the appearance of Jesus in Galilee after the resurrection, or have disregarded it entirely in writing chapter xxiv. 49.

‡ This conclusion is not, however, the unanimous verdict of criticism. See Ed. Simons, Hat der dritte Evangelist den kanonischen Matthäus benutzt? 1880. See also Davidson, Introduction, ii. p. 5 f.

that these materials were taken chiefly from one source which contained a complete biography of Jesus, since they represent all sides of his public life. This critic accordingly assigns to another source some of the sections which Wendt includes in the logia-document. There are passages which are not contained in Matthew and Mark, such as the parables of the prodigal son, the rich man and Lazarus, the Pharisee and publican, etc.* In the history of the passion there are some portions, such as the prophecy of the betrayal, the denial, the prayer in Gethsemane, and the proceedings before the council, which differ so widely from Mark, while the account of the crucifixion contains such striking additions, that the hypothesis of a combination of another source with the narrative of the second Gospel appears to be well grounded. Much diversity of opinion exists regarding the long interpolation, chapters ix. 51–xviii. 14, so called because it interrupts the chronology of the narrative of Mark, and its purpose and source have been minutely discussed. It is ostensibly an account of Jesus' journey to Jerusalem, but it does not become parallel with Mark until chapter xviii. 15. Instead of a direct journey, the narrative appears intended to relate a leisurely moving about, first in the direction of Samaria, thence from its inhospitable borders back to Galilee, again to arrive upon those borders in chapter xvii. 11. Hence Luke does not relegate the story of Mary and Martha to Bethany, wherein he is in conflict with the fourth Gospel.† The general conclusion appears to be justifiable that in this section Luke followed a source giving, perhaps, an account of the journeys of Jesus, and abounding in sayings, discourses, and parables, (some of

---

* Chap. xv. xvi. xvii. 7–10, xviii. 1–15, x. 29–37.
† Meyer, Commentar, i. 2, p. 385.

which were contained in the logia-document), differently placed, perhaps, and modified in form, but suited to the Pauline view of Christianity.

The early traditions regarding the composition of the third Gospel recognize its Pauline character, and some of them even connect Paul with its origin. Irenæus calls Luke's writing "the Gospel preached by Paul."* Tertullian says that "Luke's digest is usually ascribed to Paul."† Jerome thought that Paul referred to Luke's Gospel in the words, "The brother [Luke] whose praise is in the Gospel throughout all the churches,"‡ and said that some supposed that whenever Paul in his Epistles used the expression, "according to my Gospel," he meant that of Luke. § It would, however, be hazardous to draw from these traditions any conclusions relative to the origin of the Gospel. They appear to have arisen from a dogmatic interest to enhance the importance of the record by connecting it with an apostle; though it is, of course, impossible to say how much an early-discerned Pauline tendency in it may have had to do with their origination. While Luke does not in his prologue make any reference to Paul as one of his authorities, and connects him in no way with the writing of the Gospel, there are throughout the work certain points of contact with him and certain coincidences of language and thought which indicate an influence exerted upon the writer by the Pauline Epistles. Many extreme positions have been taken by critics in treating of this matter, some of which are little short of trifling. The Pauline account of the last supper is, however, so similar to that given by Luke that there appears

---

* Adv. Hæres. iii. 1, 1.
† Adv. Marc. iv. 2, 5. See also Euseb., Hist. Eccl. vi. 25.
‡ II. Cor. viii. 18.   § De Vir illustr. c. vii.

to be good reason for supposing the latter to be a combination of Mark's with the former. Some critics find a Pauline diction in the first two chapters which has remarkable resemblances to Romans ix.–xi.*

The historical point of view of the Gospel is quite different from that of the first, and indicates a more developed apprehension of Christianity. The writer, with his Pauline training and environment, could not towards the end of the first century produce such an account of the life and teachings of Jesus as the Jewish first evangelist had produced from his point of view twenty years earlier. Only by a miracle could he compass such a composition. In "accurately tracing up all things from the first" he could not but give the results affected by the Christian consciousness of the time as it took form in his own personality. Hence in his narrative the distinctively Jewish coloring is effaced. The Jewish state is in ruins, Christianity has become a world-religion, and at the very beginning of the record the descent of its Founder is traced as "a second Adam," from the progenitor of the race "who was the son of God." Accordingly, the messengers of Christianity are no longer merely the twelve apostles, corresponding to the twelve tribes of Israel, but the seventy, who are sent forth with no injunction limiting them to Jewish circles, but to gather the "great harvest." On the scene appear the humble publican contrasted with the self-righteous Pharisee, the Samaritan who returned to give thanks for his cure, the other Samaritan who was

---

* Davidson, ii. p. 12. Many words and phrases are used which are found only in Paul's writings, as αἰχμαλωτίζειν, ἀναλῶσαι, ἀναπέμπειν, ἀνταπόδομα, ἐνδιδώσκειν, κυριεύειν, etc. But the danger is manifest of inferring too much from such isolated verbal resemblances, a long list of which might be given.

the type of brotherly love, the sinful woman with her love and faith, the penitent thief on the cross. The legend of Jesus has had more time for development, and has not been slow to improve it. Hence expansion at the beginning in the tradition of the birth and infancy, and expansion at the end in that of the appearances after the resurrection. The personality of Jesus has increased in dignity and power. With greater majesty he moves among the scenes of his ministry, and before him Satan falls like lightning from heaven. On the cross he yields up his life with no cry of abandonment and pain, but with an assured commendation of his spirit to the Father.

The Gospel furnishes no definite indication of the place of its origin. Modern criticism has generally decided in favor of Rome, particularly with reference to the same author's Acts of the Apostles, whose Roman origin is very probable.* The author's use of the Roman Gospel of Mark is favorable to this view, and, according to Hilgenfeld, the way in which he attempts to exculpate Pilate in the matter of Jesus' execution. Köstlin decides for Hellenistic Asia Minor, and an ancient tradition points to Achaia or Macedonia. At all events, there can be no question that the Gospel originated outside of Palestine and in gentile-Christian territory. Hilgenfeld questions that Luke was the author, but gives no very good reasons for this doubt.†

Indications of a later date than that of the other two synoptics are furnished, particularly in the eschatological discourses, but the data which these furnish are not very definite. After the destruction of Jerusalem the Gospel appears certainly to have been written, and at a time when the expectation of an immediate return of Christ was no

---

* Zeller, Theol. Jahrb. 1850, p. 360.   † Die Evangelien, p. 225.

longer entertained. The Parousia is not set forth with the vividness of the delineation of the first Gospel, but with more reserve and vagueness. There appears to be a critical revision by the author of the earlier expressions regarding the advent. He does not make the disciples ask Jesus to reveal "the time of his coming and of the end of the world," but only "when these things," the overthrow of the temple, etc., "shall be." In the first Gospel the coming of Christ is placed "immediately after the tribulations" of Jerusalem's fall, but in Luke "the end is not immediately."* Luke's delineation of the destruction of Jerusalem in his rendering of the forecast of it was evidently written some time after the event, and the ill-fated city is represented as trodden down by the gentiles until their times should be fulfilled.† The persecutions of the Christians in the time of Trajan appear to be described, and among the signs of the impending final judgment is perhaps a reference to a phenomenon of the eruption of Vesuvius in the time of Titus, the "roaring of the sea and waves, men's hearts failing them for fear." ‡ The situation appears to be one of distress which must be endured under the yoke of foreign dominion, and great steadfastness and watchfulness are required. This view does not exclude a forecast by Jesus of the fate of the Jewish state, but is based on a critical judgment of the influence of the writer's historical environment upon the form of his narrative, or, in other words, is the result of a study of the record as literature. The probable date of the composition of the Gospel is about the year 90, and the reasons given for placing it later do not appear to be conclusive.

---

* Matt. xxiv., Luke xxi. † Chap. xxi. 24.
‡ *Ib.* 25, 26.

CHAPTER VII.

THE GOSPEL ACCORDING TO JOHN.

THE study of the first three Gospels has shown them to represent a definite type of the biography of Jesus both in respect to his personality and the character and theatre of his ministry. But the ordinary, uncritical reader cannot but feel, when he turns to the fourth Gospel, that he enters a different realm of thought, and approaches a unique conception of Jesus regarding his person and his manner of teaching. He will, indeed, note some points of contact with the synoptic narrative, but whether or no he construe the peculiarities with which he meets as due to a purpose to represent another phase of the character and life of Jesus, he will be unable to escape the sense of a different environment and spiritual atmosphere from that which he experienced in reading the other Gospels. To the critical reader, however, the contrast is more striking, and has been observed and expressed by the great, both among the ancients and the moderns. To Clement of Alexandria this writing was a spiritual Gospel;* to Origen the firstling of all scripture; † to Luther the only, tender, true chief-Gospel; ‡ and to Herder the echo of the older Gospels in the higher choir. § As it is the fundamental difference of this Gospel from the synop-

---

* τὸ πνευματικὸν εὐαγγέλιον, Euseb., Hist. Eccl. vi. 14.
† ἀπαρχὴ πάσης, γραφῆς. In Joh. tome i. 5.
‡ Das einzige, zarte, rechte Hauptevangelium.
§ Der ältesten Evangelien Nachklang im höheren Chor.

tic narratives which first draws the attention of the casual reader and of the critic, so it is with the consideration of it that the study of the work naturally begins. No great importance could rightly be attached to this difference if it concerned only such superficial matters as the arrangement of the material of the history, slight discrepancies as to the time and place of events, and such peculiarities as appear in the first three when compared with one another. But the facts of the case are such as to warrant the words of one of the most candid critics, which express the judgment of many scholars of great learning and sincerity : " The difference between the fourth Gospel and the other three affects the whole conception of the person and teaching of Christ and the fundamental distribution of the events of his public ministry." *

The attentive reader who passes from the study of the synoptic Gospels to that of the fourth finds his attention at once arrested by its prologue. He is taken off his feet. He has left the solid ground of history, and is caught up into the aërial regions of speculation. The oldest Gospel had introduced him to its story with the simple words : " The beginning of the good news of Jesus Christ." The next in order had proceeded at once to make him acquainted with the human genealogy of Jesus. The third had informed him concerning the historical sources by which its record was authenticated. But this Gospel ushers him into the realm of the supersensible amidst the elements of " the beginning," and tells him strange things of a Logos who was God, and was with God, through whom all things were made, who became flesh, and dwelt

* An Attempt to Ascertain the Character of the Fourth Gospel, especially in its Relation to the Three First, by John James Tayler, B.A., London, 1867.

among men. Here is no longer a simple story of the son of David with his human parentage, the representative of his people, the heir and restorer of their ancient glory, but a mystic speculation concerning a personal revelator of the Eternal, a celestial Light coming forth from the bosom of God and flashing upon the uncomprehending darkness of the world. The reverse of a historical method is this of the prologue. The reader is introduced at once into an ideal world, and led to expect a philosophical treatment of history dominated by a dogmatic conception derived from the Alexandrian speculations. The prologue justifies the reader in looking for a treatment of the evangelic material more or less affected by a "tendency," or a purpose to establish a theory, if not by invention, at least by a handling of the matter adapted to effect a predetermined conviction. He finds, in fact, such an expectation confirmed towards the end of the record where the evangelist declares with great naïveté that the Gospel has been written precisely to establish the reader's belief that Jesus Christ is the Son of God.* How different is all this from the synoptic narratives in which Jesus appears upon the open field of history without a speculative background, submitting to the baptism of John, enduring temptation in the wilderness, engaged in a real process of development, withholding Messianic pretensions until the full consciousness of his mission is attained, beginning his wonderful works by no display of almighty power, but by the healing of demoniacs and cures prompted by compassion! In these records the background of the life of Jesus is the unadorned social life of his countrymen which conspires with his personality to make him what he becomes. There is a charming conformity to nature

---

* Chap. xx. 30, 31.

in this setting of his biography. For Jesus needed, as Keim remarks, not alone a John in order to be himself, but a believing people in order that in the charm of his mind instead of mere logic and in the reciprocity with men wonders might happen, and meditative souls at his feet in order that he might climb the full height of his destiny.

This Gospel also introduces us to a new series of events. After the writer descends to the ground of reality from the region of philosophic speculation in which he moves in the prologue, he places before us things strange to us as readers of the synoptists. There are new words of the Baptist to the messengers of the Sanhedrim, of Jesus to John's disciples who had come to him; new situations, such as baptism by the disciples of Jesus as well as by John; the carrying of a common purse whose bearer was Judas; the attempt of Galileans to make Jesus a king; the visit of Greeks to him; new persons, as the Samaritan woman, the nameless man born blind, Nicodemus, Lazarus; and new localities, as Enon, Salim, Ephraim, Bethany on the Jordan. The theatre of the ministry of Jesus is quite different in this Gospel from that of the synoptic tradition. In the latter Jesus appears first in Capernaum, and is occupied during the first half of his ministry about the Sea of Galilee. The second part is employed in the northern borders, and Luke gives intimations of a journey towards the south. But in the fourth Gospel Judea is the principal field of Jesus' work. According to the synoptists Jesus made but one journey to Jerusalem after the beginning of his public ministry, and that towards the end of it. Then he cast the money-changers out of the temple. But according to the fourth Gospel, this purification of the temple was performed at the beginning of his ministry, which touched Galilee in occasional excursions mostly of short duration.* This change of theatre required a change of representation. Hence the greater part of the peculiar synoptic narratives find no place in this new arrangement of the biography of Jesus. We miss the characteristic teachings of the earlier tradition, the temptation, the numerous healings, the demoniacs, the sermon on the mount, the discourse from the boat, the thronging Galileans, the transfiguration. There is a change in time also. This new biography could not find room within the limits of the synoptic narrative with its brief Galilean episodes and its single journey to the final tragedy in Jerusalem. According to these Jesus attends but one passover, and his ministry appears to occupy but about one year, while his public ministry as detailed in the fourth Gospel extends over about double that time.

Striking characteristics in strong contrast to the older Gospels are presented in this record, in the relation which discourses and narratives hold to each other, as well as in the peculiarities of the discourses themselves. This proportion results from the purpose of the Gospel to set forth the inner essence and nature of Jesus, rather than to produce a biography. Accordingly, discourses and sayings intended to be self-revelations predominate, and doings hold a subordinate place. The history illustrates the idea, is there for its sake, and hence is made secondary to it. Often it is incomplete, as if the writer, mastered by his purpose of idealization and hurried on to a spiritual or metaphysical result, had dropped the thread of his narrative, and forgotten to take it up after he had carried the story so far as was necessary in order to furnish occa-

* Chap. ii. 12, iv. 43, vii. 1.

sion for the unfolding of the Logos-idea.* Nothing distinguishes this Gospel from the others in so marked a manner as the discourses ascribed to Jesus. In the synoptics, Jesus speaks in the popular, simple Eastern style which abounds in proverbs and parables. He speaks as a man of the people, addressing himself in homely terms to the simple-minded. But in this Gospel the profound allegory takes the place of the easy parable, and instead of the pithy, brief, but luminous sentences, with which he clothes his thought in the synoptics, there prevails here a stilted and strained style of discourse, which is often pursued at length, regardless of the capacity of the supposed hearers, and with frequently-recurring misunderstandings on their part. Often a discourse, which begins on a well-defined occasion, takes a wide range, and ends with the occasioning incident and itself hanging in the air, nothing having been accomplished but the enforcement of a doctrine of the person and work of Jesus.† We also miss in these discourses the practical interest, the direct aim at conduct, which pervades all the teachings of Jesus in the synoptic records, the admonitions to self-denial and tender mercy, the warnings against the perils of riches, worldly lust, and care, the lesson of the sower, the blessing on the poor, the preaching of the kingdom of God, and the conditions of entering it. The kingdom recedes to give place to the personality of Jesus, which is advanced into the foreground, although by no means treated in a manner adapted to the popular understanding. Weizsäcker well expresses the impression which the discourses of the fourth Gospel make upon the reader when

* For example, it is not related what was the effect on Nicodemus of the discourse which Jesus delivered to him, chap. iii. 1-22, and whether or no the Greeks attained their object, chap. xii. 20-22.

† Compare the "conversation" (?) with Nicodemus.

he says that it is one of "hardness," of a succession of glaring lights uninterrupted by any softening.*

The tendency of the fourth evangelist to glorify the person of Jesus perhaps best explains the character of his apprehension and record of the "signs" which he ascribes to him. Their difference from the miracles recorded in the synoptics is striking and significant. The compassionate, humane Son of Man who went about doing good, so charmingly portrayed in general by the synoptics, appears to have made little impression upon this writer, whose attention was enchained by his conception of the heaven-descended Logos, who performs wonderful works of the most astounding nature, who is never "unable" to compass them, who possesses marvellous insight and foresight,† knows what is in man, and is never said to have the sentiment of pity. His public ministry is introduced (in a way how different from that of the synoptists!) with the amazing miracle of turning water into wine, a miracle which appears to be entirely uncalled for, except to "manifest his glory" and become a "sign."‡ The narrative of the feeding of the five thousand is related with a manifest purpose to exalt Jesus,§ as is that of the healing of the nobleman's son, which has other features that distinguish it to the point of irreconcilability from that of the first and second Gospels. Instead of being at Capernaum, according to the latter, Jesus is at Cana, a place twenty-five miles distant. Instead of offering to go to the house to heal the son, Jesus accosts the nobleman with a rebuke. In the synoptics, the man tells Jesus not to trouble him-

---

* Untersuchungen über die evangel. Gesch. p. 250.

† Chap. iv. 64, xiii. 3, xviii. 4.

‡ σημεῖον, used by this writer, but by the synoptists only in a bad sense. The synoptic word δυνάμεις, "mighty works," he never uses.

§ Chap. vi. 5, 6.

self to go to the house, but to speak the word only, while here he supplicates him to come down ere his child die. The important incident of the nobleman's faith at which Jesus marvelled, according to the synoptics, is omitted. Jesus' marvelling at anything does not accord with the point of view of this writer. Without entering upon a discussion of the question as to the historical character of the wonders recorded in this Gospel, and waiving all considerations touching their symbolical purpose, one cannot but regard it as indicating a decided "tendency" that the man born blind should be declared to have been so born in order that the works of God might be made manifest in him (a strange teleology, surely!), and that Lazarus should be said to have died that the son of God might be glorified! The incidents connected with the death and resurrection of Lazarus all tend to the same end as the preceding accounts. Jesus is represented as glad that he was not present during the illness of Lazarus, in order that his disciples may believe. He appears to let him die in order that he may raise him, remaining where he was two days after he had heard of his illness. Though he had to be informed of his friend's danger, he knows, apparently by a miraculous prescience, that he is dead, yet, arrived at the place, inquires where he was buried. At the grave he prays "for the sake of the multitudes" "that they may believe." He calls the dead man from the tomb by a word of almighty power in order that "the glory of God" may be manifested. History all this may, indeed, be, but the conclusion can hardly be avoided that it is history subordinated to an idea.

Preliminary to the discussion of the historical character of the Gospel a consideration of its sources is important. It is in the highest degree improbable that the evangelist, whoever he may have been, composed the work by a *tour de force* of pure invention. Should the theory that he wrote it under the influence of a dogmatic purpose be established, it would by no means follow that he proceeded independently of the abundant materials for writing a Gospel which must have been within his reach, or that he was not affected in his mode of expression and even in his ideas by the existing Christian literature. The synoptic Gospels had certainly been for some time in existence when he wrote, and his use of their material to some extent is now admitted by the critics of the most opposing schools.* Along with the many sayings in honorable mention of Peter which Baur notices we are reminded of the first Gospel by the gentle beast of the entry into Jerusalem, the sword-scene in Gethsemane, Mary at the tomb, the son of the centurion, etc. There are points of contact with the synoptic narratives in the account of the cleansing of the temple, with the difference in time already pointed out; in that of the feeding of the multitude; in that of the walking on the sea, with marked discrepancies, since the account in the fourth Gospel implies that Jesus did not go into the boat; in that of the anointing at Bethany, in which there are divergencies from the older accounts; in that of the public entry into Jerusalem; in Jesus' pointing out his betrayer; and in the history of the passion and resurrection. In all this contact with the earlier records the evangelist uses the greatest freedom, and does not scruple at numerous variations in things small and great. He gives the synoptic sayings of Jesus which he uses in quite new and independent connections. The sayings regarding the destruction of the temple and

* Baur, Hilgenfeld, Keim, Ewald, Holtzmann, Godet, Hengstenberg, Luthardt, Weizsäcker, Wittichen, and others.

the naming of Peter are placed at the beginning instead of the end of the history. There appear to be some points of contact in the Gospel with the Pauline ideas and forms of expression, particularly in regard to the relation of the law and the dispensation of grace, but the resemblances are not close enough to warrant the conclusion that the writer was familiar with the Pauline thought to such an extent as to have made it his own.* The question of the sources, says Keim, leaves us undecided how we ought to explain the strong novelties and the bold deviations of the Gospel. Is it the living stream of oral tradition, is it the eye-witnessship of the author which justifies or excuses him, or must not one in many points rest in the belief that he made a free literary transformation of the history on the ground of a philosophical and religious idea which according to his own confession he would serve? †

The tendency of the modern criticism of the Gospel is towards an affirmative answer to this latter question. Baur's objections to the historical character of the Gospel from this point of view, however extreme and overwrought some of them may be, have never been entirely overcome, and their influence appears still in the judgment of moderate and conservative critics, like Weizsäcker and Wendt, who maintain some connection of the apostle John with the composition of the Gospel. In arriving at a decision as to the historical character of the record much depends, of course, on the conception of history with which one sets out. Judged by the most rigid conception of history, perhaps no one of the four Gospels could be pronounced a

---

* Holtzmann gives a long list of parallel passages which show, indeed, some greater or less similarities of thought. But one cannot decide to what extent these ideas may have been the common property of the time.

† Geschichte Jesu von Nazara, i., p. 121.

strictly historical composition throughout. But it would be manifestly improper to apply such a standard to any one of them. A history free from all ideal and legendary elements could not without a miracle have been written under the circumstances in which the Gospels originated. If, then, we take the synoptic records as representing the sort of history which one might fairly suppose would be written by Christians living near the end of the first century, we cannot but see, if we will lay aside prepossessions as much as possible, that the fourth Gospel is a widely different type of composition from even these.

Not to dwell on the speculative themes which dominate the Gospel, and must be acknowledged to be disturbing to the historical development of any composition dealing with the materials of history, it is evident to the unbiassed student that the purpose is not purely historical. The comparison of it with the synoptic narratives shows clearly a selective aim in the use of material and consequently a one-sidedness. An eclectic Gospel, as Keim remarks, is a one-sided Gospel. In passing over many parts of the history of Jesus, as we must conclude it does if we give credence to the synoptics, and adhering tenaciously to another part of it, it has, as even Weizsäcker acknowledges, presented only a "half-true picture" of his life. The impression which it makes is, besides, that of a completed work the supplementing of which from the other records would be a proceeding of great violence. To transfer to it the material, and still more the spirit, of the discourses and acts of Jesus out of the others would be to create a phantom, a hermaphrodite of unnaturalness and contradictions.*
This dispensing with, or rather downright exclusion of, a long series of correct traditions has been rightly regarded

* Keim, Gesch. Jesu, p. 122.

as inconsistent with a genuine historical aim. The theory that the Gospel was written with the design of supplementing the synoptic records is untenable on the ground that it in part repeats, and in part directly traverses, their narratives.

The subjective character of the Gospel has been repeatedly pointed out. It is not, of course, to be expected that a writer should conceal himself in composing a history; but it is evident that, just to the degree in which he obtrudes himself, in that degree is the historical character of his composition prejudiced. Now in this Gospel the personality of the writer is excessively prominent. Not only are the discourses ascribed to Jesus and the narrative portions marked by a uniformity of style and peculiar turns of expression which give them the appearance of having been cast in the same mould, but commentators find it difficult in many cases to separate the words of Jesus from the reflections of the evangelist. It is evident that the writer has put himself into the entire book to such a degree as very much to prejudice its historical character. One cannot but ask, and criticism has often asked, how the writer, even if an ear-witness, could have retained in memory these long discourses of Jesus, which are the more difficult for the memory on account of their peculiar character. That discourses which often have no point of attachment in events, are wanting in logical connection, and are suspended in the high regions of speculation, could have been accurately reproduced by the memory, is a psychological incredibility. That they could have been handed down through oral tradition, as the pithy sayings and parables of the synoptics doubtless were, may confidently be declared impossible. Even those critics who attempt to maintain the essential integrity of the discourses by the supposition that the assumed author, John, had become imbued with the teachings of Jesus, and had made his spirit and thought his own, are obliged to admit the "subjective freedom" of the writer in the construction of these long disquisitions. But, subjective freedom admitted, the question cannot but arise to what extent the historical credibility of the Gospel is affected by it. Is the mode of teaching which is here attributed to Jesus, and is so fundamentally different from that which the synoptists gathered from Matthew's logia and from the oral tradition, the actual historical method? All that is most trustworthy in the tradition of Jesus represents him as speaking in such a way that the common people heard him gladly, employing such terse, epigrammatic, and parabolic forms of clothing his ideas as go straight to the popular mind, and make a tenacious and lasting oral tradition. The long, diffuse, involved, and philosophic discourses in the fourth Gospel cannot be the historical words of the great Teacher of the synoptic tradition, if that tradition is to be accepted as essentially authentic. The "subjective freedom" of the writer appears to have been exercised to the extent that it has totally transformed the method of teaching, and, more than this, has substituted an Alexandrian mysticism for plain, practical, every-day morality. "The limpid spontaneity of that earlier teaching, with its fresh illustrations and profound sentences uttered without effort and untinged by art, is exchanged for diffuse addresses and artificial dialogues, in which labor and design are everywhere apparent."

The historical credibility of the Gospel has also been called in question, in view of its relation to Paul and the early controversies in the Church between Jewish and

Pauline Christians. Attention has already been called to the points of contact with Pauline thought in the Gospel. Whether the writer had studied the theology of Paul in the Epistles of this apostle, or had elsewhere learned it, certain it is that his representation of the attitude of Jesus towards the Jews and the gentiles is so decidedly Pauline that the opposition of the apostles and Jewish Christians generally to the tendency represented by the apostle to the gentiles is unintelligible on the presumption of the historical truth of the Gospel. Had the apostles known Jesus to have taught as he is here represented as teaching, they could not have opposed Paul, and had Paul known it, he could not have failed to appeal to such an authority. With all the spiritualizing of the law in the synoptics, Jesus there announces that he came not to abrogate but to fulfil it, and that not one jot or tittle should pass from it until all be fulfilled. No such declaration is put into his mouth in the fourth Gospel, nor does the evangelist express any such sentiment. The spirit of the record is that which belongs to a later development of Christianity under the influence of Pauline ideas. The words, " The law was given by Moses, but grace and truth came by Jesus Christ," * are quite Pauline, and imply that there was neither grace nor truth in the old dispensation. Christ is made to disclaim the functions of the law, since he came not into the world to judge it.† Eternal life comes only of *faith* in the Son.‡ The temple-worship passes away to give place to the spiritual worship, which is bound to no place.§ No more spiritual importance is attached to the Old Testament than to say that " the Jews" *think* they have eternal life in it. Indeed "the

* Chap. i. 17. † Chap. iii. 7, v. 24. ‡ Chap. iii. 36
§ Chap. iv. 23.

letter killeth, but the spirit giveth life." Moses is depreciated. It was no "true bread" that came through him.* "The Jews" appear as foreigners in this Gospel, and Jesus is made to speak to them of the law as "your law," "their law." They are of the Devil, and do the works of their father. The almost shocking declaration is put into the mouth of Jesus that all who came before him were thieves and robbers. This even surpasses Paul in downright anti-Judaism; and unless it be conceded that the "subjective freedom" of the evangelist has greatly modified the actual teaching of Jesus, so that we have here the idealization of a later time and not pure history, then the great Pauline controversy of the apostolic age remains an enigma, perhaps "a phantom, a dream, a folly."

No more striking illustration of the influence of dogmatic prepossession appears in theological literature than is furnished in the voluminous discussions of the historical evidence as to the date of the composition of the fourth Gospel. From a few data of no very complicated or obscure character the most contradictory conclusions have been drawn, and the judgments as to the time when the Gospel was first recognized in Christian literature differ by about three quarters of a century. The protracted discussion of the question has, however, tended to bring all students who are not extremists nearer to agreement, and there is ground for the hope that a correct conclusion is attainable by those who will bring an unbiassed judgment to the consideration of the matter. Truth ever escapes the partisan, pursue he never so hotly. Beginning with Papias whose writing referred to by Eusebius probably dates 130–140, we find that his New-Testament canon, if the term may be allowed, was limited to an

* Chap. v. 49.

original writing by Matthew, (the logia,) one by Mark, the first Epistle of John and the first of Peter. He also acknowledges the Apocalypse as a writing of the apostle John. It is remarkable that he makes no mention of Luke's Gospel, of Paul's Epistles, and of the fourth Gospel. Did he mention only such writings as were in his opinion traceable to the original apostles, Peter's supposed connection with the second Gospel bringing it under this category? Did he know of the fourth Gospel and omit to mention it because he did not regard it as of apostolic origin? Or was it not known to him, or, indeed, not yet in existence? Or, again, did he mention it and Eusebius fail to report his words concerning it? The affirmative of this last question is a glaring improbability, although Mr. Matthew Arnold thinks that "the good Bishop of Cæsarea" had a "very loose fashion" or "little stringency of method," and might have failed to mention so important a matter.* If Eusebius was right in saying that Papias used testimonies from the first Epistle of John, then the Gospel was probably in existence in Papias' time, since there can be little doubt that the author of the Epistle was the author of the Gospel. But Zeller tries to show that the Bishop of Cæsarea was a poor critic and made mistakes, and that he is not to be depended on in his testimony that Papias was acquainted with the first Epistle of John. Davidson, however, repudiates such criticism as "scarcely fair," while holding against the great majority of scholars that the Epistle and Gospel had different authors. The conclusion of a "fair" criticism seems to be that the Gospel was probably in existence as early as 140, but that Papias for reasons about which it is idle to speculate did not mention it.

* God and the Bible, 1883, p. 242.

The Tübingen critics, so far as they follow Baur in dating the composition of the Gospel as late as 170–180, strenuously deny that Justin (147–160) made any citations from it or was acquainted with it. Certain it is that his use of it, if he used it at all, was very slight, since, although he makes more than one hundred quotations which have striking resemblances to synoptical passages, we find very few passages which can even be called reminiscences of the fourth Gospel, and only one or two which have the appearance of quotations. When he calls Christ "the blameless and just light sent by God to man," when he employs as a favorite word $\dot{\alpha}\lambda\eta\theta\iota\nu\acute{o}\varsigma$, "true," so often used in this Gospel, and speaks of the "blood of Christ sprung not from human seed, but from the will of God,"* he appears to show a familiarity with the record in question. Familiarity with a Christological doctrine of the Gospel is indicated in the words in reference to Christ: "He was an only-begotten son of the Father, sprung from him * * * and afterwards born a man through the virgin," etc.† The term $\mu o\nu o\gamma \epsilon\nu\acute{\eta}\varsigma$, "only-begotten," here used by Justin is applied to Jesus only in the fourth Gospel. To say that it was a word already current in a certain Christian school has much the appearance of an evasion in view of the whole evidence from Justin. The fact that in the last clause of the passage Justin refers to the synoptic accounts of the birth of Jesus does not show that he had no other source nor does it require that the term "only-begotten" be explained out of the first three Gospels, since two sources may as fairly be assumed as one. In fact, the passage appears to be the product of reminiscences of the fourth Gospel and the synoptics.

* Dial. c. 63, cf. John i. 13.   † Dial. c. 105.

The most important passage from Justin is that on the new birth, and runs thus: "Christ said, unless ye be born anew ye cannot enter into the kingdom of heaven. Now, that it is impossible for those once born to enter into the wombs of those that bore them, is obvious to all men."* Now, since Justin did not derive his knowledge of the teachings of Christ from traditions, but depended on writings, the question which this citation raises is simply, from what writing did it probably come to him? Was it taken from the synoptics, from some apocryphal Gospel, or from the fourth Gospel? That the matter presents difficulties, cannot be denied. For "born anew" he does not use the words of the fourth evangelist, $\gamma\epsilon\nu\nu\eta\theta\tilde{\eta}$ $\check{\alpha}\nu\omega\theta\epsilon\nu$ but $\dot{\alpha}\nu\alpha\gamma\epsilon\nu\eta\theta\tilde{\eta}\tau\epsilon$, a word which does not occur in the fourth Gospel, nor, indeed, anywhere in the New Testament except in I. Peter i. 3, 23. Again he says "kingdom of heaven," an expression peculiar to the first Gospel, while in the fourth "kingdom of God" occurs throughout. These facts have seemed to Baur and others to warrant the conclusion that Justin did not know the fourth Gospel, but derived the words in question from the Gospel according to the Hebrews.† But the last clause of the passage is so like the words in the fourth Gospel as to leave little doubt that the whole passage is a free quotation from it, or rather an adaptation or reminiscence. Of quotations in the strict sense Justin makes none from our Gospels, and it is not necessary to suppose that he wrote these words with the fourth Gospel before him. But it is only the exigencies of a theory which can lead any one to judge that he had in mind only the passage from Matthew,

---

* Apol. i. 61, *cf*. John iii. 3–5.
† Krit. Untersuch. über die kan. Evangel. p. 352; Davidson, Introd. ii. p. 375.

"Except ye be converted and become as little children, ye shall not enter into the kingdom of heaven." Yet Tübingen critics have advocated this view. One who has no theory to serve will, however, naturally conclude that while Justin may have taken the passage from some other source, our fourth Gospel being the only one known to contain anything resembling it closely, the presumption is in favor of its existence in his time and of his knowledge of it. Baur asks why, if Justin took this passage from the fourth Gospel, he did not quote it correctly. It is surprising that any one familiar with Justin's loose way of quoting should raise this question. Baur also objects that it is improbable that if Justin knew the fourth Gospel and acknowledged it as of apostolic origin, he would have quoted so little from it.* Here lurks a fallacy. For the two questions whether Justin knew the Gospel and whether he believed it to be of apostolic origin should be kept distinct. The former can be answered with great probability in the affirmative, while for the latter the grounds are quite uncertain, if any exist at all. We have found in our study of the canon that not only Justin but also writers of a later time than his were in the habit of making liberal use of Gospel-writings without regard to the question of their origin or canonicity. As to Justin's reasons for not making more citations from the fourth Gospel, it is evident that we can only speculate about them. It is possible that its marked difference from the other Gospels known to him led him to doubt the correctness of its representation of the teaching of Jesus. Certain it is that his conception of Jesus' manner of teaching could not have been derived from this record, but only from the synoptic accounts or others similar to them. For he says: "Short

---

* Krit. Untersuch., etc., p. 353.

and concise are the sayings that came from him, for he was not a sophist, but his word was a power of God." *

The question respecting the testimony of Basilides (125–130) to the fourth Gospel cannot be so easily decided as some partisans appear to think. The work "Against Heresies" or Philosophumena, falsely ascribed to Origen and by some thought to be the work of Hippolytus, appears to state that Basilides referred to the words, "That was the true light which lighteth every man that cometh into the world," as "that spoken in the Gospels," and that he used many other passages which resemble words contained in the fourth Gospel. There is, however, some doubt whether the author of the work refers to Basilides or his school. The work was written about the beginning of the third century, and if the reference was to the followers of Basilides it would, of course, establish nothing as to the existence and use of the Gospel in the first half of the second century. It appears that the writer of Philosophumena was careless as to the use of the verb "says," † without a definite subject, so that it is not easy to determine whether he refers to Basilides or his school. Sometimes he speaks of Basilides and his son, and other Gnostics, and "the whole choir of these" or "the whole school of them," ‡ and then quotes them with the verb "says." It is remarkable that nowhere in his work does he mention John, except as the author of the Apocalypse. It is difficult to pronounce positively on this question, although Matthew Arnold and Ezra Abbot are positive against Tayler, Davidson, and the great majority of the critical

---

* βραχεῖς δὲ καὶ σύντομοι παρ᾽ αὐτοῦ λόγοι γεγόνασιν, οὐ γὰρ σοφιστὴς ὑπῆρχεν, ἀλλὰ δύναμις θεοῦ ὁ λόγος αὐτοῦ ἦν. Apol. i. 14.
† φησίν.
‡ πᾶς ὁ τούτων χόρος, πᾶσα ἡ τούτων σχολή.

school that Basilides is quoted. So much, at least, is certain, that if Basilides is quoted in this work, his testimony establishes no more than that the Gospel was in existence and approved by a Gnostic soon after the first quarter of the second century; but that it was written by John is not established, nor is anything made known regarding its origin.

The earliest account that we have in Christian literature of the composition of this Gospel is contained in a fragment in the canon of Muratori, which has already been quoted in the chapter on the canon, where its legendary character was pointed out. Towards the end of the fourth century Epiphanius preserved the tradition connecting John with the authorship of the Gospel. He says that John wrote last, reluctantly, and because he was constrained to write, and that he wrote in Asia at the age of ninety. Athenagoras, who wrote his " Plea for the Christians " and " The Resurrection of the Dead " about 177, has some passages which bear a very strong resemblance to Johannine thought. He as well as Justin held the doctrine of the Logos, but since it was current in the thought of the time, and may be traced to Philo, the fourth Gospel was not necessarily its source. He speaks of " the one God who made all things through the Word proceeding from Him," but he makes no definite reference to John or the Gospel. The first Epistle to Diognetus is " deeply imbued with Johannine thought," such as, " He sent His Son in love, not to judge," and " They are not of the world, as I am not of the world." But there is no indication of the source of these sayings. Tatian, too, a pupil of Justin, appears to have been acquainted with the Gospel, although he does not expressly refer to it. About the year 180, Theophilus of Antioch, in a writing addressed to Autolychus, makes the first distinct reference to the Gospel, and attributes it to John, although he does not say the apostle John. He classes it among the holy Scriptures, and calls its author "inspired," * thus giving him a place among canonical writers.

The conclusions regarding the external evidence for the Gospel appear to be that there is a strong probability of its existence soon after the first quarter of the second century; that it was perhaps known to Papias, though not used by him so far as our data enable us to judge; that it was known to Justin, but very sparingly used by him for reasons which we can only conjecture; that any earlier use of it is doubtful; that there are very strong indications of its use by Athenagoras and the author of the Epistle to Diognetus; that there is a legendary tradition as to its Johannine authorship and its revision by certain associates of John, which dates from about the last quarter of the second century (canon of Muratori); that prior to this latter date there is no evidence of any kind which connects John with its composition or makes any reference to its authorship; and finally that about 180 appears the first distinct expression of the opinion that John was the author and that the Gospel was regarded as canonical. The cautious and unbiassed student of the early Christian literature soon learns, however, not to place too much reliance upon tradition, particularly when he meets with it in the legendary form in which that of the canon of Muratori presents itself. He feels in need of precisely the sort of confirmation which in most cases is not to be had, the grounds on which this or that writer based his assertions regarding the origin of books, a knowledge of the evidence which was before him, if, indeed, there was any, and he did not

* πνευματόφορος.

proceed upon mere rumor credulously accepted. The student, for example, would like to know the sources of the information on which Theophilus makes the assertion that John wrote the fourth Gospel. Since, according to a very good tradition, there were two Johns, he naturally asks which of them Theophilus had in mind; how Theophilus knew that the writer of the Gospel was a $\pi\nu\epsilon\upsilon\mu\alpha\tau\acute{o}\varphi o\rho o\varsigma$; whether or no he had informed himself regarding the composition of the Gospel so as to be able to tell whether the John in question actually wrote the Gospel himself or was somehow indirectly connected with its authorship; and finally, what sort of a man this Theophilus intellectually was. A fair view of the matter appears to be that of Matthew Arnold: "Tradition may be false; yet it is at least something * * * in a thing's favor that men have delivered it. But there may be reasons why we cannot believe it." If, then, there be reasons why we cannot believe the tradition respecting the authorship of the fourth Gospel by the apostle John, at least if we are to understand it as testifying to his immediate, personal composition of it, these reasons must be found in the Gospel itself, and we are remanded to a study of it as the only, if not altogether satisfactory, means of settling the question, so far as it is capable of definitive settlement.

In pursuance of this aim and in view of the limits within which the treatment of the subject is here confined, it becomes necessary to omit a consideration in detail of the question of the relation of the fourth Gospel and the Revelation with reference to the problem of authorship. On the theory that the apostle John wrote the Revelation, and his authorship of this work is better attested externally than his authorship of the Gospel, it has been argued with great cogency that the same person could not have written the Gospel. The difference of the two writings is so great in spirit, point of view, aim, and language that identity of authorship is most improbable. The writer who in the Revelation shows himself a true "son of thunder," as John is designated in the synoptic narratives, could not have produced the spiritual, gentle fourth Gospel. On the other hand it has been argued that the two writings have resemblances which indicate identity of authorship. Again, some of the ablest scholars have contended that there are not sufficient grounds either external or internal to support the Johannean authorship of the Revelation, while they find arguments which appear to them conclusive that the "beloved disciple" was the author of the Gospel. Others hold that John wrote neither of these works, and Keim and Lützelberger deny altogether the story of his residence in Asia Minor. The most recent criticism of the Revelation makes it a composite work containing Jewish and Christian elements assignable to dates separated by a period of sixty or seventy years, and completed as late as the year 136.* But the question of the authorship of this book is not of essential importance in the consideration of that of the Gospel, although its solution would throw light upon some of the problems involved. To waive, then, the investigation of a matter so complicated will simplify without seriously prejudicing the discussion of the subject of immediate concern.

Among matters internal to the Gospel bearing on the question of authorship, belong the passover-controversy and the divergence of this record from the synoptics as to the day of the crucifixion. The synoptists expressly

* The subject is discussed with considerable fulness in Martineau's Seat of Authority in Religion, 1890, p. 217-227.

state that Jesus partook of the passover-supper which was eaten, "according to the law," on the evening of the 14th of the Jewish month Nisan. Accordingly, he must have been crucified on the 15th of the month. The fourth Gospel is equally explicit in the statement that when Jesus was brought before Pilate the passover-supper was still in the future, for the writer says, that the Jews " went not into the judgment-hall lest they should be defiled, but that they might eat the passover." * It follows that according to this record the crucifixion was on the 14th Nisan, or one day earlier than according to the synoptists. There is no question that there is here an irreconcilable difference between the fourth Gospel and the others as to the day of the crucifixion. The attempts of extreme partisans like Hengstenberg and Wieseler to reconcile the discrepancy have been shown to be futile by Bleek, who maintained the genuineness of the Gospel. All attempts to make it appear that this evangelist is correct to the prejudice of the synoptists have failed. But the matter does not end with a discrepancy between the records. The question whether or no the 14th Nisan was the day on which Jesus ate the passover with his disciples was contested in the second century between the Eastern and Western branches of the Church, or rather a controversy arose which turned upon this question. This has been called the passover-controversy. It appears that the churches in Asia were accustomed to celebrate on the 14th Nisan, a feast of the " passover of salvation," or a communion in commemoration of the last paschal meal of Jesus with his disciples. Eusebius says: " The churches in Asia, guided by a more ancient tradition, supposed that they ought to keep the 14th day of the moon as a

* Chap. xviii. 28.

festival of the passover of salvation, on which day the Jews were wont to kill the paschal lamb." * The 14th Nisan was accordingly observed as a festival-day by the partaking of a supper in the evening.

The Roman Christians, breaking away from bondage to all rites which had a connection with Judaism, ignored the passover-feast, and transferred their memorial of the Saviour to the day of his resurrection, that is, to Easter Sunday, which they celebrated as a yearly festival uniting the ideas of a crucifixion- and resurrection-passover.† Those who observed the 14th Nisan were called quartodecimans. Now, in the course of the long controversy between the Eastern and Western churches over this question which was finally settled by the council of Nice in favor of the Roman usage, it is important to observe that appeal was made by the former to the practice of the apostle John in regard to the celebration in dispute. This was not far from the middle of the second century, when the Gospel was probably in existence, which places the crucifixion on the 14th Nisan. Yet the Romans did not appeal to its authority, although it would have favored their view. On the contrary, in the discussion between Anicetus of Rome and Polycarp of the East, we find that the latter maintained his position on the strength of John's custom of observing the 14th of the month as the day on which Jesus ate the passover-supper, while according to the fourth Gospel that supper, if eaten at all, must have been eaten on the evening of the 13th, since the crucifixion was on the 14th. Polycrates (190) writing as Bishop of Ephesus to Victor of Rome, appeals to the practice of the " great lights " of the Eastern Church who

* Hist. Eccl. v. 23.
† A πάσχα σταυρώσιμον and a πάσχα ἀναστάσιμον.

"observed the genuine day," and among them to "John who rested upon the bosom of our Lord," and to Polycarp, "both Bishop and martyr." All of them, he says, "observed the 14th day of the passover, according to the Gospel," *i.e.*, of course, the synoptical records. Accordingly, these "great lights" can have recognized this account only as correct, and even John followed it in opposition to that of the fourth Gospel. How, then, knowing that Jesus partook of the last meal with his disciples on the evening of the 14th, and was crucified on the 15th, could he have written the chapter of the fourth Gospel which is directly contradictory to these facts? No more glaring contradiction can be conceived than that a man should have written thus of the day of the crucifixion and have joined the quartodecimans in keeping the passover-feast on the 14th of the month, particularly when his views are expressed by Hippolytus to the effect that, "Christ celebrated the passover on that very day (the 14th), and I, therefore, must do as the Lord did."

The fourth Gospel was not, however, wholly out of the controversy, for one writer at least, Apollinaris (170), in a fragment of his work on the question in dispute, not only indicates the discrepancy between it and the other records, but places in a true light the real nature of the issue. Writing in opposition to the quartodecimans, he says: "They say that on the 14th the Lord ate the lamb with his disciples, and suffered himself on the great day of unleavened bread; and they explain Matthew as stating the matter in accordance with their own ideas. Hence their notion is irreconcilable with the law, and according to their views the Gospels seem at variance." * These

---

* The evils resulting from the quartodeciman theory are thus said to be two: a contravention of the law which enjoined that the paschal lamb and, *à fortiori*, Christ, should be sacrificed on the 14th of the month, and by the words of Apollinaris: "They (the quartodecimans) say that on the 14th the Lord ate the lamb with his disciples," appear to set forth the actual question in dispute, to settle which the example of John was cited. Unfavorable are they, as well as those of Hippolytus previously quoted, to the theory advocated by some scholars that the paschal controversy had regard not to the subject of the festival, but only to the day; that the Christians of Asia Minor in carrying out an originally Jewish-Christian practice had attached themselves to the Jewish law, and established an analogous festival on the same day on which the Jewish passover fell; but afterwards, in order to show the propriety of connecting with this Christian festival of salvation the commemoration of the institution of the last supper, had maintained the like practice of Jesus according to the synoptists.* With all the difficulties of the problem it appears pretty certain that at the time of the passover-controversy there was no question of a celebration of the passover in general, but of an event of the Gospel-history connected with it; of the institution, in fact, of the Lord's supper at the last passover-celebration by Jesus. But if the festival of the Christians of Asia Minor concerned this institution it stands in insoluble contradiction with a Gospel which cuts off its roots, since it formally excludes a last passover-meal of Jesus with his disciples. †

acceptance of the synoptic account, an introduction of discord between the two narratives. Apollinaris seems to imply that in his time the statement of the fourth evangelist regarding the last supper was already received by certain persons. From this problem of the variance of the records, Dr. Routh shrinks: Difficillima quæstio, cui me virum pusilli ingenii interponere noluerim. Relig. Sacra, i. p. 168. Tayler, Fourth Gospel, p. 108.

* Lücke, Gieseler, Bleek, De Wette, Riggenbach, Hase, Schürer, Luthardt, Weiss, Ezra Abbot, and others.

† Holtzman, Einleit.; Baur, Schwegler, Zeller, Keim, Scholten, Hilgenfeld, Davidson, Matthew Arnold, Martineau, Tayler, and others, to whom

The echoes of this discussion have long since died away, and it is no longer a matter of importance to Christians whether Jesus was crucified on one or another day of the month. The sole interest in the question is now a critical one, and relates to the authorship of the fourth Gospel. Two questions must, however, be kept distinct: Is it probable that the apostle John wrote a Gospel, against an important statement in which he stands historically committed? and Is the position of those critics tenable who hold that the writer of the Gospel, whoever he may have been, composed it with the object in part of exerting an influence in the paschal controversy against the identification of the last supper with the Jewish passover? It is evident that the affirmative of the former question does not at all necessitate that of the latter. The purpose of the writer, however, to represent Jesus as the true paschal lamb cannot be doubted, and probably accounts for the discrepancy.*

If we begin the search for the author of the Gospel with a study of the intimations as to his personality contained in the work itself, we are first impressed with a vague presence which rather conceals than manifests itself. In the body of the Gospel there appears three times a personage otherwise undefined than as the disciple whom Jesus loved, and in the appendix (chapter xxi.) he is expressly pointed out as one who was to survive the second coming of Christ. But it is nowhere intimated that this disciple was John. Of the Word (Logos) that became flesh the evangelist says: "We beheld his glory, a glory as of an only-begotten of a

with Hausrath and Pfleiderer acknowledgments are due for suggestions for this chapter.

* Martineau, Seat of Authority, etc., p. 233.

father," [*] thus including himself among those who had beheld a certain supersensible manifestation "full of grace and truth," which he calls a "glory." The nature of this seeing is indeterminate, and may be a spiritual intuition of which one might thus speak who had enjoyed an experience of the "grace and truth" of Jesus, as "ye have seen the Father," and "the world seeth me no more, but ye see me." [†] In another place the evangelist refers to a witness in confirmation of a statement: "And he that hath seen this hath borne witness, and that one knoweth that he saith what is true, that ye also may believe." [‡] The improbability that a writer should refer to himself as "that one" [§] has led Ewald to conjecture that John, whom he supposes to have been the author, employed a young friend as amanuensis who inserted these words! Certainly, the only natural explanation of the passage is that the author refers in it to one who has already borne testimony which he uses, and wishes to assure the reader to be trustworthy. An author writing of himself could neither say "that one" nor "hath borne witness." In the appendix the disciple previously mentioned is declared to be the one that "hath written these things." If this chapter was written by the author of the Gospel it is evident that he was, or wished to pass for, the vague disciple whom Jesus loved, whoever he may have been. But it is generally conceded that the twentieth chapter is the proper and natural ending of the Gospel, and that the twenty-first was added later. The authorship of the chapter is too uncertain to warrant any

[*] Chap. i. 14.

[†] The same word for "see" is used in all these passages and in chap. i. 51, "Ye shall see the heaven opened and the angels of God ascending and descending on the Son of Man."

[‡] Chap. xix. 35. [§] ἐκεῖνος.

conclusions from it as to that of the Gospel itself. Suspicion is thrown upon it by the last verse which has a decidedly apocryphal character: "And there are also many other things which Jesus did; and if they were to be every one written, I suppose that not even the world itself could contain the books that would be written." This verse is textually well authenticated, being found in all the oldest manuscripts except the Sinaïtic. Tischendorf's rejection of it is quite arbitrary. Widely different opinions have been held as to the veiling of the voucher for the narrative in these passages on the assumption of John's authorship of the Gospel, according as it is thought to indicate a delicate modesty, or especially in the characterization of the disciple as one whom Jesus loved, an ambiguous and artificial manner of introducing him,* if not a presumptuous self-exaltation,† or vanity,‡ or a piece of offensive self-glorification,§ or an unendurably conceited self-designation.‖ These difficulties disappear, however, with the rejection of an immediate Johannine authorship.

Since, from the critical point of view, the Gospel must be regarded as the product of a human personality, the question naturally arises whether the Galilean fisherman, John, the son of Zebedee, surnamed "the son of thunder," was a person likely to produce it. From the synoptics we learn that he was of an ambitious, fiery, and vindictive nature. He aspired to sit beside the Son of Man in his glory, and would call down fire from heaven on the inhospitable Samaritan village. It should be remembered that the portrait of the disciple whom Jesus loved is painted only in the fourth Gospel, and is not

---

* Holtzmann.   † Weisse.   ‡ Scholten.
§ Keim.   ‖ Schmeidel.

there intimated to be that of John. According to our knowledge of him from the synoptics, he was much better qualified to write the fierce and fiery Apocalypse than the love-breathing Gospel. Paul represents him as one of the " pillar-apostles " who maintained the legalistic attitude of the original apostles, and preached the Gospel only to those of the circumcision,* in a word, as " the natural continuation of the disciple of the synoptic Gospels, called among the first to be a follower of Jesus." Now, the fourth Gospel represents a phase of universalism which even surpasses that of Paul, as has already been pointed out, a phase of the development of Christianity to which the world is the field, to which a universal spiritual worship is preferable to rites and ceremonies in Jerusalem or on Gerizim.† The writer of this great work has left far behind him all national limitations and the meagre ingathering through Jewish proselytism; recognizes " other sheep " than those of the fold of Israel; beholds with prophetic eye " one flock and one shepherd "; represents the great Martyr as dying " not for the nation only, but that he may also gather together in one body the children of God that are scattered abroad," and introduces Greeks to see Jesus in the solemn hour of preparation for the sacrifice which was to " bear much fruit." ‡ Here one sees no longer traces of " the violent separation of the new faith from the mother-religion "; there are no echoes of the pathetic complaint of Jesus over his people; § the voice of Paul is not heard in sympathy for his " brethren according to the flesh "; no word of promise or of prophecy for the reprobate nation is spoken, but rather one of irrevocable condemnation; ‖ the

* Gal. ii. 7–12. ‡ Chap. x. 16, xi. 52, xii. 20 f.
† Chap. iii. 16, 17; iv. 23, 24. § Luke xix. 41–44.
‖ Chap. xii. 38–40.

glowing hope of Paul for the conversion of "all Israel" finds no place in the sombre picture depicted in the ominous prophecy, "Ye shall die in your sins."*

This is evidently not the point of view of a Jewish-Christian writer of the apostolic age. Not to charge the author with a wholesale invention, one cannot but see that he has given the biography of Jesus such a setting, has used his material in such a way, as to indicate unmistakably the time of the waning of Judaism and the growing supremacy of Pauline ideas. The Judaism which he has before him is that of the beginning of the second century, and the Christianity which he represents is that of the same period, with its theological ideas, problems, disputations, and refinements of speculation. It would be difficult to conceive of the synoptists representing Jesus as entering into a discussion with the Jews on the problem how he could be one with God and represent the Father without overthrowing the monotheistic doctrine.†
Such speculations were as remote from their time and foreign to their thought as they were native and familiar to the first quarter of the second century. It is also questionable that the author's point of view indicates familiarity with the Jews of the time of Christ, their country, state, and institutions. He speaks of their customs in such terms as a foreigner would employ—for example, of "the manner of purifying of the Jews," "the Jews' passover was nigh," "as the manner of the Jews is to bury," etc. This style is peculiar to him among the evangelists. The judgment of Matthew Arnold appears just, that "it seems almost impossible to think that a Jew born and bred—a man like the apostle John—could ever have come to speak so." "A Jew talking of the Jews'

* Chap. viii. 24. † Chap. x. 30-37.

passover * * * is like an Englishman writing of the Derby as the English people's Derby." As to "Bethany beyond Jordan,"* it is well known that Origen's personal investigation on the spot failed to find such a place, and that, finding a Bethabara there, his influence prevailed in establishing that reading temporarily. The oldest and best manuscripts, however, read Bethany.† It is only the exigencies of a theory that can lead scholars to conclude that there must have been such a place, though it has never been found.‡ A geographical error of this kind could not have been committed by an apostle of Jesus. Again, a writer familiar with Jewish institutions would not write of Caiaphas as "High-priest of that year," as if the office were a yearly one. It is likely that, writing in Asia Minor, the custom prevailing there was before his mind.§

Objections against the Johannine authorship of the Gospel have been urged with great cogency, on the ground of the theological point of view of the author and of his manner of dealing with the philosophical problems which he introduces. While his limited vocabulary shows the narrowness of his range of thought, this range of

---

* Chap. i. 28.

† Davidson's remark is at least obscure: "We assume that Bethany, not Bethabara, is the true reading, as Origen attests; with the approval of Lachmann and Tischendorf"! Introduction, ii. p. 427.

‡ Meyer and De Wette. Matthew Arnold's judgment is that the author's "Palestinian geography is so vague * * * that when he wants a name for a locality he takes the first village that comes into his remembrance, without troubling himself to think whether it suits or no," and that, knowing the Bethany where Lazarus lived, he hastily took it as the place where John baptized! To Baur this Bethany is a pure invention, made in order to have Jesus' work begin and end at Bethany! Such are some of the vagaries and follies of criticism.

§ "The High-priest of the new temple in the province appointed from year to year." Mommsen. Holtzmann.

thought betrays itself as anything but that of primitive Christianity, and rather indicates a contact with Gnostic ideas. It has been suggested that perhaps that which, for Gnosticism, was separated into a plurality of Æons, is, in the Johannine Logos-doctrine, combined in the form " the only begotten of a father," in whom dwelt all the of fulness of the Godhead.* Some of the author's philosophical principles are far too much like the dualistic speculations of the Gnosis to be classed with primitive-Christian conceptions without a manifest anachronism. Such are the ideas of a fundamental opposition between the kingdom of God and that of the world,† between God and the Devil, light and darkness, truth and falsehood, and that of the helpless spiritual condition of those who are of the " world." ‡ Not only does the Time-spirit thus cast a " dualistic shadow upon the Gospel," but its terminology of the school is more prominent than the language of the unsophisticated religious consciousness. The mysticism, also, which is a unique feature of the Gospel, is very questionably of Jewish or early-Christian origin.§ In its doctrine of salvation the emphasis is laid upon the incarnation of the Logos, ‖ a speculative doctrine wholly foreign to the original conception of soteriology. The sensuous, external conception of the judgment, which is expressed with great fulness in the earlier Gospels, finds incidental expression, it is true, but it is evident that the author's idea of the world-judgment is that of an inward separation by recognition or rejection of the Logos, or a

* Chap. i. 14, *cf*. I Tim. i. 4, Col. ii. 9.
† Chap. viii. 23, xv. 19, xvii. 14, 16.
‡ Chap. viii. 44-47, i. 4, v. 10, iii. 19-21, xii. 35, viii. 43, 44, 47, x. 26, xii. 37-40.
§ Chap. xiv. 17, xvii. 9, xiv. 23, xv. 4-7, xvii. 23.
‖ Chap. v. 28, 29, xi. 50-52, xvii. 19, i. 9-13, viii. 12, xvii. 4-8.

judgment in the modern sense of the word.* The original notion of a resurrection of the dead is transformed into that of an inward, eternal life, beginning upon the earth, and never to be extinguished.† The visible return of Christ from heaven, the great and inextinguishable hope of the early Christians, which is perhaps once intimated in the body of the Gospel, and is clearly expressed only in the spurious appendix, is changed into an enduring spiritual fellowship, and even into the dissemination of his spirit among men.‡ Not less characteristic is the gentle but unmistakable setting aside of the belief which is supported by miracles and of external institutions in baptism and the Lord's supper.§ In all this there has been generally recognized the latest and ripest development of theology in the New Testament, but it should not be overlooked that it is a form of it which deviates most widely from the original, and that it cannot be accounted for apart from the speculations of the second century. An evolution it is, indeed, but not an evolution which could take place in the inward experience of an apostle of Jesus. It has, accordingly, been well observed that one must make the disciple greater than the Master, and ascribe to him a growth surpassing the possibilities of individual human development, if one will suppose such ideas to have been ripened in the mind of the aged man who, in his best years, stood beside James and Peter as one of the "pillar-apostles" of the Jewish-Christian Church.

* Chap. v. 28, 29, xii. 48, iii. 18–21, v. 24, xv. 22–24.

† Chap. vii. 39, 40, 44, 54, xi. 24, viii. 51, xi. 25, 26.

‡ Chap. xiv. 3, xxi. 22, 23, xiv. 18–23, xvi. 16–23, xiv. 16–18, xv. 26, xvi. 7, 13–15.

§ Chap. ii. 23–25, iv. 39, 42, 45, 48, x. 38, xx. 29, iii. 3–8, vi. 63. The institution of the Lord's supper is not mentioned. Holtzmann Einleit.; **Hausrath,** Neutestamentliche Zeitgesch.

That out of the circle of the original apostles could proceed two such radically different and even contradictory representations of the person and nature of Jesus as that of Matthew's logia and the preaching of Peter, or the Gospel of Mark, which are the basis of the synoptic records, and that of the fourth Gospel, is quite incredible. The Christology of the latter is a complete transformation of that of the former. The descendant of David, the son of a carpenter, a young man belonging to a family of the people, his brothers named and his sisters known, who uses the common speech of the lowly, and draws lessons from the lilies and the birds, according to the synoptists, becomes in this record the incarnation of a pre-existent essence, the Philonic Logos become Messiah, the divine being, heaven-descended, without whom nothing was made, who was in the beginning with God, and was God. His entire discourse and conduct are represented in accordance with this conception of him. He speaks of a glory which he had with God "before the world was."*
What he declares is that which he *has seen*, which the Father *has told* him, *has commanded* him. His divine existence is an eternal present; "before Abraham was, I am,"† he says. Not only are the secrets of heaven an open book to him, but the secrets of the human heart also. He needs not that men should tell him anything, for he knows what is in man,‡ recognizes Simon as the "rock"§ at a glance, without testing him as did the Jesus of the synoptists; miraculously sees Nathaniel at a distance under the fig-tree; ∥ knows preternaturally the previous life of the Samaritan woman;¶ foreknows his betrayer, the death of Lazarus, and the time of his own

* Chap. xvii. 5.   † Chap. viii. 58.   ‡ Chap. ii. 25.
§ Chap. i. 42.   ∥ Chap. i. 49.   ¶ Chap. iv. 16.

death.* He knows no limitations, works miracles as with omnipotent power, heals a man at the distance of a day's journey, turns water into wine, and by a word calls a dead man already putrescent from the grave. He has but to command, and it comes to pass, for the Father has put all things into his hands. No traces of human growth, wrestling, and struggle mar this wonderful portrait of a divine one incarnate. The great Logos has no part in the baptism of John, no awful days and nights of conflict with temptation in the wilderness. Satan does not venture to approach him. The final tragedy is only a means by which the heaven-descended one may return to the world above, and he has no need to falter and writhe and watch. "Shall I say," he cries, " Father, save me from this hour?" If his soul is for a moment "troubled," there is no protracted struggle, no bloody sweat, and no need of an angel to strengthen him. On the cross he speaks no words of heart-broken despair, but, with godlike majesty, proclaims, "It is finished!" Finally the master-hand that has drawn this great picture sweeps from the heavens the apocalyptic paraphernalia of the synoptic second coming, as a Jewish conception, or rather a dream, unfitted to a world-religion and incongruous with a later philosophy.

It does not, however, by any means follow from the foregoing considerations that this Gospel is for the most part a work of pure invention, a fancy-piece, written to serve the exigencies of a theological system, and devised with consummate art to bring to the support of that system the assumed teachings of Jesus. Granting that the internal evidences are decidedly unfavorable to the Johannine authorship, we are by no means under the necessity

---

*Chap. vi. 64, xi. 1-13, xii. 23, xiii. 1.

of adopting this "rigorous" theory. As to the author's being "a consummate artist," Matthew Arnold has shown by a process of fine literary criticism that it is no true art which he employs, because "it does not manage to conceal itself." The unlikeness of his Jesus to the Jesus of the synoptists is "too glaring." "The redaction and composition of this Gospel show literary skill, and indicate a trained Greek as their author, not a fisherman of Galilee. But it may be said with certainty that a literary artist capable of inventing the most striking sayings of Jesus to Nicodemus or to the woman of Samaria would have made his composition as a whole more flawless, more artistically perfect than the fourth Gospel actually is. Judged from an artist's point of view it has blots and awkwardnesses which a master of imaginative invention would never have suffered his work to exhibit."* The Gospel, then, remains to be accounted for, and any theory of its origin must reckon with the fact of its unmistakable spiritual character, which we have seen was recognized by the ancients, and must offer an explanation of the great sayings attributed to Jesus in it and of the qualities unique and beautiful which made it appear to Luther and even to Baur "the only, tender, true chief-Gospel." The theory of the composition of the Gospel which will stand the test of criticism must also take account of the tradition which connects its origin with John. While tradition is not blindly to be received, it does, as we have seen, count for something, and should not be arbitrarily set aside. An acceptable hypothesis cannot disregard the fact that the Gospel was received without dispute in the latter part of the second century as a Johannine account of the life and teachings of Jesus, and took its place in the canon early

---

* God and the Bible, p. 247.

in the third century along with the other Gospels. No theory of the Gospel can, however, be expected to stand which does not have a strong support in the record itself, which is not, in a word, sustained by the internal evidences.

Now, that there are internal indications of the composite character of the Gospel can hardly be denied by a careful and unbiassed reader of it. It is a work of striking incongruities. Whoever reads it attentively finds himself now charmed and stirred by passages of great beauty and spiritual profoundness, now shocked and perplexed by enigmatical words and by sayings hard to reconcile with a conception of the unity and consistency of the whole. The problem which these internal phenomena present has received various solutions, according to the point of view of different investigators. Schweitzer[*] regarded the accounts of the Galilean ministry of Jesus as later interpolations. Tobler,[†] Ewald,[‡] Hase,[§] and Weizsäcker[‖] have attempted to explain the mingling of authentic or apostolical with spurious or unapostolical elements in the Gospel by the hypothesis that an evangelic oral tradition of the apostle John, which had come down without definite form, was recorded in it with many modifications by one of his disciples. On the other hand, Weisse[¶] maintains that the basis of the Gospel was a writing by John containing certain discourses of Jesus which received a historical revision by a later hand. Weisse's hypothesis has recently been assumed in its general features by Wendt.[**]

[*] Das Evangelium Johannes nach seinem inneren Werth und seiner Bedeutung, etc., 1841.
[†] Die Evangelienfrage, etc., 1858.
[‡] Die Johanneischen Schriften, 1861.
[§] Geschichte Jesu, 1876.   [‖] Untersuchungen, etc., 1864.
[¶] Die Evangel. Gesch., 1838 ; Die Evangelienfrage, 1856.
[**] Die Lehre Jesu, i. 1886.

and defended with much acumen and in critical detail. According to this view, the fourth evangelist held a relation similar in general to that of the first evangelist to the logia of Matthew, and the marked difference of the former from the latter work is due in part to the character of the logia of Jesus preserved by John and in part to the point of view of the writer who gave them a historical setting. It is maintained that one can hardly find the differences difficult to explain when one takes into account a half-century's development of Christianity, the Alexandrian philosophy, the influence of Pauline ideas, and the point of view of a Greek-Christian writer in Asia Minor.

But all the critical acumen which has been applied to the development of the Weisse-Wendt hypothesis does not succeed in freeing it from grave difficulties and an appearance of arbitrariness. The literary unity of the Gospel is so generally admitted by critics of opposing schools that it can hardly be regarded as a contested question. Now, the joining of a logia-document of any considerable extent written by a Jewish-Christian apostle to the composition of such a writer as the fourth evangelist must have been, so as to produce a work like the fourth Gospel, is in the highest degree improbable, is perhaps a literary impossibility. Wendt, it is true, does not oppose the unity of the Gospel in the sense of contesting its unitary redaction in its present form; but he cannot be said to have overcome the difficulty which is presented in the supposition that a writer of the Johannine school should have taken such liberties with an apostolic logia-document as to give it the impress of his own individuality and the coloring of his theological opinions to the extent of making it unrecognizable as apostolic. Besides, as we have already seen, it is in the discourses of Jesus as set forth in this Gospel that some of the principal objections to its Johannine authorship appear, and the difficulties are not overcome by the arbitrary elimination which Wendt makes of certain objectionable portions of them. Such a piece-work as this theory would make it, the Gospel certainly does not appear to be. Neither is any considerable participation of the apostle John in its composition made to appear probable by the quite gratuitous assumption of a radical change of his opinions and shifting of his point of view in later life under the influence of gentile-Christian and Pauline ideas in Ephesus. That in this environment he should gradually have "put off many remnants of Jewish-Christian limitations," that "the portrait of his Master should have been transfigured in him," "removed from the human sphere, and surrounded with a divine splendor,"* is anything but "probable." A companion of Jesus in youth and "pillar-apostle" in middle life could scarcely be transformed into an Alexandrian philosopher and Pauline universalist by any magic likely to have been operative in the Ephesian environment.

That the problem of the authorship of the fourth Gospel is one to be solved off-hand by radical criticism, or to be pronounced upon *ex cathedra* by conservative dogmatism, no sound critic will maintain in view of a century's discussion of it. A criticism which has a savor of spiritual discernment will not cast this remarkable work aside as an invention of second-century Gnosticism, containing only "the arid mysticism of the schools of Alexandria." If the external evidences are indecisive of its early origin, if from internal grounds we cannot regard it as the work of an apostle; if it plainly has a composite character, then

---

* Schenkel, Das Charakterbild Jesu, 1864.

the unbiassed critic may still be just to the ancient tradition of the Ephesian church and to the profound spiritual sayings of the Gospel in holding that, while on any hypothesis of its origin many critical problems remain unsolved, there is at least a strong probability for a Johannine nucleus in the book, for frequent "words of the Lord" (λόγια κυριακά) handed down from the apostle without connection, probably, and without a historical setting, which have in this remarkable work found a literary embodiment in the midst of much mysticism, it is true, and overlaid by Greek-Christian, second-century speculations, but distinguishable from these by their unique quality and surprising originality. The attentive reader finds on almost every page of the Gospel words which are probably genuine Johannine logia of Jesus. They have been now skilfully, now awkwardly, connected with the narratives, and embodied in the discourses, and are recognizable by their profound spirituality and by that gnomic character which is stamped upon the synoptic tradition of Jesus. A prudent criticism will perhaps refrain from the somewhat hazardous attempt to distinguish these logia in detail from the rest of the record, as well as from venturing conjectures as to the form or way in which they may have come to the writer. Inventions these quickening words surely cannot be, unless the Jesus of the synoptists, who taught "as one having authority," was also an invention of Galilean fishermen. If these logia descended from the Ephesian apostle, and so much at least ought to be accorded to the tradition, then the Gospel which contains them may well be entitled that "according to John."

Since Baur placed the date of the composition of the Gospel at about the year 170, the tendency of representatives of the critical school has been towards the assumption of an earlier period, the variations extending through about a quarter of a century. The precise date is manifestly indeterminable, but the opinion which assigns it to the second quarter of the second century is probably correct. Idle are all speculations as to its author. Worse than idle is the charge that he intended to forge a Gospel in the name of an apostle. That he wrote with sincerity is as evident as that he wrote with a purpose. His relation to John is somewhat analogous to that of the first evangelist to Matthew, though he doubtless handled his materials with much greater freedom than the latter. Like the author of the second Isaiah, he remains, and will forever remain, a great Unknown. This incomparable Gospel is a monument to a great genius, and we may well believe that no one would be more ready than he to acknowledge his indebtedness to his greater Master.

CHAPTER VIII.

THE ESCHATOLOGY OF THE GOSPELS.

THE sayings ascribed to Jesus regarding "the last things," and particularly regarding his own participation in certain events which were believed to be the final scenes of the Messianic drama of the then "present age," present some of the gravest problems with which the criticism of the Gospels has to deal. That Jesus should have had so much faith in the vitality and the transforming power of his doctrine as to look forward with unshaken confidence to its gradual but certain triumph; that he should have believed his word destined to judge men by separating between good and evil, light and darkness; and that by a bold figure of speech he should have connected himself with this triumph and judgment, are natural inferences from his personality and history. Little doubt, indeed, can exist that he did more than once speak prophetic words of such spiritual import. These words present no serious difficulties to interpreters of insight and literary sense. The real difficulty in the eschatological sayings ascribed to him begins, as Schenkel has pointed out,* with the passages in which Jesus announces his personal return to the earth, and this in immediate connection with the judgment on Jerusalem. All attempts in an apologetic interest to deny that the synoptists wrote of such a coming of Christ in such a

---

* Das Charakterbild Jesu, p. 280.

connection are not in accordance with a sound hermeneutics, and do not deserve refutation. The real problem to be solved, then, it is not difficult to state. For most modern interpreters of note agree that in the synoptic eschatological discourses the Parousia is represented as a personal visible reappearance of the Son of Man in the life-time of the generation then living for the establishment of his kingdom and for judgment, and also that this return is often, particularly in the great discourse concerning the last things in the thirteenth of Mark and its parallels, connected with the abomination of desolation and the judgment on Jerusalem.* The chief divergence of opinion arises on the question whether the notion of a return in the form in which it lies before us is to be put to the account of Jesus, with the error and self-deception involved, or to that of his disciples who may have misunderstood him and to that of the evangelists who recorded the misunderstanding.

The only explanations of the passages in question worth seeking or considering are such as proceed from a historical and critical study of the Jewish-Messianic beliefs and expectations and of the relation of Jesus to these. The purely exegetical process which is usually unfruitful must be especially so in this case. Only when the Gospels are studied as products of the Jewish race in a particular phase of its historical development can many of the problems which they present be rightly solved. The true criticism is historical criticism. Not until Jesus is apprehended in his relation to the ideas and history of his nation can his life be truly written. For the solution, then, of the problem before us we must go back to the

* So Bleek, Meyer, De Wette, Baur, Holtzmann, Schenkel, Weisse, Wendt, Hase, Weizsäcker, Keim, Pfleiderer, and many others.

original Jewish-Messianic expectations, and follow them down to the time of Christ. In the next place must be considered the relation which Jesus regarded himself as sustaining to Jewish Messianism. Finally we must study in the light which we may hope to get from these investigations the principal Messianic or eschatological sayings which are ascribed to him in the Gospels.

Out of the books of Hebrew prophecy speak no wavering, uncertain voices. The Hebrew, being an intense believer in the providential mission of his nation, never lost his faith in the future triumph of Jahveh's chosen people and their cause. In the predictions of the prophets this faith finds glowing expression. It is enfeebled by no disaster, it is quenched by no adversity. The Hebrew warriors shall ultimately triumph over the enemies of the nation on whom the Most High will pronounce judgment. The oldest of these prophets whose visions have been preserved, Joel, towards the middle of the ninth century B.C., depicts in fine poetry the great day of Jahveh, which shall be announced by dreams of old men and visions of young men, by " wonders in the heavens and in the earth, blood and fire and pillars of smoke." "The sun shall be turned into darkness and the moon into blood." All nations shall be gathered in the valley of Jehoshaphat for the judgment of Jahveh on account of His people, whose scattered captives shall be brought back, while they who took them away shall be sold into slavery. Jahveh shall roar out of Zion, the heavens and the earth shall shake, Egypt shall become a desolation, and Edom a wilderness for their violence towards Judah, but " Judah shall dwell forever." * Micah, after announcing the fearful judgments which shall fall upon the chosen

* Joel, chap. ii. iii.

people for their sins, Zion plowed as a field and Jerusalem become heaps, proclaims that "in the last days" the mountain of the Lord's house shall be established, and "many nations" shall come up to it, and shall learn of the ways of the God of Jacob who shall judge among many peoples, and shall rebuke strong nations afar off amidst universal peace, the beating of swords into ploughshares and spears into pruning-hooks.* The prophets exhaust the resources of imagination in painting the splendors of "the age to come," the blessed, Messianic time. Tears and weeping shall be no more. There shall be no old man who does not fill out his days, and the child shall die a hundred years old.† Nature shall be renewed, and rejoice in a new heaven and a new earth.‡ The house of Jacob shall be restored, the captives brought home, the ten tribes reconciled to Jerusalem to form one people and one realm § in which "the iniquity of Israel shall be sought for, and there shall be none."‖ The foreign peoples who have oppressed the holy nation shall be terribly chastised, while the Jews shall found a vast empire, and the vanquished shall pay them tribute.

The Hebrew prophets did not, however, stop with the delineation of an indefinite, kingless future. The golden age of the reign of David, the great conqueror, the compeller of peace, the ideal prophet-king, furnishes the keynote of many prophecies. This great theocratic prince, this Charlemagne of Israel, this man after God's own heart, was never to be without a descendant on the throne of his people. The idea of a personal Messiah of the Davidic line, who should restore the ancient glory

---

* Micah, chap. iii. iv. † Is. lxv. 20.
‡ Ib. 17. § Zech. x. 6-11, Is. xi. 13.
‖ Is. l. 19, 20.

of his race, does not, however, appear in full vigor until towards the middle of the eighth century before Christ, when Samaria was already ruined, and the decadence of Jerusalem had begun. Isaiah and Micah, Jeremiah and Ezekiel (about 720–600 B.C.), are the principal prophets who associate the Son of David with their hopes of the future.* These have been called "the royalist-prophets," while of their successors, who lived during or after the Babylonian exile, the unknown author of Isaiah xl.–lxvi. and Malachi do not speak of a descendant of David nor of any visible chief of the theocracy which was to be restored. Sometimes David appears to stand for the dynasty in general, as, "I will be your God, and David shall be your king forever." Again, a single king only seems to be in view, a descendant of David, as when Zechariah designates the Messiah as a Branch who shall build the temple and sit upon the throne.† From Bethlehem shall this king come forth, under whose sway "the remnant of his brethren shall return unto the children of Israel." He shall also be "great unto the ends of the earth," and shall deliver the people "from the Assyrian when he cometh into our land." But the future of all the visions of the prophets is near at hand. In "a very little while" shall the Branch of Jesse appear, who shall overthrow the enemies of Judah and bring the exiles from Assyria and Egypt.‡ The descendant of David who was to appear from Bethlehem should be "peace" when the Assyrian should come into the land, and, turning against these enemies, should make Israel as a lion, and rebuild the temple. The writer of the second Isaiah is occupied with an early restoration from the Babylonian exile, and

---

* Micah v. 1–4 ; Is. ix. 5, 6, xi. 1–5 ; Jer. xxx. 5, 6, 15–17 ; Ezek. xxiv. 23, 24, xxxvii. 24, 25.
† Zech. iii. 8, vi. 12. ‡ Is. xi. 1–5, 11–13.

sees the hope of the future in the theocratic and pious remnant of the people which had been "bruised for the transgressions of many." A peculiar trait appears in Malachi, who announces that, before the great and terrible day of the Lord, Elijah, who had, according to an early tradition, been translated, should be sent to "turn the hearts of the children to their fathers," lest the earth be smitten in the divine wrath "with a curse." This prophet is not announced here as a forerunner of Messiah, of whom Malachi does not speak, but of Jahveh, who is to come for the great judgment upon the idolatrous nations and upon Israel. This strange fancy has been characterized as "the first fantastic element which is joined to hopes hitherto so simple and natural."*

The presence of "fantastic elements" characterizes the Jewish apocalyptic literature of a later period. The point of view of the Maccabean age is represented in the book of Daniel, written probably about 167 B.C., to encourage the Jews in their conflict against Antiochus Epiphanes. Here, however, no descendant of David, no personal Messiah appears. The natural order gives place to a cataclysmal development. The "one like the son of man," whose appearance "with the clouds of heaven" is declared with genuinely apocalyptic features, is not a personal Messiah, but represents the kingdom of collective Israel, whose distinguishing qualities are set forth in this way to contrast it with the preceding visions, as the noble human characteristics are superior to those of beasts.† The human ruler of the kingdom of God does

---

* Colani, Jésus-Christ et les Croyances Messianiques de son Temps, 2me ed. 1864, p. 16.

† Hitzig, Das Buch Daniel erklärt, 1864, p. 115 ; Holtzmann, Judenthum und Christenthum im Zeitalter der apokryphischen und neutestamentlichen Literatur, 1867, p. 198.

not appear in this book. The overthrow of the enemies of the nation is to be consummated by supernal forces, when "the great prince which standeth for the children of thy people," the archangel Michael, "shall stand up," and those "found written in the book" shall be delivered.

In the book of Enoch, written about seventy years after that of Daniel, in the name of the Old-Testament worthy who "walked with God," the Messiah appears as no earthly prince or scion of a king, but as one who before the world was created dwelt in the bosom of God. He is called "the Elect," "the Just," "the Anointed," "the Son of Man," "the Son of a man," "the Son of a woman." Concealed at present in the heavens, he shall at length appear, the elect shall stand before him, and the kings of the earth shall fall at his feet.* Here the time of the catastrophic end is near, when the oppressors of the Jews shall fall, and after the judgment the Messiah shall reign. In Hebrew prophecy and Jewish apocalyptics the end of the travail-pains ($ὠδῖνες$) and of the tribulations ($θλίψεις$) is always near. The apocryphal writings of the Old Testament are, for the most part, contemporary with the apocalypse of Enoch. But they are silent as to the person of the Messiah. They give expression to what may be called a Messianic hope, that is, a hope of the return of Israel to Palestine, the perpetuity of the nation, the conversion of the heathen, the chastise-

* "If this delineation is pre-Christian, it shows how, in certain narrow circles at least, the apprehension of the Messiah had begun to be formed by means of the idea of the Son of Man in Daniel, and consequently as a preexistent celestial being."—Holtzmann, Judenthum, etc. Dillmann regards the entire book as a Jewish production, Das Buch Henoch übersetzt und erklärt, 1853. Hilgenfeld maintains the Christian origin of a part of it, and finds thus an explanation of the Messianic titles, "Son of a man," "Son of a woman," Die jüdische Apokalyptik, 1857. Dillmann, in article "Henoch" in Schenkel's Bibel-Lexicon, reaffirms his former position.

ment of the enemies of the Jews, a bodily resurrection of the dead, and the assembling of the dispersed people in Jerusalem. Power is given of God to David " forever," and Elijah shall come to appease the divine wrath before the judgment.

As we approach and enter upon the Christian era, we find the Jewish conception of the personality of the Messiah again well defined. There appears to be a return to the ancient prophetic point of view in the Targums and the Gospels. The Messiah is the anointed of God, the son of David, the king of Israel,* the one who is to come, he who cometh in the name of the Lord, he that cometh of the seed of David and from Bethlehem,† then disappears, and returns suddenly without that anyone knows whence he comes.‡ He shall have as forerunners Elijah and other prophets, particularly the one foretold by Moses.§ His office is to be at once religious and political, and his reign is called the kingdom of the Messiah, the kingdom of David, and the kingdom of God.‖ He shall separate the wheat from the chaff; he shall pray for the sins of his people; he shall take away the sin of the world; he shall establish the kingdom of Israel by bringing back the ten tribes, and deliver the Jews from their enemies; he shall gain a victory over Gog, the personification of the pagan power, and the Jews shall share in the spoils.¶ The expectation of the Messiah was, then,

---

* Luke ii. 36 ; Mark xii. 36 and parallels ; John i. 50.

† Luke vii. 19 ; Matt. xxi. 9 ; John viii. 42.

‡ Targ. Jonath., Micah iv. 8.

§ Mark ix. 11, vi. 15 ; John i. 21, vii. 40.

‖ Targ. Jonath., *ut supra ;* Mark xi. 10 ; Targ. Jonath., Is. xl. 9 and Micah iv. 7.

¶ Matt. iii. 12 ; Targ. Jonath., Is. liii. 11 ; John i. 29 ; Targ. Jonath., Zech. x. 4 ; Luke i. 74 ; Targ. Jonath., Is. xxxiii. 23.

the expectation of the consolation of Israel and the redemption of Jerusalem.* History shows the prominence of political hopes in this earnest awaiting of the Messiah. Josephus can explain the bold insurrections of the Jews against the Roman power only by an "oracle," which had predicted for them the empire of the world.† The monarch was to be the son of David, and the seat of empire Jerusalem. Those disciples of Jesus were, accordingly, consistent Jews who asked of him a place as viceroys in his Messianic reign.‡

The form which Jewish Messianism assumed towards the end of the first century of our era appears in the fourth book of Esdras, written probably by a Jew about A.D. 96. The nation, overthrown, deprived of political and military power, had no hope but in the supernal powers. The author beholds Messiah rise from the sea, and fly with the clouds of heaven, while the earth trembles wherever he turns his glance. He abides in heaven with Enoch, Moses, and Elijah, who had been removed from the earth without death, until at the end he comes forth in order from Mount Zion to slay with his flaming breath the heathen who were besieging it, to bring back the ten tribes and enter upon his reign over the elect. But he is not appointed to preside at the final judgment. Rather Jahveh declares by the mouth of Uriel that the heavens and the earth were made by Him, and by Him shall be their end. It thus appears that from the time of Joel to the end of the first century of our era Jewish Messianism underwent great modifications. The judgment of the valley of Jehoshaphat becomes a terrible world-catastrophe to which the teachings of the Persian religion have

---

* Luke ii. 25, 38. † De Bello Jud. v. 5, 4.
‡ Mark x. 35 and parallels.

added the resurrection of the dead to take part in the great assize. The personal Messiah, the son of David, disappears in the political decadence of the nation, with a priestly aristocracy for two centuries at the head of affairs, with the Maccabeans in power, descended not from the tribe of Judah, but from that of Levi, and with the spiritualizing of the Messianic idea which prevailed during the period of the apocalyptic literature. Finally, later Judaism, with its closed canon of sacred Scripture, its veneration of the letter, its fine-spun interpretations, its allegorizing, brought back the original Messianic conception, and restored the effaced image of the son of David, which was hailed with joy by the helpless and oppressed people of the era of Jesus.

In studying the relation which Jesus regarded himself as holding to Jewish Messianism, it is not necessary to enter upon a discussion of the question at what period he openly made this relation known. This question appears to be complicated by the different points of view of the evangelists. It is sufficient for our purpose to say that it appears on a fair interpretation of the Gospels that he regarded himself as in some sense the Anointed, the Christ. The terms employed by him to designate the principle that he came to establish are the ones which were familiar to the Jews of his time as Messianic expressions, the kingdom of God and the kingdom of heaven.*
John the Baptist is said to have announced the approach of the kingdom of God, that is, of the Messiah; and Jesus during a part of his Galilean ministry speaks of it in the same way as future, although he does not represent

---

* Matthew generally employs the latter term, Mark and Luke use only the former. These terms appear, however, to be sometimes used synonymously with our expression " the life to come."

it with the terrible features which his forerunner gives it, but rather as the "good news."* Later he speaks of it as already come. His works show the advent of the new reign.† This kingdom cometh not with visible signs, as the Jews suppose, but is already in their midst.‡ The new life of renunciation, peace, and joy which he has brought to the world is the veritable kingdom of God. It is Christianity itself, "a treasure," a "pearl of great price." In order to enter this kingdom one must become as a little child.§ Blessed are the poor, the persecuted, the weary and heavy-laden, for to such belongs the kingdom, while the rich will hardly enter it. Far from being limited to Israel, there is danger that it be taken from this people and given to others.‖ It is evident, then, that one has not to read far in the Gospels to find that the Messianic conception of Jesus was widely different from that of the Jews of his own or of any previous time. "In making supreme the spiritual character of his kingdom he removed the confusion of the temporal and the spiritual, the visible and the invisible, which inhered in the Hebrew theocracy." It is safe to say, in spite of the Judaistic coloring which has been given to some of his words, particularly by the first evangelist, that he recognized no special national claims to or rights in his kingdom. His word is a leaven which is to transform human society by a process of development, and not by violence and convulsions. As the Jewish national Messiah, as assuming the rôle of that expected person, he could not have spoken as he did without conscious deception or superlative folly.

---

* Mark i. 15.
† Matt. xi. 4–6, xii. 28.
‡ Luke xvii. 20.
§ Mark x. 14, and parallels.
‖ Matt. xxi. 43.

This conclusion is confirmed by the relation which Jesus assumed towards the popular Messianic titles of his own and previous times. "Son of David" he never calls himself, and when the blind men, the woman of Canaan, the beggar, and the multitude hail him with this title, he pays no attention to it. Adopting the rabbinical exegesis, he once shows by a forcible *argumentum ad hominem* that according to the terms of a Psalm, probably erroneously ascribed to David, the Messiah cannot properly be called the son of that king. The conclusion of this remarkable argument appears to be that he regarded the Messiah as greater than a temporal monarch, not to be compared to the greatest of earthly kings, and not a son even of David, the grand Messianic type of his nation.*
The appellation, "Son of God," was undoubtedly a Messianic title current among the Jews previously to and at the time of Christ, and the evangelists employ it in this sense. They report that a voice from above proclaimed it at the baptism and the transfiguration, and Mark reports that the demoniacs accosted Jesus by this title. At Cæsarea Philippi Peter's celebrated response, "Thou art the Christ, the Son of the living God," was gladly accepted by Jesus according to the account of the first evangelist.† Before the High-priest Jesus acknowledged himself to be the Christ, the Son of God.‡ These latter words are not, in the first place, very well authenticated, since it does not appear that any one of his disciples was present at the scene, Peter alone being mentioned as hav-

---

* Matt. xxii. 42-45 ; Mark xii. 35-37. See Meyer *in loc.*
† Matt. xvi. 16. According to Mark, Peter's answer was simply, "Thou art the Christ," while according to Luke it was, "Thou art the Christ of God." These record no commendation of Peter for the answer.
‡ Matt. xxvi. 63, 64.

ing followed him at a distance, and as being, according to one account, "outside in the court," and according to another, "below in the court."* At all events, when we take into account his repeated and undoubtedly genuine declarations of the spiritual and unworldly character of his kingdom, we are constrained either to reject all that appear to have a contrary meaning, or to modify them to accord with the former. The fact appears to be that Jesus intentionally avoided applying to himself the standard Messianic title, "Son of God," and that he chose the simple appellation, "Son," to express what was deepest in his consciousness, his spiritual relation to God, the Father. He teaches, it is true, that all men are children of God; that even prodigals are still sons; that prayer should be addressed to God as our Father, and that there is a special sense in which men may become sons of God on certain conditions.† Yet there can be no doubt that he claimed for himself a pre-eminence among the sons of God which entitled him to call himself "the Son."‡ He is reported as claiming for himself an especial knowledge of God and the function of a pre-eminent revelator of His will.§ When he calls himself "the Son," then, he appears to speak out of the profound consciousness of the indwelling of the Father, of intimate communion with Him, and not at all to wish to be understood as claiming to be the Messiah in the Jewish sense of the word, but rather the Son of God in "the mystic and Christian meaning" of the term.

There remains to be considered the term by which Jesus usually designated himself, "the Son of Man," while

---

* Matt. xxvi. 58, 69; Mark xiv. 54, 56.   ‡ Mark xiii. 32.
† Matt. v. 9, 45.   § Matt. xi. 27; Luke x. 32.

neither the people nor the disciples apply it to him. The reasons for believing that he did not by this appellation wish to declare himself as the expected **Messiah are very strong, although some noted exegetes have not been convinced by them.*** **In the first place this was not a common** designation of the **Messiah among the** Jews before Christ nor in his time. **It appears, indeed,** in the book of **Daniel and in the Apocalypse of Enoch. In the former it is employed in connection with apocalyptic visions of a Messianic character in the general sense of the** word. The fact that the hope in a personal Messiah is foreign to the apocryphal books of the Old Testament, as it is to Obadiah and Malachi, furnishes a strong presumption against a personal reference in the passage in Daniel in which one appears "*as* **the Son of** Man." Rather, **as has already been said**, the term is here applied **to a kingdom** which the writer represents under the symbol **not of a beast, but of the noble** human figure. † As to the book of Enoch, **the appellations, " Son of** Man **" and " Son of a man,"** there employed **of the** Messiah may be **of** Christian origin, and if they are not, this single instance of their use is of little importance. It is hardly to be supposed that Jesus would have borrowed the term from such a writing. **The** language used by Jesus at Cæsarea Philippi shows **that he did not** intend by the term to designate himself as the Messiah, **and that he** could not have supposed the disciples **to understand it in** that sense. The words: "Who do **men say that I, the Son of Man, am?"** cannot mean, who do men **say that I, the** Messiah, **am?** Jesus

---

* **Particularly** Meyer, Commentar, **i. 1.** p. 223 f, and Keim, Geschichte Jesu, ii. p. 570.

† Hitzig, **Das** Buch Daniel, **p. 116 ;** Colani, **p. 112 ;** Weisse, Die Evangelienfrage, pp. 101, 102.

could not thus have put into Peter's mouth the answer for which he commends him, and of which he declares that it came by a revelation of God. It is probable, then, that Jesus chose for himself this by no means current and popular designation of the Messiah with the design not of saying directly that he was that expected one, but rather to mark himself, in opposition to the splendid Jewish-Messianic expectations, as Man, as one who completely participated in all that is human, *qui nihil humani a se alienum putat*.* It appears, too, according to Mark,† that notwithstanding Christ's repeated use of the term, the people had not prior to the event at Cæsarea Philippi recognized him as Messiah, but had thought him to be John the Baptist or one of the prophets, and that not even his apostles would have known him without the special revelation granted to Peter. Again, the claim which Jesus made of the authority as Son of Man to forgive sins,‡ is not set up as pertaining to Messiah, otherwise he would probably have employed instead of "Son of Man" an unambiguous term, as "Son of God," or "Son of David." Rather he speaks of himself as specially commissioned to represent the human race, and accordingly as authorized to pronounce the judgment of forgiveness on human transgression. This son of Mankind, this archetypal Man, sprung from the race "crowned with glory and honor," is endowed with the highest human dignity, and clothed with a divine prerogative.

If, then, Jesus did not regard himself as the Messiah in the sense of the term current among the Jews and generally set forth by the ancient prophets, in what sense did he apply that title to himself? It appears, according to a

---

* Baur, Vorlesungen über neutestamentliche Theologie, 1864, p. 81.
† Chap. viii. 27. ‡ Matt. ix. 6.

tradition which there seems to be no good reason for doubting, that at Cæsarea Philippi he at least allowed the Messianic appellation to be applied to himself, whether, according to Matthew he received it with approval, or, according to Mark, passively and in silence. Now, familiar with the literature of his nation as he must have been, Messianism could have been no strange idea to him. It is not improbable that he had been profoundly impressed with the religious features of the golden age, the Messianic future, which abound in many of the prophetic delineations. The proposition is by no means hazardous, is, in fact, psychologically grounded, that he apprehended the Messianism of the ancient seers in accordance with his nature, his religious genius. May not he who treated the law with so much freedom have also transformed the prophets? One cannot think of him as associating the advent of the Messianic age with scenes of carnage and "garments rolled in blood," nor with apocalyptic imagery and cataclysmal terrors. He could no more be a Judas Maccabeus or a Simon Bar-Cochab, than he could imagine himself as ushering in the Messianic kingdom by a catastrophic descent with the clouds of heaven. To such a soul as his the " future age " of Israel's glowing prophecy and indestructible hope must have presented itself as a "restitution of all things " in a moral and spiritual sense, a veritable kingdom of God whose subjects should love one another as he loved men, and practise his gentleness, humility, patience, and obedience to the Father. But too much emphasis cannot be laid upon the fact that to Jesus this " future age " ($αἰὼν\ μέλλων$) was not a far-off epoch. Its hour had already struck. No need of apocalypses and visions to herald it ! The kingdom of God was already in the midst of a people slow of heart to apprehend it. The stone which the builders rejected was already laid at the corner of the world's Messianic temple. In declaring himself to be the Messiah, then, Jesus, with a consciousness of his moral and spiritual superiority, with a sublime confidence in himself as a king of men, places himself at the head of this new kingdom of God, and stakes its entire fortune upon the enthusiasm and love which his personality may inspire.

In greeting with approval, then, Peter's confession at Cæsarea Philippi Jesus accepted the Messiahship according to his own apprehension of it, that is, in a transformed sense. Now the die is cast. The momentous step is taken. But he who has made the high resolve does not think of himself as a triumphant Messiah, marching at the head of conquering legions to restore the fallen fortunes of the line of David. Rather with a heavy heart and in the shadow of the cross he proceeds towards Jerusalem. In the language of the evangelist, from that time he "began to show his disciples that he must go to Jerusalem and suffer many things from the elders and chief priests and scribes, and be put to death." Transformation of the traditional and current Messianism could not be more radical than this. A Messiah who should suffer at the hands of the elders and chief priests, who should give himself up to his enemies, who should be put to death, was so contrary to all that the prophets had taught and the people believed of this person, that it is no wonder that the Jews have never accepted him as their Messiah. How complete was the transformation of the Messianic conception may be seen in the Epistles of Paul, in which he labors to make acceptable to Jews the idea of a suffering Messiah. Whence, then, did Jesus derive his Messianic conception? It has already been intimated that one will

not greatly err if one answers that he derived it from his
own nature. But we are led to think of an Old Testament
source when we recall the impressive scene in the synagogue at Nazareth when he read from the second Isaiah
the beautiful words about preaching the glad tidings to
the poor, proclaiming deliverance to the captives, the
recovery of sight to the blind, to set at liberty the oppressed, to proclaim the acceptable year of the Lord.
That Jesus, when he had read these words, and said:
"To-day is this scripture fulfilled in your ears," applied
to his own office and ministry to men the terms which the
prophet used in reference to himself, is by no means improbable. The fifty-third of Isaiah, then, that pathetic
"hymn to grief," in which the great prophet of the
Babylonian age represents the hope of his nation as cen-
tred in the pious, theocratic remnant of the people, "the
servant of Jahveh," "oppressed and afflicted," "brought
as a lamb to the slaughter," must have found a quick
response in his mind, and, if it did not suggest his mission
to him, must have confirmed his antecedent conception of
it.* But apart from suggestions found in the prophets,
the transformation of the Messianic type, one would say,
must have been inevitable in a mind like that of Jesus.
Conscious of a mission of Messianic import to his nation
—that is, a mission of salvation, of deliverance,—one of
his clear insight could not but see the hopelessness, the
folly, of their temporal expectations, and realize that the
only Messiah that could help them, the only Messiah that
God would ever send to them, must be such a one as himself, the moral reformer, the religious teacher, the Anointed
of the divine Spirit, the man who could sacrifice himself
for them.

* See Colani, *ut supra*, to whom acknowledgments are due for suggestions
and interpretations.

If, now, Jesus actually used the language ascribed to him by the evangelists (and it is open to grave doubts that he did so), in which he represents himself as fulfilling prophecies in his death, if we can without a shock think of such a character as going to his death "in order that it might be fulfilled" which was spoken by any oracle whatever, then we must believe that he set aside all the prophecies of the royalist-Messianic sort, and, by a spiritualistic interpretation not at all uncommon in his age, read his fate in that of the humble "servant of Jahveh" who was "bruised for the iniquities" of the people. If one will, let one call this proceeding by which a word is retained whose meaning has been radically changed, "an accommodation to the weakness of his disciples." A conscious deception it certainly was not, since immediately after his acceptance of Peter's confession at Cæsarea Philippi Jesus began to speak of his humiliation. If the disciples were mistaken in their apprehension of the nature of his Messiahship, it was because of that dulness which made it impossible for them during their association with him to comprehend the spiritual character of his kingdom. Rather we have here the transformation which a great soul gave to an effete idea, a vain expectation; a transformation which the literalists of his own time could not understand, a transformation at which the literalists of all subsequent ages have stumbled.

This spiritual apprehension of his mission and his Messiahship is the incontestable fact from which the consideration of the relation of Jesus to the apocalyptic eschatology of the synoptic Gospels must proceed. From this point of view the probability amounts almost to a demonstration that he cannot by any express word or intimation have encouraged the expectation which the evangelists certainly entertained that he would descend to the earth surrounded by angels to establish the kingdom of God. There would be some reason for charging this expectation to him if it did not admit of another explanation. Now, its explanation is found in the fact that the early followers of Jesus were Jews, and must have cherished the Jewish-Messianic hopes and doctrines. In spite of all his teachings to the contrary, they believed, even after his death, that he should have been a temporal Messiah, and saw all their hopes shattered by the tragedy of Calvary. To believe in Jesus was for them to believe that he was the Jewish Messiah who would establish the longed-for theocratic kingdom. They could not continue to believe in him, and relinquish the expectation that he would yet be a veritable Messiah, coming in glory and power to efface the ignominy of his humiliation and death. Hence the affinity of Jewish and Christian apocalyptics. Out of what slowness of heart to comprehend the nature of Jesus, out of how fundamental a misconception of him did this idea spring! It is one of those dreadful contradictions which dulness always perpetrates when it attempts to interpret greatness. A belittling apocalyptic attachment is joined to the greatest career in history which had been finished with sublime grandeur on Calvary, and Jesus, in his earthly existence, is made a mere precursor of himself, his life "a Christian preface to a Jewish poem."

That the Jewish-Christian Messianic expectations should have found expression in the Gospels is antecedently probable on the presumption that these writings are the products of their times, and not infallible oracles dictated through supernatural intervention; and one cannot long hesitate when one must choose between this hypothesis and the doctrine that Jesus actually spoke of a second

coming as the evangelists represent. At about the time when the synoptists wrote Christians were intensely occupied with the expectation of a near return of Christ to the earth. We know this from the book of Revelation in which the second advent is depicted with the vividness and materialism of Jewish apocalyptics, and from the Epistles of Paul in which the "groaning creation" and the ardent longing for the Parousia are by no means subordinate features. Whether the form which is given to the expression of the expectation in the several passages be charged directly to the evangelists or to well-intentioned alterations of the text, it does not seem too much to say that "it were a veritable miracle if these feverish beliefs had left no impression upon our Gospels." But we are not left to conjecture as to the freedom of the evangelistic handling of the matter. The third Gospel which was written subsequently to the capture of Jerusalem by Titus shows what liberties an evangelist allowed himself with the text of the celebrated discourse ascribed to Jesus on the destruction of the city and the "last things." Besides omitting the passage in which Jesus acknowledges his ignorance of the time of the catastrophe, he rejects that concerning the abomination in the holy place, probably because he knew that no pagan idol had been set up there, and adds details from his own knowledge of the events occurring in the investment of the city, the destruction of life and the captivity of the people.*
It is significant, too, that he strikes out the words which Matthew puts into the mouth of Jesus to the effect that the second coming will take place "immediately after" the overthrow of Jerusalem, doubtless because he knew that events had not confirmed them.

* Chap. xxi. 24.

What sort of eschatological sayings were ascribed to Jesus in good faith, no doubt, by the early Christians may be seen in the celebrated account of the luxuriant growth of grapes to be expected in the Messianic kingdom, which Irenæus took from Papias' work on the sayings of Christ. Now this good Bishop, Papias, as we have seen, was a diligent collector of information regarding the teachings of Jesus, not from writings, which he held in small estimation, but from the "living voice" of oral tradition. This account of the wonderful vineyards which the saints should enjoy after the second coming of Christ and the attendant renewal of the "creation" he says he obtained from the apostle John, and Irenæus gives it as an example of Christ's teaching.* In the times of the Messianic reign, it appears, there will grow vines having ten thousand shoots, and each shoot ten thousand branches, and each branch ten thousand twigs, and each twig ten thousand clusters, and each cluster ten thousand berries, and the juice of each berry will make twenty-five measures of wine! Now, while no one will claim that Jesus ever said anything of this kind, it must be admitted that the external authentication of the prophecy is remarkably good. Besides being directly referred to John, it is confirmed by the oldest and most important witness to our first two Gospels. Its sensuousness bears a strong resemblance to the New-Jerusalem prophecies of the Apocalypse. As to the question of its origin there can be but one answer. It sprang from the second-advent expectations of the early Church. The fact that it was believed by disciples of the apostles to be an authentic saying of Jesus lends strong support to the hypothesis that some words regarding his second appearance ascribed to him in the

* "Quemadmodum docebat Dominus et dicebat."

Gospels find their most probable explanation in the same source.

The foregoing considerations prepare us to look in the Gospels for a more or less free handling of the words of Jesus in accordance with the Jewish-Christian Messianic expectations which were current and dominant in the early Church. What is more natural than that to the solemn injunction at the close of the parable of the ten virgins: "Watch, therefore, for ye know not the day nor the hour," tradition should have added the words, "wherein the Son of Man cometh"?* They stand in many manuscripts, but Tischendorf omits them. It does not, indeed, appear improbable that Jesus should have enjoined watchfulness and fidelity upon his disciples, and have employed terms applicable to all men in view of the uncertainty which belongs to all human calculations. He may, indeed, have said that the lord of the servant will come in a day when the latter is not looking for him. But he could hardly have said that the kingdom of God is comparable to a state of things in which men are watching for the coming of the Son of Man with the clouds of heaven. Such words imply a limitation and degradation of this kingdom, and give it a temporary and apocalyptic character quite incompatible with his exalted spiritual conception of it. The critical judgment cannot but attach suspicion to such formulas as "wherein the Son of Man cometh," especially in view of the probably liturgical formula which has been added to the Lord's prayer, "for thine is the kingdom," etc. Irreverent as this suspicion may appear to some devout minds, we must entertain it if we will preserve many of the fine parables of Jesus from a merely apocalyptic application, and accord to them

* Matt. xxv. 13.

that universal scope which alone agrees with the general character of his teachings. The reverence, however, which it is of the greatest importance to us to cultivate and preserve is a reverence for Jesus rather than a reverence for his biographers. No one can read without profound emotion the words of Jesus to his disciples in Gethsemane: "Watch, lest ye enter into temptation." We feel that it would be a great loss if they were struck from the record. But the apocalyptic words ascribed to him about coming with the angels on the clouds move no one, unless it be those misguided people who still look for him so to come, and set the day of his return; and there are not a few who would experience a sense of relief if it could be made to appear probable that they were not spoken by him at all.

It does not, however, at all follow that, if Jesus neither himself indulged in nor gave encouragement to apocalyptic visions of the Jewish sort, he made no forecast of the future fortune of his kingdom on the earth. His faith in the success of his word is expressed in the parables of the leaven and the grain of mustard. If, however, any one should object that the subject is regarded in this chapter from a subjective, *a-priori* point of view, let that one consider the manner in which three of the evangelists, the synoptists, have reported one of these prophecies of Jesus. The first evangelist, after making him declare that the Son of Man is to come in the glory of his Father with the angels, puts into his mouth the words: "Truly do I say to you, there are some of those standing here who will not taste of death till they have seen the Son of Man coming in his kingdom."* Mark reports the words as follows: "There are some of those standing here who will not taste of death till they have seen that the king-

---
* Matt. xvi. 28.

dom of God hath come with power."* But Luke says: "Till they have seen the kingdom of God."† The passages are almost verbatim the same, except in the closing words. Plainly, no one can tell precisely what Jesus said on this occasion. According to the first synoptist certainly, and perhaps according to the second, he employed the terms of Jewish apocalyptics. According to Luke, he simply foretold the spiritual development of his kingdom. Did the writer of Matthew add the apocalyptic words, or did some copyist add them? The fact that Luke, who wrote last, omitted them, favors the hypothesis that he exercised precisely the sort of critical discrimination which is in question in the present discussion. It is not by any means, however, to be maintained that Jesus employed no figurative language in speaking of his future relation to his cause. It is plain that he identifies his work and himself: "Lo, I am with you always"; "Where two or three are gathered together in my name, there am I in the midst of you." That he used very strong figures of speech on occasion is apparent from such passages as Luke x. 18, 19. There can be no doubt, too, that with the insight of a true seer he foresaw that the welfare of the Jewish people depended on their acceptance of his teachings, on abandoning their wild Messianic dreams, on rendering to Cæsar the things that were Cæsar's and to God the things that were God's. The particular case of the Galileans whom Pilate had massacred calls forth from him a pathetic prophecy upon the nation: "Except ye repent, ye shall all likewise perish." ‡

An examination of some of the passages in the synoptic Gospels in which the second coming of Christ is men-

---

* Mark ix. 1. † Luke ix. 27.
‡ Luke xiii. 3, *cf.* xx. 15, 16.

tioned will show the application of the principles set forth in the foregoing discussion of the subject. Let us take first a passage found in the first Gospel only : * "And when they persecute you in one city, flee to another. For truly do I say to you, ye will not have gone over the cities of Israel till the Son of Man hath come." It has already been pointed out in a foregoing chapter that this discourse in its main features is wholly out of place in this early period of the ministry of Jesus, when the disciples are sent out on a missionary journey. It belongs undoubtedly to a later period of his work.† But in any case it is irreconcilable with the saying ascribed to Jesus in another place ‡ that before his second coming the Gospel will be published throughout the whole world. Later experiences of persecution and flight probably gave its existing form to the passage, experiences in which was mingled an ardent expectation of the coming of Christ to put an end to the trials of his followers. The occasion of the flight of the Jewish Christians from Jerusalem to Pella § to escape the persecutions of their compatriots, when they doubtless consoled themselves with the hope that the advent would take place before they should be entirely driven from their country, furnishes the most probable explanation of the origin of the words.

Another passage peculiar to Matthew contains words which it is very improbable that Jesus can have spoken.∥

---

* Chap. x. 23.

† Meyer, Commentar *in loc.* Weiffenbach, Der Wiederkunftsgedanke Jesu, 1873, p. 300 ; Colani, p. 105.

‡ Matt. xxiv. 14.

§ Eusebius, Hist. Eccl. iii. 5.

∥ Chap. xix. 28. Peculiar to Matthew in this connection. See Luke xxii. 30, where the words are extremely inappropriate after the supper, and "surcharge the picture with a new Judaistic coloring."

Peter, having asked what the disciples who had left all to follow Jesus should have, this evangelist makes Jesus answer: "In the renovation" ["the restitution of all things," or the Messianic reign], "when the Son of Man sitteth on the throne of his glory, ye who have followed me shall sit on twelve thrones judging the twelve tribes of Israel." These words are not at all necessary to the sense, for those which follow them here, as well as in the other synoptists, are an answer to the question. Besides, the passage is in flagrant opposition to the refusal of Jesus to assure to the sons of Zebedee places of honor in his kingdom: "Ye know not what ye ask, for to sit on my right hand or on my left is not mine to give." He does promise them, indeed, that they shall drink of his cup and be baptized with his baptism. Here is a true word of Jesus evangelic and profound. It is a psychological improbability that the author of these words can have spoken the others also. Let him who pronounces this criticism an arbitrary dealing with the text reflect that Luke is equally arbitrary in omitting the words in question in this connection, and that Mark omits them altogether. Let the student, with the alternative before him that either these words are genuine or an interpolation, decide which of the two suppositions is the more probable, that Jesus actually made to his disciples a promise like this, which has never been fulfilled, a promise whose materialism must have excited the most unspiritual hopes and ambitions in their breasts, or that the thought originated in the apocalyptic Messianism of the early Church, and found expression through the evangelist or the hand of an interpolator.

Two of the synoptists ascribe an apocalyptic saying to Jesus before the High-priest,[*] while a third, Luke, modi-

[*] Matt. xxvi. 64; Mark xiv. 62.

fies it in the interest of a spiritual apprehension.* The first evangelist reports him to have said: "Henceforth ye will see the Son of Man sitting on the right hand of power and coming in the clouds of heaven." Mark gives the same words after suppressing the adverb "henceforth" (ἀπ' ἄρτι). But Luke's version is: "From this time the Son of Man will sit on the right hand of the power of God." It cannot be denied, in the first place, that some weight must be allowed to Volkmar's remark that the disciples, being absent from the scene before the High-priest, the words cannot be well authenticated.† But Weiffenbach's attempt to parry this objection by observing that "such a characteristic (?) word, which in the Sanhedrim led to the outbreak of fearful horror and to the definitive sentence of death, could not remain within the four walls of the hall of judgment, but must fly with stormy force from mouth to mouth,"‡ only tends to strengthen it. A word which flies as with the wings of the storm through an excited multitude has small chance of being correctly reported. One may, indeed, say with Keim that Jesus before the Sanhedrim (High-priest) may have made a confession "by which he out of the heart's blood of his faith maintained the claims of his Messiah-ship apparently lying in ruins"; § but our chief concern is with determining what he really said there. If, then, the account of the first evangelist represents, as it probably does, the earliest form of the tradition, who will not choose to follow Luke in his critical revision of it, since a choice must perforce be made between the two records?

* Luke xxii. 69. Luke's account is confused, the scene being changed to the "council."
† Die Evangelien, oder Marcus und die Synopsis, etc. 1870, p. 588.
‡ Der Wiederkunftsgedanke Jesu, p. 206.
§ Geschichte Jesu, iii. p. 335.

In the great eschatological discourse recorded in Mark xiii., Matthew xxiv., and Luke xxi. the application of the critical method in question is indispensable to a rational solution of the problems presented. The hypothesis appears to have great probability in its favor that in Mark xiii. 5–31 and parallels we have a fragment of Jewish-Christian apocalypse which was written and in circulation shortly before the overthrow of Jerusalem, perhaps the very "oracle" to which Eusebius refers as inciting the Christians to the flight to Pella.* The section is evidently an interruption of the narrative, since the answer of Jesus to the question of his disciples is only given at the end of the apparent interpolation. The words which the first evangelist preserves. "Let him that readeth understand," belong to a writing, and are manifestly unfitting in a spoken discourse, and "Pray that your flight be not on the sabbath," cannot have come from Jesus.† Eusebius says that the chief men of the church received an oracle which commanded them to emigrate. If this oracle was regarded by the Christians as having come to them "through revelation," as Eusebius says, its incorporation in the record is not difficult of explanation. If anywhere in the Gospels the apocalyptic-Messianic expectations of the early Christians have found expression, it is certainly in this section that they exist in a most pronounced form. All the traits of apocalyptic writings appear here, and so evident are they that even Keim, who holds that Jesus believed in and explicitly taught his second personal coming to the earth, finds himself compelled to admit the apocalyptic origin of these words. ‡

* Hist. Eccl. iii. 5. So Keim, Holtzmann, Weizsäcker, Colani, Weiffenbach, Wendt, and many other critics of the first rank.
† See Luke xiii. 15, xiv. 5.
‡ Geschichte Jesu, iii. 199 f.

To this eschatological discourse as recorded by Mark and Luke the first evangelist adds a dramatic scene of general judgment which is to be enacted " when the Son of Man shall come in his glory and all his angels with him." * Then " all nations " will be gathered before him, and he will " separate men from one another as a shepherd separateth the sheep from the goats," rewarding and punishing them according as they shall have fed and clothed and visited in prison or neglected the least of these his brethren, that is, the Christians. The attention of the critical reader of this passage is first drawn by the incompatibility which it presents with some of the other sayings concerning " the last things " ascribed to Jesus by the evangelists. Evidently this coming of the Son of Man must be regarded as the same coming referred to in previous chapters and declared to be impending, to be consummated, in fact, in the life-time of the existing generation. Yet this judgment on " all nations," this world-assize, presupposes the proclamation of the Gospel to all mankind. If it be a judgment on Christians only, as some exegetes suppose, they must be gathered from all nations, while if, according to other interpreters, it be a judgment on unbelievers with reference to their treatment of the " brethren " of the judge, the existence of Christians among all peoples is implied. The time-limit here required is plainly far beyond the life of the generation living in the time of Christ. One cannot but recall here the incompatibility previously pointed out between the declarations that the disciples shall not have gone over the cities of Israel before the Parousia, and that the Gospel must be preached to all nations before that event. These facts furnish incontestable evidence of the modification of the eschatological expectations of the early

---

* Chap. xxv. 31–46.

Christians. They show, too, that these expectations in the form in which they are expressed in the synoptic Gospels, with all their fantastic and inconsistent features, find their most probable explanation in the intense Messianic hopes which prevailed among Jewish Christians when these writings were composed. Besides, the words which open the section in question, and represent Jesus as coming in his glory " with the angels " and sitting " on the throne of his glory," are not more strange and improbable from his lips than is the doctrine here set forth of his office of judge of the nations. In no other place in the synoptic Gospels is he so represented, and this passage, standing alone, as it does, can hardly establish the doctrine as his. To Paul must be charged this bold innovation in Jewish Messianism, which never recognized the Messiah as a judge.* How unfitting, too, to a delineation of a world-assize is the judgment here described which takes into account no conduct but that springing from good-will or indifference towards the " brethren "! A strange world-judgment, surely, is this which consigns to age-lasting punishment men of " all nations " for not visiting in prison, clothing, and feeding " the least " of the believers, and leaves out of account all other sins of omission or commission! It is, then, in the highest degree improbable that this section in its present form can have come from Christ. Some genuine words of his, such as Matt. x. 40–42, may have lain at the basis of it, or it may originally have been a parable which later received this apocalyptic form and coloring.

Serious and insuperable objections lie against all other explanations than the one here proposed of the eschato-

---

* I. Cor. iv. 5. Here the judgment follows the return of Christ, ἕως ἂν ἔλθῃ ὁ κύριος. See also II. Cor. v. 10.

logical sayings ascribed to Jesus in the synoptic Gospels. The most of these explanations proceed upon the presumption that he has been correctly quoted, a presumption which a critical comparison of the records shows to be unfounded. The doctrine that Jesus employed the extravagant language in question to indicate his spiritual coming and presence in his church,* involves the conclusion that he used words to which his disciples must have given a sensuous interpretation, words, in fact, which could not but be misleading. This explanation proceeds from a dogmatic interest, and has nothing to commend it to a sound hermeneutical judgment. One might with equal propriety maintain that the account of the marvellous Messianic vineyards recorded by Papias may fairly be in like manner "spiritualized." But happily this did not make its way into the Gospels, and has accordingly been spared such a hermeneutical treatment. The popular orthodox interpretation which finds in the language under consideration a prophecy of the coming of Christ in a future general judgment and catastrophic "end of the world," † is untenable in view of the explicit and repeated statement that the generation then living would see the Parousia.

That Jesus put forth no claim to the Messiahship in any sense appears to be the view defended with great force and acumen by Martineau,‡ who urges with good reasons that in the eschatological discourses the term "Son of Man," evidently employed in the Jewish-Messianic sense, expresses an afterthought of the evangelists, and not a conception of Jesus himself. In interpreting the scene at

* Immer, Neutestamentliche Theologie, 1877, p. 143 f.
† Dorner, System of Christian Doctrine, 1885, iv. p. 87.
‡ The Seat of Authority in Religion, pp. 326–358.

Cæsarea Philippi, however, Martineau repudiates, without giving a reason for doing so, the report of the first evangelist that Jesus explicitly accepted the appellation "Christ," or "Messiah," with the declaration that Peter's insight was by a revelation of God, and regards the result of the great episode as a "disclaimer" on the part of Jesus of all Messianic pretensions. A disclaimer of the Messiahship in the popular, Jewish sense, probably also in Peter's sense, who had spoken better than he knew, there certainly was in Jesus' rebuke of the solicitude which could not tolerate a suffering Messiah. But the injunction of silence does not justify the conclusion that he did not assume in any sense a Messianic mission to his nation, and regarded the Messiahship as " a *private* prerogative which could be clandestinely held." Evidently nothing could have been more repugnant to Jesus, nothing more imprudent, than to suffer this inflammatory word " Messiah " to be thrown out upon the common air, changed from the esoteric, spiritual meaning in which he held it, and perverted to a revolutionary watch-word. While perhaps the critical study of the original evangelic tradition shows that Jesus made no announcement of himself as Messiah prior to the scene at Cæsarea Philippi, and then reservedly and not at all as the expected Son of David, there appears to be a very decided implication of a Messianic mission in the frequent declarations that with him the kingdom of heaven was ushered in. The sense in which he employed this Messianic term is clear to us, though it was veiled to his disciples. His kingdom was not of this world. It is open to grave question, then, whether the theory under consideration does not tend to invalidate a central and well-authenticated portion of the tradition of Jesus.

There remains to be considered the theory that Jesus

spoke touching his return to the earth essentially in the terms of the records, and thereby expressed his own expectation of an actual, personal Parousia to be early realized for the consummation of his mission in the founding of the Messianic kingdom. "As death without revival was a downright burial of his Messiahship, so life without return abolished upon the earth his Messianic work, the world-kingdom, the kingdom of heaven," says Keim.* From this point of view the expectation of a personal Parousia was incidental to the humanity of Jesus. "There is nothing more certain than that on the ground of a human consciousness he could find only this adjustment and no other, if he bound the salvation of the world not alone to the spiritual truths which he announced, but also to his person and to the Messiahship, his Messiahship, and that on the same human ground especially the catastrophe of Jerusalem must appear in general as the limit at which his Messiahship should attain to honor and power upon the earth." † It is evident that the self-deception of Jesus, perhaps even his fanaticism and folly, cannot but be implied in this hypothesis. It is hardly necessary to say, in view of the results of the criticism of the Gospels, that it is idle to maintain this theory on the ground of the testimony of the synoptists to the sayings in question, when the variations and inconsistencies of that testimony are taken into account. Ineffectual, too, it is to urge that if we discredit these eschatological, apocalyptical sayings ascribed to Jesus we invalidate the entire record. For the dilemma in which we are placed is either to conclude that the synoptists have misrepresented Jesus by giving to his words the coloring of the Messianic expectations of their time, or that he in the most solemn terms prophe-

* Geschichte Jesu, iii. p. 566. † Ib. p. 219.

sied a coming on the clouds with a retinue of angels, and was, accordingly, a self-deceived apocalyptist. That he should have believed that his mission could only be accomplished by founding a "world-kingdom" and presiding in person over it, is in most flagrant contradiction to his spirit and aim as made known in words of his which have the unmistakable stamp of genuineness. It is a doubtful confirmation of the Gospel as a whole to establish the correctness of the record at the expense of the trustworthiness of Jesus. By this sort of criticism criticism itself is dissolved.

If, now, it results from the criticism of the Gospels that Jesus left to mankind no word respecting a second coming in person to take place either in the first century or at a remote "end of the world"; that he taught nothing concerning a general judgment and a dramatic scene of a separation of men from one another "as a shepherd separates the sheep from the goats"; that he rather left the consequences of human conduct to be inferred from the general principles of his teaching than depicted them by means of apocalyptic imagery; that, in a word, his real Gospel, when freed from Jewish-Christian accretions, is not at all a Book of Revelation disclosing celestial arcana, then is not the loss great in losing all that we lose by this critical sifting, unless it be for those who in religion "want the materialism of the apocalypse," and while "gazing up into heaven" miss the earthly footprints of the Master.

In accordance with the "spiritual" point of view of the fourth Gospel, we should expect to find in it an eschatology different in important particulars from that of the synoptics. While the doctrine of a visible return of Jesus to the earth was well adapted to the materialistic popular conception, it evidently maintained itself with difficulty. We have seen that in the first Gospel it is to take place "immediately" after the judgment on Jerusalem. In Mark the determination is not so definite, and Luke inserts the indefinite period of the "times of the gentiles." At the time of the composition of the second Epistle of Peter, probably in the last half of the second century, the writer of it finds "scoffers" who ask "when is the promise of his coming?" and consoles himself with the thought that "one day with the Lord is as a thousand years." Some traces of the persistent popular notion remain even in the fourth Gospel. We find here a "last day" of resurrection both for those who have done good and those who have done evil.* Many mansions are to be prepared, and Jesus will come to receive the disciples to himself.† The prominent and peculiar eschatological feature of the Gospel is, however, a spiritualization of the Parousia and the judgment. All sensuous traits of a second coming are banished in favor of a spiritual presence. The judgment is "now," and the condemnation of men is in their rejection of the "light" that has already come into the world.‡ The true judgment is the separation between those who love the light and come to it, and those who hate the light and remain in darkness. He who believes in the Son is not judged, but he who does not believe is judged *already*. Eternal life is attainable here and now, for he that believeth *hath* it, while on the unbeliever the wrath of God *abideth*. He who thus passes from death into life has experienced the real resurrection, which is a spiritual transformation. They who eat the flesh of the Son of Man and drink his blood have eternal life. To them

---
* Chap. v. 29.   † Chap. xiv. 3, 18, 28.   ‡ Chap. iii. 19.

he *is* the resurrection and the life. The doctrine that the second coming of Christ passes over in this Gospel into that of the pouring out of the Holy Spirit, the sending of the Paraclete, who should lead the disciples into all truth, and bring to their remembrance all things that Jesus had taught them, has the weight of Hausrath's authority in its favor, who finds in the thought of the evangelist an identification of Christ and the Paraclete.*
Oscar Holtzmann sees in this identification a reproduction of a Philonic doctrine, and the dependence, accordingly, of the fourth Gospel upon the Alexandrian philosophy.†

* Neutestamentliche Zeitgesch. iii. p. 579.
† Das Johannesevangelium, 1887, p. 78.

CHAPTER IX.

DOGMATIC "TENDENCIES" IN THE GOSPELS.

MR. MATTHEW ARNOLD'S genial criticism of the theories of "vigor and rigor" has exposed some of the excesses committed by Baur and his followers in supporting the hypothesis of doctrinal "tendencies" in the writers of the Gospels. To the celebrated Tübingen critic and many of the adherents of his school, the Gospels were pre-eminently tendency-writings.[*] Their writers were advocates. They had taken sides with reference to the great question which is supposed to have been agitated in their time; they were friendly or hostile to the Pauline doctrine, and wrote the Gospels to support their individual partisan convictions. We have already seen to what extremes this theory was carried in the Tübingen criticisms of the fourth Gospel, a considerable part of which the exigencies of it required to be regarded as inventions in the interest of a preconceived doctrine. In the place of downright invention this criticism sometimes assumed, however, a modification and arrangement of the materials of tradition by the evangelists in order to subserve a dogmatic purpose. It may well be conceded to Mr. Arnold, and maintained in the name of sane criticism, that many of the procedures of these learned scholars are very questionable; that they suppose in the evangelists a *finesse* which they in all probability did not possess; and

[*] Tendenz-Schriften.

that they require conclusions of vast import to be drawn from very slender premises. Of this sort is the "ingenious conjecture" of Schwegler made in support of the theory that the third Gospel was written in the interest of the Pauline or gentile-Christian view of Christianity, that the impenitent and penitent thieves who were crucified with Jesus were intended to represent respectively the Jews and the gentiles, the former rejecting, the latter accepting Christ. If, however, there is in this account a tendency or a conscious intention of the writer, one can hardly decide which is the more to be admired, the skill of the evangelist in concealing it or the ingenuity of the German critic in discovering it. In the same Gospel it is related that Peter fishes all night and catches nothing, but when at the command of Jesus the net is once more let down, a great multitude of fishes is caught, and the net breaks. Volkmar discovers that in this narrative the writer meant to contrast the barren result of preaching the Gospel to the Jews with the fruitful result of preaching it to the gentiles.* But the surprising ingenuity which could make this discovery is surpassed by that which finds the more advanced Paulinism of the author of the fourth Gospel proved by the fact that in his account of the same miracle, which he places after the resurrection, he declares that the net was not broken, and thereby indicates that the heathen may be brought in "without any such disruption of the church as to his faint-hearted predecessor had seemed inevitable"! The fourth evangelist's mention of only one boat engaged in this fishing instead of the two of the third Gospel is, again, an intimation

---

* This strange fancy appears to have been adopted by J. Estlin Carpenter in The First Three Gospels, their Origin and Relations, second edition, London, 1890, p. 330.

that the co-existence of a Jewish and gentile Christianity is no longer satisfactory to the religious consciousness which now demands a catholic church, one and indivisible!

It is evident, however, that neither the extreme statement of a theory nor extravagances committed in its defence do by any means invalidate the essentials of the theory itself. A fair test of the tendency-doctrine, accordingly, requires an examination of the Gospels in some detail with reference to its assumptions. We may well begin, then, with the first Gospel, which is regarded by the Tübingen school as originally written in the interest of Jewish Christianity and with intentional opposition to the Pauline doctrine. It cannot, indeed, be denied that the Gospel contains some passages which, taken by themselves, appear to favor this theory. Among these may be mentioned the declarations ascribed to Jesus that he came not to destroy, but to fulfil, the law; that in his coming again with the angels he will "reward every man according to his works," in assumed opposition to the Pauline doctrine of salvation by faith; that if one will enter into life one must "keep the commandments"; and that the disciples ought to do whatsoever the scribes and Pharisees enjoin.* The deprecation of a flight from Jerusalem on the Sabbath also appears to represent the Jewish superstitious reverence for that day.† The injunction not to give that which is holy unto the dogs might be regarded as a thrust at Paulinism if any support could be made apparent for Hilgenfeld's gratuitous reference of "dogs" to the gentiles.‡ In the sending out of the apostles the injunc-

---

* Chap. v. 17 f., xvi. 27, xix. 17, xxiii. 2 f.
† Chap. xxiv. 20.
‡ Chap. vii. 6; Hilgenfeld, Die Evangelien, p. 114.

tion is given to them not to "go into the way of the gentiles," but rather "to the lost sheep of the house of Israel," and it is declared that the consummation of all things will come before they will have gone over the cities of Israel, thus apparently excluding a ministry to the gentiles.*

On the other hand, the Gospel contains many passages which an interpreter interested in detecting in it a Pauline "tendency" would find favorable to his theory. Jesus is made to declare, for example, that one cannot enter into the kingdom of heaven unless one's righteousness exceed that of the scribes and Pharisees, and in connection with this anti-Jewish saying he announces strikingly liberal modifications of the teachings of those "of old time." † The spiritualizing of the law to the extent of declaring all its requirements to be fulfilled by doing as we would be done by indicates rather a tendency to Paulinism than to Judaism. A similar tendency appears in the disparagement of external forms in the explanation of the parable concerning defilement, "To eat with unwashed hands defileth not a man," and in the declaration that on the two great commandments hang all the law and the prophets.‡ The prophecy that many will come from the East and the West, and sit down in the kingdom, while the children of the kingdom will be cast into outer darkness,§ shows certainly no leaning to Judaism, and scarcely leaves room for so much hope for the chosen people as Paul expressed more than once. In a similar vein are the declaration that before "the end come" "the Gospel will be preached in all the world for a witness unto all nations," and the commission to the disciples to go out and teach all nations.‖ The refusal by Jesus of the re-

---

* Chap. x. 5 f. † Chap. v. 20 f. ‡ Chap. xv. 20, xxii. 40.
§ Chap. viii. 11, 12. ‖ Chap. xxiv. 14 (see also xxvi. 13), xxviii. 19.

quest of the woman of Canaan on the ground that he was sent only "to the lost sheep of the house of Israel" has, indeed, an anti-Pauline appearance, but is neutralized by his final granting of the petition.* The Messianic title, "Son of David" is, indeed, much more frequently applied to Jesus in this Gospel than in the others, but only as the popular designation.† On the occasion of the triumphal entry into Jerusalem Jesus is hailed by the multitude as the Son of David, and appears to acknowledge the title, and thereby to place himself at the Jewish point of view. ‡ There can be little doubt that the scene is an integral part of the Gospel, and the problem presented is whether or not it was enacted as recorded in this Gospel. The fact that Jesus argued from one of the Psalms to prove that the Messiah could not be the son of David § renders his acceptance of the title on this occasion very doubtful. Baur, accordingly, thinks that the scene of the entrance into Jerusalem as here recorded is one of the problematical events of the Gospel-history, since it is as easily explicable how such a narrative might arise out of the Jewish-Messianic idea as the assumption is difficult that the thing can have occurred as here related. ‖ The fact that the first evangelist accepted either intentionally or without objection the tradition with this cry of "Son of David" which Luke omits may indicate a Jewish-Christian tendency, or may be put to the account of mere naïveté. That the first Gospel as a whole does not appear to be the work of a partisan in the Pauline controversy is evident from the foregoing review of texts in which two tendencies are strongly represented. Hilgenfeld accordingly maintains

---

* Chap. xv. 24.   ‡ Chap. xxi.
† Chap. ix. 27, xii. 23, xv. 22, xx. 30, 31, xxi. 9, 15.   § Chap. xxii., 41-45.
‖ Kritische Untersuchungen, etc., p. 611.

with much acumen that the original form of the Gospel was of the Judaistic tendency, and that the Pauline passages were added by a reviser.* But it is very improbable that a Pauline reviser, who can have had no scruples at taking liberties with the text, would have left the passages standing in his revised edition which are as decidedly anti-Pauline as his supposed additions and modifications are Pauline. Baur, whose intellectual greatness and rare critical discrimination saved him from many of the vagaries into which some of his disciples have fallen, acknowledges that since the Gospel in many passages indubitably bears testimony to the universality of Christianity, one cannot charge it with representing a limited Judaism. The anxiety, he adds, with which the other Gospels, in order not to concede too much to Judaism, have omitted or changed certain passages is a far more distinguishing criterion of a definite tendency-character than the naïveté with which the author of the first Gospel has taken them up from the tradition, and left them standing by the side of others which apparently contradict them.

That the first Gospel, however, represents the Jewish-Christian conception of the Gospel-history can hardly be denied by any unbiassed student of it. In this respect it has a "tendency," and is, in the phraseology of the Tübingen school, a "tendency-writing." This concession does not at all, however, carry with it the conclusion that the tendency in question is of such a nature as seriously to affect the plan and composition of the writing and subvert its historical credibility, however much this may be prejudiced by it. The type of Gospel-writing which we have in this record is a natural and necessary result of the historical connection of Christianity with Judaism. Jesus

---

* Die Evangelien, pp. 100-120. See Baur, *ut supra*.

declared, indeed, that he came not to annul the law and the prophets, and this artless record of his teachings and ministry shows only too well that he did not in fact destroy them, and reveals with what tenacity the most tenacious of religious beliefs held his divine word in its inflexible grasp. The law and the prophets constitute without doubt the point of view from which the writer of this Gospel regards the mission of Jesus and the evangelic tradition. The Old Testament is his point of departure. He finds that the Gospel was contained in it from the beginning, and makes it no small part of his task as an evangelist to show how the former may be explained out of the latter. The frequent reference to the Old Testament and the application of passages from it to the events of the life of Jesus constitute a peculiarity of this writer which has given rise to the remark that one does not sometimes know whether the history is there for the sake of the citation or the citation for the sake of the history. Throughout the Gospel, and particularly in the first two chapters, the tendency is manifest to find in the events of the life of Jesus the fulfilment of prophecies of the Old Testament. Jesus is born of a virgin, and "all this took place in order that it might be fulfilled which was spoken by the Lord through the prophet."* He was born in Bethlehem according to a prophecy, and the flight into Egypt took place in order to fulfil a word of Hosea.† In the slaughter of the children by order of Herod a saying of Jeremiah found its fulfilment, ‡ and when the parents of Jesus on their return from Egypt take up their residence in Nazareth with the

---

* ἵνα πληρωθῇ τὸ ῥηθὲν, κτλ, cf. Is. vii. 14.

† Chap. ii. 6, cf. Micah v. 2 ; chap. ii. 15, cf. Hosea xi. 1.

‡ Chap. ii. 18, cf. Jer. xxxi. 15. For a discussion of these quotations from a hermeneutical point of view see the next chapter.

child, this also happened in order that a prophecy might be fulfilled, which said that he should be called a Nazarene.* John the Baptist is "the voice of one crying in the wilderness," spoken of "through Isaiah the prophet." When Jesus dwells for a time in Capernaum "in the borders of Zebulon and Naphtali," it is that a saying of Isaiah "might be fulfilled." † This "pragmatism" dominates the evangelist's entire conception of the history, so that he appears unable to regard any act or experience of Jesus otherwise than from the point of view of prophetic announcement and fulfilment. No sooner does he begin to relate the healing of the sick and the casting out of demons by Jesus than he "pragmatizes" about these works by declaring that they are done "in order that" what Isaiah had foretold might come to pass; and even Jesus' direction to those whom he had healed not to make him known is said to be given for the same reason. ‡ The parabolic method of teaching is employed by Jesus in order to fulfil a prophecy of Isaiah, and the people who are slow of heart, and hearing hear not, also have a share in the fulfilment, whose monotonous recurrence betrays the persistent predilection of the writer. § Not only are the Pharisees denounced as hypocrites, but they were prophesied of by Isaiah. ‖ The preparations for the triumphal entrance into Jerusalem are made in order to fulfil a prophetic word of Jeremiah, and the shouting multitude proclaim the Messiahship of Jesus in the words of a Psalm.¶ In the history of the passion it is declared that the disciples will

---

* Chap. ii. 23.
† Chap. iii. 3, cf. Is. xl. 3 ; chap. iv. 14, cf. Is. ix. 1, 2.
‡ Chap. viii. 17, cf. Is. liii. 4 ; chap. xii. 18, cf. Is. xlii. 1–4.
§ Chap. xiii. 14, 35, cf. Is. vi. 9, Ps. lxxviii. 2.
‖ Chap. xv. 8, cf. Is. xxix. 13.
¶ Chap. xxi. 4, 5, cf. Zech. ix. 9 ; chap. xxi. 9.

forsake Jesus, "for it is written, I will smite the shepherd, and the sheep of the flock shall be scattered."* When the chief priests bought a potter's field with Judas' thirty pieces of silver, "that was fulfilled," we are told, "which was spoken by Jeremiah the prophet." †

Without entering here upon a discussion of the hermeneutical method according to which these Old-Testament passages receive the application which the writer of the Gospel makes of them, it is evident that the wearisome citation betrays a tendency to "Judaize" which, while not peculiar to him, is his marked characteristic in comparison with the other evangelists. It is difficult to believe, in view of this unquestionable tendency, that he wrote with no other object than to set forth the life and teachings of Jesus. Rather the evidences of an ulterior design are as unmistakable as that design itself is probable. We have already seen how hard it was for Jews to believe in a Messiah who had not fulfilled the national Messianic expectations, and how Paul found it necessary to argue vigorously against this prejudice of his countrymen. Now a Jewish writer, whether apostle or evangelist, could not leave the life and teachings of Jesus standing by themselves as sole and sufficient evidences of his Messiahship, but thought it necessary in writing for Jews to appeal to the only holy Scriptures acknowledged by himself and his readers, the Old Testament. No other evidence lay so near his hand; and not to employ it would have been un-Jewish, unnatural. But to use it liberally, even if somewhat soberly in comparison with some of the uncanonical early writers, to press the Old Testament in the interest of the demonstration in question is precisely the

---
* Chap. xxvi. 31, cf. Zech. xiii. 7.
† Chap. xxvii. 9, cf. Jer. xviii. 1, 2, Zech. xi. 12, 13.

sort of proceeding which a true historical divination would look for in a writer like the author of the first Gospel. For historical divination expects a writer to reflect the prepossessions of his age and to write from its point of view. When it does not find him altogether doing so it rightly assumes some influence of an environment, and proceeds to inquire of what nature it was. The critical and historical judgment cannot, then, approve any other method of interpretation than that known as the historical, and is offended by a hermeneutical procedure which goes upon the presumption that a Jewish-Christian writer, living towards the end of the first century, could at all view the life of Jesus much as a Christian of the nineteenth century views it. Although criticism may be obliged to leave without an entirely satisfactory solution the problem which is presented by the appearance, side by side, of Pauline and anti-Pauline elements in the first Gospel, it cannot at all be in doubt that this is in a very real sense a "tendency-writing," conceived and executed in the interest of establishing for Jews the Jewish-Christian Messianic office of Jesus. We have already seen that the eschatological portions of the Gospel find their most probable explanation in the Messianic expectations of the writer and his contemporaries, and if the tendency in question is such as is *a priori* to be expected, it appears to be established by reason as well as by the evidence furnished by the texts which have been quoted.

Since the second Gospel offers little that calls for consideration under the title of this chapter, and the tendency of the fourth Gospel has already been pointed out in Chapter VII., there remains only the third Gospel to be studied with reference to the matter in question. Mention has already been made in Chapter VI. of the recognition by early traditions of the Pauline character of this Gospel, and if we accept the principle with regard to tradition that "it is something in a thing's favor that men have delivered it," we shall have the presumption to begin with that in studying Luke we have to do with a writing which has a tendency more or less unequivocal. It is very much in favor of this tradition, in the first place, that modern criticism since Gieseler has confirmed it so far as the character of the Gospel as a whole is concerned, though reaching quite different conclusions in some matters of detail. Extreme defenders of the tradition, on the one hand, have argued for a direct or indirect share of Paul in the writing of the Gospel.* The so-called "broad centre" of theology finds in Luke a modification of the common material of the history conditioned by Pauline traditions and points of view.† According to the Tübingen school the Gospel is a blending of Pauline and Jewish-Christian elements in a conciliatory manner, indeed, but essentially in the interest of a moderate Paulinism. ‡ Some of the critics of this school, however, show not a little favor to the extreme theory of the Saxon Anonymous § in regarding the Gospel as a thoroughly Pauline partisan writing, which expresses hatred for the Jews, satirizes Peter, etc.‖ Finally, the attempt has been made to reduce to a minimum or entirely to dissipate the Paulinism of the Gospel. ¶

* Thiersch, Aberle, Godet, and H. H. Evans.
† Bleek-Mangold, Holtzmann, Schanz, Schenkel, Weiss, and others. Renan's point of view is essentially the same.
‡ Baur, Hilgenfeld, Keim, Overbeck, Hausrath, Holsten, Pfleiderer, and others.
§ Die Evangelien, ihr Geist, ihre Verfasser, und ihr Verhältniss zu einander, etc. 2te Ausg. 1852.
‖ Hasert and Volkmar, the latter more moderate.
¶ Schwanbeck, Reuss, Ritschl.

It is certainly fair to judge this Gospel as to the matter in question by the explicit statement which the writer makes of his object in the introduction. Here he says that he writes for the instruction of Theophilus as to the "exact truth" in regard to those things in which he had been instructed. Now as Theophilus was doubtless a Greek-Christian, and as history brings Luke into relation with Paul, the presumption of a Pauline point of view in the Gospel appears to have at least probability in its favor. But it goes without saying that one is not warranted by these data in looking in it for an obtrusive propaganda of Paulinism, for great *finesse* and cunning art, or for downright invention of situations and doctrines in the interest of a theory. We have reason probably to look for precisely that setting and coloring of the history which are due to the writer's environment and point of view, and are denoted by the word "tendency." To more than this the writer's situation could hardly have been favorable. The observation of Holtzmann appears to be well grounded that at the time when the Gospel was written the material of the Gospel-history was so fixed in the consciousness of the Church that its transformation according to Pauline principles could not have been thoroughgoing, and must have been confined to slight modifications in the way of transpositions, omissions, and insertions.* The way in which the twelve apostles are sometimes referred to does not necessarily, as Davidson † thinks, following the Saxon Anonymous whom Baur takes to task for his excesses,‡ indicate a disposition to depreciate and ridicule them, or rather "to give them a lower place than Matthew assigns them."

* Einleit. p. 400. † Introduction, ii. p. 45.
‡ Krit. Untersuch. p. 526 f.

It is true that the writer mentions once a strife among them as to who should be greatest, and several times their slowness of heart in understanding Jesus.* But he may have found the narrative as he gives it in his sources. Not every variation in the Gospel-narratives indicates a tendency. Besides, a writer cannot fairly be charged with intentional opposition to the twelve who apparently with design passes over such passages as Christ's rebuke of Peter and the account of the latter's profanity.† If such a procedure renders it impossible that the writer should be regarded as an "anti-Petrine," remarks Holtzmann, much less can he be called an anti-Judaist in view of the facts that the great discourses against the leaders of the people contained in the first Gospel, the threats and woes of the anti-Pharisaic philippics, the cursing of the fig-tree, the execration of the entire people, are partly passed over by him, and partly robbed of their effect by distribution at different points.

A decided inclination towards a broader and more liberal apprehension of Christianity than that of the Jewish Christians is, however, unmistakable in this Gospel, and is indicated by several traits. Luke alone has the account of the appointment and mission of the seventy, whose large number as compared with the twelve may very well be supposed to indicate an enlargement of the field of labor so as to include the gentiles. Accordingly, certain passages of a Jewish-Christian tendency in the first Gospel are omitted in this Pauline record, such, for example, as the injunction to the twelve not to go to the gentiles nor to the Samaritans, and the saying of Jesus that he was not sent except to the lost sheep of the house

---

* Chap. ix. 45, 51–56; xviii. 34; xxiv. 25.
† Matt. xvi. 22, 23; xxvi. 74.

of Israel.* Certain accords with Pauline expressions indicate a familiarity with the thought if not with the Epistles of Paul.† The account of the institution of the Lord's Supper appears to be in part copied from Paul.‡ In the discussion of Jesus with the Sadducees on the resurrection the words, "for all live to Him," are added apparently from Paul. § In the explanation of the parable of the sower an expression is added to the other synoptic accounts in accordance with the Pauline doctrine of salvation through faith. ∥ The saying respecting the first and the last in the kingdom appears to refer to the relations of Jews and gentiles. ¶ Pauline is the prophecy put into the mouth of Simeon.** The genealogy which goes back to Adam is in significant contrast to that of the first Gospel which stops at Abraham. The scene in the synagogue at Nazareth has an addition in the Pauline interest.†† In the parable of the supper is allegorically expressed the Pauline thought that the gentiles are called into the kingdom in the place of the indifferent Jews.‡‡ Not without significance are the story of the good Samaritan, who may be regarded as a representative of the gentile world, and the fondness of the evangelist for narratives and parables representing forgiveness and love for sinners. §§ The love born of faith is emphasized in the touching story of the anointing, and on the publican's cry for mercy the blessing of justification is pronounced.

---

* Matt. x. 5 ; xv. 24.
† Chap. x. 7, 8, *cf*. I. Cor. ix. 5, 14 ; x. 27.
‡ Chap. xxii. 19, 20, *cf*. I. Cor. xi. 23–25.
§ Chap. xx. 38, *cf*. Rom. vi. 11 ; xiv. 18.
∥ Chap. viii. 12, $\emph{ἵνα μὴ πιστεύσαντες σωθῶσι}$, *cf*. I. Cor. i. 21.
¶ Chap. xiii. 30.
** Chap. ii. 31–34.
†† Chap. iv. 25–27.
‡‡ Chap. xiv. 21–24.
§§ Chap. x. 30–38 ; vii. 36–50 ; xv. 11–32.
∥∥ Chap. viii. 15–24, $\emph{δεδικαιμένος}$, "justified," the Pauline terminology at least.

As a merely dogmatic composition, however, the third Gospel cannot fairly be regarded. Its generally conceded tendency towards Paulinism is not at all incompatible with its claim to as great a degree of credibility and as truly historical a character as belong of right to either of the other synoptic Gospels. Its slight Judaistic coloring bears testimony to its fidelity to the original tradition, while its breadth and liberality show the influence of the great Pauline idea by which alone the mission of Jesus received its true, world-historical interpretation.

CHAPTER X.

THE OLD TESTAMENT IN THE GOSPELS, OR THE HERMENEUTICS OF THE EVANGELISTS.

THE criticism of the Gospels must not only take into consideration the fact that the evangelists quote largely from the Old Testament in the endeavor to place the mission of Jesus in a relation of dependence on Jewish prophecy, but it must also investigate the principles of interpretation according to which these quotations are made, and study the phenomena in question in the light of a scientific hermeneutics. It is not necessary for the purpose in view in this chapter to enter into an examination in detail of all the citations of the kind which are made in the Gospels, and the present inquiry will accordingly be limited to a few taken from the first and fourth Gospels. For an account of the general character of the citations from the Old Testament made by the first evangelist the reader is referred to page 180. The question naturally arises at the outset whether the quotations to be considered may fairly be regarded as interpretations of the Old Testament, since some of them are "free" quotations, others are made from the Septuagint version, which is notoriously inaccurate, and few if any show certain evidences of a careful reference to the original Hebrew. It must be conceded that these conditions furnish a decided presumption against a real interpretation, and present in a strong light the absurdity of the pretension of the evangelists to show in the history of Jesus the fulfilment of prophecy. Now, it is precisely this pretension to give a real interpretation of Old-Testament passages that gives rise to the problem. For if the quotations in question were only applications of passages from the Old Testament by way of illustration, or mere literary embellishments, it is evident that the case would be quite different from that actually before us, and that there would be no occasion for calling in question the hermeneutics of the evangelists.

That the formula with which many of the quotations are introduced indicates a serious purpose to interpret the writers so quoted does not admit of question. Such a purpose could not be more explicitly announced than by the words: "Now all this took place in order that it might be fulfilled which was spoken by the Lord through the prophet."* Winer says of this expression and of all expressions of the same import that "it cannot be doubted" that "when used in reference to an event which has already occurred" they have "the more precise sense of in order that it might be fulfilled"—that is, that the Greek particle ἵνα has the "telic" and not the "ecbatic" sense.† The highest authorities in lexicography and the most distinguished commentators agree with the eminent grammarian.‡ Now, an examination of a few passages in which the quotations occur will suffice to show the hermeneutical method of the evangelists.

* τοῦτο δὲ ὅλον γέγονεν ἵνα πληρωθῇ τὸ ῥηθὲν ὑπὸ κυρίου διὰ τοῦ προφήτου, Matt. i. 22.

† Grammar of the Idiom of the New Testament, etc., 1869, p. 461.

‡ Grimm's Wilke's Clavis Novi Testamenti, Thayer's translation, 1887, sub voce ἵνα, and Fritzsche, Olshausen, De Wette, and Meyer on the passages. The ecbatic (ἐκβατικός) sense of ἵνα as ita ut, "so that," in these passages is rejected by the best authorities, although it has been advocated in a dogmatic interest.

Attention has already been called in Chapter V. to the fact that the first evangelist,* in interpreting the passage, Is. vii. 14, as a prophecy of the miraculous conception of Jesus, made the quotation from the Septuagint translation, which incorrectly renders the Hebrew word for marriageable young woman by παρθένος, "virgin." A reference to the prophet quoted shows the incongruity of the application which the evangelist makes of the passage.† The birth of the child is announced as a "sign" to Ahaz. This child shall eat butter and honey, that he may know to refuse the evil and choose the good, for before he shall have reached the age of such knowledge the land abhorred by Ahaz shall be forsaken of both her kings. Nothing more than this is indicated or intimated in the original passage and its connection. A passage from Hosea‡ is interpreted as a prophecy which was fulfilled by the flight into Egypt, or rather by the return of the parents of Jesus with the child out of that country. Here the translation of the Septuagint did not suit the purpose of the evangelist, and he has correctly rendered the Hebrew text.§ But the prophet had in mind Israel as a people, and evidently nothing else: "When Israel was a child, then I loved him, and called my son out of Egypt." A prophecy of Jeremiah is said to be fulfilled in the lamentation over the children slaughtered by the order of Herod,∥ a free quotation according to the Septuagint, Cod. Alex., probably.¶ The words of the prophet relate, however, to the Babylonian captivity. It is said that Joseph took up his abode in Nazareth "in order that

---

* Chap. i. 23.   † Is. vii. 14.   ‡ Hosea xi. 1, Matt. ii. 15.
§ The septuagint renders the Hebrew בני, "my son," by τὰ τέκνα αὐτοῦ, "his sons."
∥ Jer. xxxi. 15, Matt. ii. 18.   ¶ Credner, Beiträge, ii. p. 146.

it might be fulfilled which was spoken through the prophet: He will be called a Nazarene."* No such prophecy, however, occurs in the Old Testament.† John the Baptist is said to have been **foretold by Isaiah in the words** of the great prophet of the restoration **spoken in** reference to the **return of the Jews from the captivity in** Babylon.‡ **The statement is** explicit: "For this **is he that was spoken** of through Isaiah **the prophet**," etc. In Is. ix. 1, 2, the prophet declares that the people **who were in the** darkness of the Assyrian captivity "**have seen a** great light" in the hope **of restoration to their** country; but the **first evangelist regards Jesus'** residence in Capernaum as a fulfilment **of these words. The** citation is one **of the freest, and is a distortion of** the original apart **from the incongruous** application. It cannot be referred to the Septuagint and is nearer the Hebrew **text.**§ Credner remarks that the old translations, **the variants in** the Septuagint, and **the old explanations show that the** passage was a cliff **to the expositors which they did not** know how **to sail around; but that if the sense was so in**definite and ambiguous **it was so much** the **more** allowed to give, **as does the** evangelist, a Messianic interpretation to the obscure words and **with** their help **to** contest the unbelief in a Messiah **from Galilee.**‖ Twice also does the first evangelist apply to Jesus words spoken by the second Isaiah in reference **to** the pious remnant of the people of the Babylonian captivity, the remnant true **to the** theocratic religion in whom was the hope of the nation.¶

According to the theory of the authorship of the fourth Gospel set forth in Chapter VII. its citations from the Old

---

* Chap. ii. 23. † See page 183, Note *.
‡ Matt. iii. 3, cf. Is. xl. 3. § Chap. iv. 14, 15.
‖ Beiträge, ii. p. 139.
¶ Chap. viii. 17, xii. 17, cf. Is. liii. 4, xlii. 1–4.

Testament should be found to be made from the Septuagint, through which alone the writer probably knew the Hebrew sacred Scriptures. They are, in fact, made from this translation, sometimes accurately, and sometimes with great freedom, in order to adapt the words quoted to the purpose in view. This writer leaves no doubt in the reader's mind that he believed in an explicit and intentional reference to Christ by the prophets. Though Jesus wrought many "signs," he says, the Jews did not believe in him, " in order that what was spoken by Isaiah the prophet might be fulfilled: Lord, who hath believed our report?" etc.* Then he adds: "For this cause they *could not believe*, because Isaiah said again: He hath blinded their eyes, and hardened their heart, lest they should see with their eyes, and understand with their heart, and turn from their ways, and I should heal them." Finally he establishes the telic sense of his Greek particle, ἵνα, by adding: "These things said Isaiah because he saw his glory and spake of him." † Here we have two passages brought into connection which originally had no relation to each other, and are in fact from two different writers, the first and second Isaiah. They are not in any sense prophecies, and require no fulfilment. The first Isaiah hears "the word of the Lord to the people, 'See ye, indeed, and perceive not,'" etc., and "Make the heart of this people fat, and make their ears heavy, and shut their eyes, lest they see," etc. Then the prophet asks, "How long?" The answer is, "Until the cities be wasted * * * and the land be desolate." ‡ In the other passage the prophet of the restoration simply complains that his word is disregarded. There is nothing in the passages

* Chap. xii. 38, *cf.* Is. liii. 1.   † Chap. xii. 40, 41, *cf.* Is. vi. 10.
‡ Is. vi. 10 f.

or their context to indicate a reference by their writers to events future to their own times. Again, the treachery and the fate of Judas are represented as a fulfilment of prophecy.* But the Psalm to which reference is made for the words, "My own familiar friend who did eat of my bread hath lifted up his heel against me,"† contains complaints of the writer purely personal to himself, and if any part of it is applicable in the way of prophecy to Christ, a sound interpretation requires that all of it should be applicable to him. Yet no one would allow that the words, "Heal my soul, for I have sinned against Thee," can properly be so applied. The typology on which apologists depend for the vindication of the hermeneutics of the evangelists almost always breaks down when the connection of the Old-Testament passage is taken into account. There is in fact no passage in the Old Testament which by the most strained allegorizing can be made out to be a prophecy of the person or the fate of Judas.

It is unnecessary to proceed further in the examination of these quotations. One hazards nothing in saying that in all the Gospels there is not a single application of a so-called prophetic passage from the Old Testament to the history of Jesus which can be justified by a scientific interpretation. The hermeneutical method of the evangelists was a false method, and it is fruitless to attempt its defence. Nothing can be more absurd than the frantic efforts of apologists to make it appear to be good hermeneutics, unless it be to set up the claim that the evangelists were "inspired" grammarians and hermeneuts, and were miraculously preserved from error in their interpretations of the Old Testament. Their method was the allegorical, which from the Epistle to the Hebrews to the

---

* Chap. xiii. 18; xvii. 12. † Ps. xi. 1.

Speaker's Commentary has vitiated the greater part of biblical interpretation in the Christian Church. It owes its origin and maintenance to the exigencies of a dogmatic interest.* In order to support a given doctrine by appeal to a writing supposed to be authoritative passages are quoted from this scripture, and if by a correct historical and grammatical interpretation they do not yield the desired sense they are allegorized (ἄλλα ἀγορεύειν, to say other things), or made to say what they do not really mean. Now, as has been shown in Chapter IX., the first evangelist wrote in a dogmatic interest. He wished to make it appear that the history of Jesus had been foretold by the Hebrew prophets. He could not do this without allegorizing, and since allegorizing was the fashion of his time, he resorted to it in perfect naïveté and good faith. But Christian interpreters who ought to have known better, in whose justification in fact naïveté cannot be pleaded, have avenged upon the writings of the evangelists their unsophisticated torture of the law and the prophets.

It is precisely this fact that the hermeneutical method of the evangelists was the one in vogue in their time which furnishes a reason for their procedure and the only apology that can be made for it. The allegorical and typical interpretation by which any sense that a dogmatic interest required could be obtained from a biblical passage, and the extreme literalism which pressed a text or a word regardless of its original meaning and its context, were characteristics of the Palestinian-Jewish exegesis.† Had the evangelists' been superior to the influences of their age in this regard, they would have presented a truly surprising phenomenon, and given, perhaps, evidence of miraculous guidance and inspiration. That they

---

* See Essays, etc., by Fifteen Clergymen, Boston, 1889, p. 140 f.
† Immer, Hermeneutik, p. 28.

employed this method, however, far more sparingly than many of their contemporary writers is an evidence that they possessed those qualities of soberness and good judgment to which it is largely due that their writings were reckoned among the classics of the Christian literature of the first two centuries, or in other words became canonical.* It was inevitable that from the rabbinical literature and from Philo, the great Alexandrian allegorist, who employed it freely in the interest of eliminating from the Old Testament certain ethical teachings and historical statements which offended Hellenic culture, this method of interpretation should pass into the Christian Church. We should expect to find it pervading the New Testament from our knowledge of the antecedents and environment of its writers. Of these says Bleek, the cautious representative of a "mediating" theology, that in their conception of single passages in the Old Testament they are more or less dependent on an earlier exegetical tradition as it had taken form in the schools of the Jews, as well as on the entire condition of exegesis in their time among that people; and since we are not justified in presupposing that the Jewish exegesis of the time rested either in general or in particular on perfectly correct principles, and was employed in a manner wholly right, we cannot but expect that this fact should have so influenced the New-Testament writers as to lead them to apprehend this or that Old-Testament passage in a sense which, in a greater perfection of exegetical science and skill, and with a more harmonious application of all the auxiliary helps, would not prove to be entirely correct and accurate.†

---

* See p. 30.

† Ueber die dogmatische Benutzung alttestamentlicher Aussprüche im neuen Testament, etc., Studien und Kritiken, 1835, p. 447. See also Döpke, Hermeneutik der neutest. Schriftsteller, 1829, p. 189 f.

Accordingly, we are not surprised to find the author of the Epistle to the Hebrews* referring to Christ the words of a Psalm, "Thou art my son, this day have I begotten thee," which in the original are addressed to a Jewish king, and making a similar use of allegorical interpretation in many other passages. The exegesis of the apostle Paul, too, shows the influence of his rabbinical training, for he is quoted as employing this same passage in a similar way, † and throughout his Epistles he treats the Old Testament allegorically and typologically. To him Adam was a type (τύπος) of Christ, and various events of Hebrew history happened as "ensamples" (τυπικῶς, τύποι) for Christians. The two wives of Abraham were "an allegory," and prefigured the old and the new covenants. ‡ The rock smitten by Moses prefigured Christ, and was a "spiritual rock" (πέτρα πνευματική), typical of the source of "living water." He presses the collective singular, "seed" (σπέρμα) in order to show that by it only the one Christ can be meant, § as if it were at all allowable to say that a promise was made to the "seeds" of Abraham! If the author of the Epistle of Barnabas and Justin Martyr descend to a more trivial typology than the writers of the New Testament employ, their offence is different in degree only and not in kind from that of the latter.

To refer the question of these quotations to typology and leave it there, as many expositors do, ‖ is quite unsatisfactory from the critical point of view. For criticism cannot but inquire into the grounds of typology, and see whether or no it have any justification, and if there be

* Chap. v. 5, *cf.* Ps. ii. 7.   † Acts xiii. 33.   ‡ Gal. iv. 24.
§ Gal. iii. 16. See Immer, Neutestamentliche Theologie, p. 252.
‖ Even Meyer. See his commentary on the passages.

any, of what sort it is. Now typology in the only sense in which it can have any significance for theology involves prophecy, or, in other words, it implies that a person or an event written of by an author in some past age is intended to prefigure a person or an event which in some future age shall be a fulfilment of the type. The only real antetype, then, is something which is prophetically seen and intentionally expressed in the terms by which it is assumed to be indicated. According to this canon the paschal lamb can only have been a type of Christ, or the emigration of Israel from Egypt typical of Jesus' return from that country, if the writers in whom these supposed types are found intended to convey such a prefiguring. On no other principle can the typological interpretation be guarded against perversion by unlimited caprice and fancy. If a certain thing or event may be a type of any other thing or event subsequently happening to which a writer turning the leaves of history to find "ensamples" may see fit to apply it, then there is manifestly an end of all typology except that of the imagination. To prefigure nothing in particular but anything in general is really not to prefigure at all. Now, if we apply this canon to the Old Testament we shall find in it no types at all. For it does not appear that in any of the passages in it which are applied in the Gospels or Epistles to events in the history of Christ the writers had any remotely future circumstances or personality in mind, but only matters in or very near their own time.

If we interpret the Old-Testament authors in accordance with the principles which we apply to the interpretation of other writers, we do not find that their words explained in their natural or grammatical and historical meaning appear to prefigure events which were to happen several hundred years after their time. Whence then are the types? Plainly, they are the invention of a false, rabbinical exegesis. No one would ever have thought of them but for the refinements of this perverted hermeneutics. Those who applied this exegesis to the Old Testament made the discovery of types, because they wished to find in writings assumed to be authoritative the confirmation of certain doctrines, and being unable to find it in any other way, resorted to the process of exegetical pressure. If one will seek to defend typology by the doctrine of a "double sense," then with that doctrine let it stand or fall. If the Old-Testament writers conveyed the type in a "hidden" or "deeper" sense of their words, then it is not allowable to say that they were conscious of it, since we have no right to affirm that one is conscious of a particular thing which one does not express. But if the type is "hidden," who will undertake to furnish a rule for finding it out? The only means of certainly determining what it is in each case would appear to be an inspired hermeneutics, of which history furnishes no examples. The theory that the prophets of the Old Testament were not conscious of indicating types, but prophesied "better than they knew," is altogether trivial and absurd. He who prophesies better than he knows, or, in other words, what he does not know, cannot be said really to prophesy at all. The alleged prophecies are afterwards interpreted into his writings, and may be one thing or another according to the fancy of the interpreter. The only application of type, then, which appears to be permissible is that which Diestel calls the "logical"[*] and Immer seems to approve.[†] It is, however, emptied of all theological sig-

---

[*] Article "Vorbild" in Schenkel's Bibel-Lexicon, v. p. 620.
[†] Hermeneutik, p. 133 f.

nificance, since it rests upon mere historical analogy, or similarity of circumstances or fortune in different ages. In this sense, according to Immer, the "servant of Jahveh" in the second Isaiah may be a type, though not a prophecy, of Christ. But it is evident that from this point of view the application might be made to any person who should be "afflicted" on account of the transgressions of his people. But in no such trivial sense did the evangelists understand and apply the prophecies of their sacred books, and the rationalizing which so perverts their serious intention is very unjust to them. They undertook, as has been shown, a real interpretation, and no mere literary embellishment. If their exegesis was faulty, and faulty it certainly was if there exist any valid principles of interpretation, it is because they were true children of their race and age, and thought and wrote in entire sincerity in accordance with the standards and the point of view then and there recognized and in vogue.

CHAPTER XI.

THE GOSPELS AS HISTORIES.

THE decisive test to which the criticism of the Gospels is subjected lies in its conclusions respecting their historical character. It cannot shrink from answering the questions which are here pressed upon it not only by the devout, by the Christian consciousness, by the Church, by eighteen centuries of Christian history, but also by scepticism itself. For these questions concern the interpretation of history and the rationality of thinking. They regard the problem, whether the most fruitful moral and spiritual impulse in the world's history proceeded from a fact or a dream, from a great personality or a phantom. The criticism of the Gospels must, then, answer whether these writings are the artless productions of sincere men containing the tradition of Jesus of Nazareth in its essential features, or artificial creations, religious romances, dominated by ideal aims and "tendencies" in which history is dissolved. Questions of this sort are rightly addressed to the critic of the Gospels, not because the Gospels are the source of Christianity, not because there was not a Christian religion before there were Gospels, and a century of Christian history before they were recognized as canonical, but because they are the revered and most ancient documents of Christianity, and contain and preserve the tradition of Jesus. Now, although the invalidation of the Gospels would not, indeed, destroy

Christianity, for it is indestructible, he who subjects them to a free handling and reconstruction may well be called upon to give an account of his results, whether there remain a kernel or a husk.

That a kernel and not a husk remains as the result of the critical sifting of the Gospels is at length the almost unanimous verdict of criticism whose real function it is, indeed, to preserve the kernel and cast the husk aside. It is a significant fact in the history of the criticism of the Gospels that extremists, of whatever school, have not exerted a permanent influence, have not well maintained their ground. The vagaries of Bruno Bauer, and the negative criticism of Strauss, though put forth with great learning and acumen, find no advocates among the distinguished scholars of the present day, and the tendency in the Tübingen school has been steadily towards the recognition of the historical element in the synoptic Gospels, and a more conservative view of the history of the canon. After having apparently exhausted all the possibilities of forming hypotheses, examined with infinite patience all the facts in the case as well as innumerable fancies and theories, analyzed the records with the most unsparing scrutiny, and illuminated them with the widest and most accurate historical and linguistic learning, Gospel-criticism appears to have run its course, and to have ended in entirely defensible, conservative conclusions. The so-called source-criticism of Eichhorn advanced by its author at the beginning of this century with the design of "establishing the internal credibility and truth of the Gospel-history," has, though rejected in his particular application of it, continued to grow in favor, and has established itself as the only method which can produce satisfactory results. The relation of this source-criticism to the historical character of the Gospels is apparent from the conclusions of the preceding chapters which have been devoted to a study of the synoptics from that point of view. It is manifestly of the greatest importance to the question of the historical character of the synoptic Gospels, which will alone be considered here, that the writers all appear to have depended in a greater or less degree on one original source, which may be clearly traced in these records, if not reconstructed from them. The logia, or sayings of Jesus,* the first collection of which Papias ascribes to Matthew, undoubtedly composed the principal part of this source. These pithy, aphoristic sayings of Jesus which, as Strauss remarks, could not be dissolved by the flood of oral tradition, in however different ways they may have been combined by the synoptists, may be regarded as constituting the historic kernel of their narratives. Had Papias' Exposition of the λόγια κυριακά been preserved we know not what strange and improbable sayings would have been found in it attributed to Jesus. For the oral tradition on which he depended for his collection must, in the nature of the case, have been a precarious source. That this source had perils for the evangelists, too, so far as they depended on it, cannot be denied. The fact, however, that Matthew committed his collection of the logia to writing is of the greatest importance, and the extent to which the historical credibility of the synoptics is due to it is perhaps inappreciable. But it should be kept in mind in considering the perils to which the synoptists were exposed from oral tradition or from any other source that they appear to have been men of exceptionally sound and sober judgment. This quality is evinced by the nature of their writings, and is a factor in the historical

* τὰ λόγια τοῦ κυρίου, λόγια κυριακά.

character of these which cannot be too highly estimated. Had they been such men as the good Bishop Papias, their records might have contained the account of the famous vineyards of the Messianic age, and we do not know what fantastic and absurd stories besides.

The assumed lapse of time between the event and the record is evidently an important consideration in the study of the historical credibility of the Gospels. Not to be too precise in the matter of dates, we may place the composition of the synoptics between forty and sixty years after the death of Christ. It would appear at the first glance that after the life-time of from one to two generations histories in the proper sense of the word could not reasonably be expected to be produced under the then existing circumstances. There is room for grave question at this point, and due weight should be allowed to the doubt to which these conditions give rise. It should be borne in mind, however, that the synoptists based their records on antecedent writings, one of which can be traced without doubt to Matthew, and found in various fragments in all three narratives. Of this we know, indeed, with certainty, nothing more than that it contained certain sayings of Jesus. Criticism is unable precisely to determine its extent, and has no means of fixing its date. Of other writings mentioned by Luke, and probably used by him, it knows nothing, and is not at unity with itself as to his use of our first Gospel. This situation evidently presents a difficulty which is not at all relieved by the fact that the evangelists did not proceed in the manner of modern historians, perhaps we may say in the manner of historians proper of any age, and inform their readers of the sources of their narratives. The difficulty is, however, somewhat relieved by the character of the central figure in the history, the personality of Jesus as we know it from the records themselves. That he made a very profound and lasting impression upon his generation, and in particular upon his immediate followers, there can be no doubt. The simple grandeur of his character, and the easily remembered teachings which he left, sententious, aphoristic expressions, according to the synoptic records, must have produced a tradition of great vividness and vitality to which history probably furnishes no parallel. If we add to this the fact which is generally conceded, that the tradition of Jesus constituted the substance of the preaching and teaching of the apostles and their followers for a considerable time after his death, we have conditions antecedent to the writing of the Gospels not at all unfavorable to the composition of writings entitled to be called historical, so far at least as the essential teachings of Jesus and the portrait of his character are concerned. The concession of Köstlin, a Tübingen critic, is noteworthy in this connection : " The narratives of the synoptists date from a time which was near enough to the facts reported by them to enable them to hold them in memory, and to remain in accord with the historical situation, even in regard to those important features of it, as the beginning and end of the public ministry in Galilee, in connection with which attempts had already been made in a symbolic and poetic way, and through ideal narratives and Old-Testament prototypes representing his earthly person and history in the splendor of Messianic glory, to set forth the greatness and dignity which belonged to Jesus as the Messiah, and the blessings which would flow from him to his people."

The source-criticism according to which Mark's Gospel is the oldest, and has been substantially taken up into the other two synoptics, finds confirmation in the fact that that record approaches more nearly a genuinely historical character than these. It is tolerably free from legendary narratives, and is throughout well arranged and self-consistent, though not always presenting a strictly chronological order. Of "tendency" and disturbing dogmatic interests there is almost no trace. The proclamation of the kingdom is the prominent theme, and the personality of the Founder is subordinated. As has been pointed out in Chapter III., the Messianic title and claims of Jesus are not thrust forward at the beginning as in the first Gospel, but a cautious and steady progress is indicated which is consistent with the great scene at Cæsarea Philippi. This historical plan corresponds with the probabilities of the case, and is so far favorable to the credibility of this Gospel in a very important part of its contents. For nothing is more improbable than that Jesus should for any considerable time have journeyed about Galilee in the face of the Roman authorities under the banner of the "Son of David" and the "King of Israel." Besides, the frequent and sometimes awkwardly-placed injunctions of silence even in the first Gospel show the persistence of the tradition as Mark has in general apprehended it. This Gospel, however, which was not written until after the first generation from the death of Christ, could not entirely escape the influences of that legendary period in which some unhistorical features were stamped upon the tradition of Jesus.

That the oral proclamation of the Gospel, naturally occupied no doubt very largely with a repetition of the sayings and doings of Jesus, should have taken on a fragmentary, disconnected form was natural and inevitable. No change in this form except for the worse could result from the delivery of the message of the Gospel by others than the original witnesses, by wandering preachers and ecstatic speakers "with tongues." How the evangelic tradition was affected to the prejudice of historical accuracy and continuity by the way in which it came to those who finally gave it a fixed form in writing is shown in the Gospels themselves, particularly when their narratives are critically compared with one another. The separate scenes of the life of Jesus are placed in a loose connection, so that one is puzzled to tell whether a given arrangement is made with intention, or because the writer found difficulty in handling his material. Sayings of Jesus are grouped in masses or dispersed apparently according to a purpose or a fancy of the evangelist, and frequently an aphorism receives from its setting now one application and now another. The chronological sequence is often indeterminable, as when the first evangelist connects the preaching of John the Baptist immediately with the return from Egypt by the words, "In those days," etc. The relation of the records to one another is of such a nature that the arbitrary and violent procedures of the harmonists could not but be abandoned as soon as the doctrine of the inspiration of the evangelists was found to be untenable. Yet in the midst of all the chaotic elements which the flood of oral tradition rolled along is clearly discernible an historical grouping of salient facts, the appearance of the Baptist, the Galilean ministry of Jesus, the healings, the teachings, the travels with the disciples, the gathering multitudes, the conflicts, Cæsarea Philippi, the fateful journey to Jerusalem, Gethsemane, the trial and the tragedy, the consternation of the little flock, and the mysterious birth of a great hope.

As history, however, pure history in the proper sense of the word, the Gospel-narratives can by no means be regarded. Of vivid, immediate impressions of the life and teachings of Jesus they are not, and in the nature of the case could not be, the record. The historical interest and motive, with all the prominence which they hold throughout, are not unmixed with motives and interests which check and wrest their proper development. To apply to these records the canons of historical composition were an error only less misleading than that of regarding them as the speculations of artful "tendency" philosophers, or collections of myths intended to interpret the life of Jesus through prototypes of Old-Testament history or legend. The constructions of apologists and the hypotheses of Strauss are alike broken in pieces against these unique productions of love and legend. That the tradition of Jesus, in the absence of a fixed and definite form, should have undergone no modifications in passing through the media which it traversed before it was recorded in the Gospels is incredible to any one who regards the conditions from an historical or psychological point of view. That cold and critical research rather than the transfiguring imagination should have been occupied with it is improbable and contrary to all the facts in the case. Accordingly, the picture of Jesus which the evangelists have produced is not a photograph nor a reproduction from memory, but rather a reconstruction at which faith, hope, and legend wrought. The prominence of the biographical interest is not more evident in their records than is the want of material for a real biography. In the chronological confusion the subject-order often takes the place of the time-order, and there is a painful absence of important dates. Information regarding the youth and education of Jesus there is none, and even his birth-place is questionable.

That the Gospels are historical writings, then, is true;

but the affirmation is only a half-truth. The whole truth is that they are different from histories, more than histories. They contain historical reminiscences of Jesus, vivid pictures of his life, striking sketches of his character, above all, authentic reproductions of his great teachings. But what a generation or two of Jewish Christians had believed about him and hoped from him as the national Messiah; what construction Pauline Christians had put upon some of his words; what reverence, faith, and wonder had wrought of transformation in his tradition; and what the glamour of poesy had woven into his legend, these are also discernible in them. If the tradition of the Founder of Christianity had a natural, historical development, its product in the synoptic Gospels must inevitably have been what it is, an account not only of what he was in himself as Jesus, but of what he was believed to be as Christ. Human love, veneration, faith, could not so guard it that it would not take such a course. Nothing short of a supernatural intervention, a suspension of psychological laws, a reversal of history, could have compassed a different result. The tendency to subordinate the spiritual and essential teachings of Jesus to materialistic and apocalyptic ideas and hopes was not less strong, certainly, in the first century than it has been since to the great detriment of Christianity. Accordingly, of the three great principles of the early creed, "Jesus was the Messiah; he is risen; he will come again in glory," two were doubtless not taught by Jesus at all. Their appearance in the Gospels is only explicable on the theory that these writings are the deposit not alone of the actual tradition of Jesus, but of the beliefs, meditations, and hopes concerning him which occupied the first generation or two after his death. That the form and contents of the Gospels must have been to some extent determined by the tendency to group the sayings of Jesus around the two ideas, Jewish Messianism and the glorious return of the Messiah with the angels, needs no other proof than these writings themselves furnish.

That the Old Testament should have been read in a new light by Jews who had accepted Jesus as their Messiah, was the inevitable consequence of an entirely changed point of view. But whether there was "a veil upon their heart," or upon that of their brethren who did not so accept Jesus, is a question on which Paul and the scientific hermeneut are not agreed. The tendency, however, to search the Old Testament for events typical of what Jesus should be as the Messiah could not but affect the reconstruction of his tradition, in connection with the belief that he ought to fulfil, if not surpass, what had been prefigured, as was thought, by the great prototypes. When by this new hermeneutics the Old Testament had been so far transformed that its image of the Messiah-king was converted into that of the suffering servant, so that "the cross ceased to be a stumbling-block,"* the tendency once established could not but lead by an inherent necessity to an exploitation of Hebrew history and legend in the interest of showing various fulfilments in the sayings and works of Jesus. Strauss shed a new light upon the Gospels when he showed how many events recorded in them have their prototypes in the Old Testament. But it is doubtless an error to regard the records of the evangelists as the products of the cool reflection of intentional myth-makers. Rather they show how these writers had become accustomed to think about Jesus under the influence of the Old Testament, to idealize

* Gal. v. ii.

actual occurrences, and sometimes to intensify them into a miraculous form. To say nothing of the wholesale appropriation of the ancient Hebrew poetry in the prehistorical portions of Luke's Gospel by the author in sayings ascribed to Mary and Simeon, it is certainly not without significance that there appear so evident reminiscences of words of psalmists and prophets in the accounts of the miracles on the lake, the stilling of the tempest and the walking on the water. In some of the accounts of miracles wrought upon external nature it is difficult to determine whether an actual occurrence, or an allegory or parable, lay at the basis. If Luke appears to have found in his sources the cursing of the fig-tree as a parable, it is certainly neither incredible nor improbable that the account of the feeding of the multitude may originally have had this form. Weizsäcker's arrangement of the synoptic narratives into groups of doctrinal tenets * intended to exhibit the life and teachings of Jesus as they historically were, or were apprehended to be from an idealistic point of view, throws much light upon accounts of this sort. "The feeding of the multitude shows Jesus upon the heights; he assembles the people, and has gifts for all; all are filled." † The natural reaction from the mythical theory and the growing influence of an historical apprehension of the Gospels have led even conservative critics to recognize a mingling of history and idealizing representations in the synoptic narratives. "In detail," says Holtzmann, "these transitions from historical recollection and Old-Testament legendary form can scarcely be followed with certainty. Only the beginnings and ends of the entire movement can still be established, that is, the

---

* Lehrstücke.
† Das Apostolische Zeitalter, 2te Aufg., 1890, p. 411.

support which a legendary representation has in the events of the actual life of Jesus, and the definite direction in which, in consequence of guidance supplied by the Old Testament, the delineation and the enhancement into the miraculous must proceed."*

How far the demonstrable "tendency" of the evangelists affected the historical character of the Gospels is a question of importance in this connection. Very much of the tendency which appears in the Gospels originated in Messianism, and expresses itself in the attempt to adjust the life and character of Jesus to the Jewish-Messianic ideal. Jesus being believed to have been the Jewish Messiah, it is to be expected, it may even be said to be inevitable, that his tradition would assume a Messianic coloring. Then by a modification of the original Messianic type the attempt would be made to shorten the distance that actually separated the real Jesus of Nazareth from the ideal Messiah, the Son of David, the King of Israel, to abolish the difference between them as far as possible, and bring them into a unity satisfactory to thought. It is evident that one cannot fairly judge such a writing as our first Gospel, for example, by the principle that it must be throughout historical or not historical at all. It betrays an absence of historical and literary sense to apply to such a composition the rigid rule, *falsus in uno falsus in omnibus.* If the tradition out of which it sprang was affected by dogmatic tendencies, by pragmatism, if the writer was affected by these, it by no means follows that the tradition did not bear the truth, and the writer record it. If the first two chapters are unhistorical, if Jesus did not announce a second coming on the clouds, and if the dead did not come forth from their graves and

---

* Hand-Commentar zum neuen Testament, 1889, i. p. 19.

walk the streets of Jerusalem at the crucifixion, it does not at all follow that Matthew's logia are not incorporated in the book, and that the parables are all inventions. The Zeit-Geist has much to reveal to men if they would only listen to him; but if men can hardly interpret the spirit of their own time, it is no wonder that that of past ages with difficulty reaches their minds. To those who are deaf to the revelations which the Time-Spirit of the first century has to make, and blind to whatever his busy invention wove into the tradition of Jesus, the Gospels are in some parts written in an unintelligible language. They are not fitted to be interpreters of these writings as a whole, and would do well to confine their reading of them to the parables and the sermon on the mount.

It is evidently of the greatest importance to observe that so far as the tendency of the first evangelist led him to regard the history of Jesus from the point of view of Jewish Messianism, this tendency could not, and in fact did not, affect the essentials of the history as he has recorded it. The narrative contains its own correction in such sayings as "my kingdom is not of this world," and in all the words of vast spiritual import whose authentication is the more striking, since they stand out in bold relief against all the temporal limitations and all the apocalyptic imagery of the record. The correction of history applied to the narrative will also show that Jesus was in no sense the national Messiah of the Jews. Besides, it has already been shown that the hermeneutical correction when brought to bear upon the passages in question leads to the same result. The remarkable words of Baur may well be quoted here: "All the concessions which must be made to the mythical view, as well as all that which may be placed to the account of the evangelist's pragmatism, can in no way put in question the substantial, historical, fundamental character of the Gospel; and there follows hence only the necessity of the requirement ever more sharply to distinguish as much as possible by a continuous critical investigation of its contents the two elements, the historical and the unhistorical, which have blended in their growth."* The same may be said of Luke's Pauline tendency. For this does not affect the essentials of the history. A distinction must be made between the teachings of Jesus and an interpretation of them which was made in the first century in the exigencies of the Pauline-Jewish controversy. If anything is unquestionable as to the character of his teachings it is that they were intended for mankind, and not for the Jews only, that they were not national and limited, but universal. This character, as we have seen, was so impressed upon the logia that it is clearly discernible even in the Jewish first Gospel, while the third evangelist was so faithful to the tradition that he appears to have left some things standing in his record which are unfavorable to his predilection.

That theophanies and angelophanies do not belong to the domain of history is a proposition which does not require demonstration for one who has the elements of the historical sense. To treat them as historically verifiable is as unreasonable as to hold that their invalidation invalidates the entire record in which they are found. The whole scene in Gethsemane does not even become a poetic representation, nor the words spurious, " Pray, lest ye enter into temptation," because Luke brings an angel upon the scene. The angelophanies in the account of the resurrection do not convert that event into a myth, any more than the story of the resurrection of the

* " Krit. Untersuch., p. 604.

saints in the first Gospel renders the crucifixion unhistorical. If, then, the divine overshadowing and the appearances of angels cast suspicion on the prehistorical narratives of the birth and infancy of Jesus in the first and third Gospels, it is because these supernatural phenomena constitute a part of the texture of the accounts. These narratives are, however, prejudiced as to their historical validity by the absence of verification and by internal improbabilities and incongruities. They are not contained in the oldest and most historical Gospel, and formed no part of the original writing by Matthew. The subsequent history far from confirming tends to cast doubt upon them, the kernel of it showing no trace of this "wonder-world of the childhood." The contemporaries of Jesus know him as the carpenter's son, Joseph's son,* and of Mary herself is recorded no intimation of a knowledge of the mysterious birth. On the contrary, surprised at the effects of his ministry, she with her sons comes to Capernaum to get possession of him as of one who was "beside himself." † The synoptists represent Jesus as furnished at the baptism with the spirit and power requisite for his ministry, and in all his conflicts with questioning, opposing enemies he never refers to a birth-miracle as an authentication of his claims. In what is said of him by Peter in the Acts and by Paul in his Epistles there is no hint of this astounding mystery which could not have failed of mention and comment in the earliest writings had it belonged to the original tradition.

The internal incongruities of the two prehistorical

---

* Matt. xiii. 55 ; Luke iv. 22.

† ὅτι ἐξέστη, Mark iii. 21, 31. The two passages are to be interpreted in connection as relating to the same event. See Meyer, "Commentar," i. 2, p. 49 f. *Cf.* John vii. 3.

accounts indicate a legendary origin and character. In the first Gospel the birth of Jesus at Bethlehem is spoken of as though that city were the residence of his parents, and Nazareth is mentioned as if it were a place previously unknown to the family, in which, though apparently intending to go back to their home in Judea after the flight into Egypt, they took up their residence, "in order that it might be fulfilled," etc. The author appears to know nothing of the previous residence in Nazareth from which Luke's narrative proceeds. According to Luke, the family returned to "their own city Nazareth" after a few weeks' sojourn in Bethlehem and the presentation of the child in the temple, which does not appear to have excited Herod's suspicion notwithstanding the Messianic announcements of Anna and Simeon. This is irreconcilable with the first evangelist's account, which requires time here for the journey of the magians from the East, the flight into Egypt, and the return. The order of Herod to slay all the children "from two years old and under, according to the time which he had ascertained from the magians," shows the time required by this account. Again, the first evangelist's account of Joseph's suspicions and the angelic message to allay them does not presuppose, but rather excludes, the celestial announcement to Mary which Luke records. For that Mary after such a revelation should have made no communication of the great mystery to Joseph would be, as Meyer remarks, "not less psychologically unnatural than in violation of her relation and duty as his bride." Psychological and moral impossibilities of this sort are the work of legend, not of history. In the one instance in which Luke appears to touch really historical ground he commits an error, for his statement that there was an imperial census under Quirinius at the time of the birth of Jesus is pronounced incorrect by conservative critics.* The eminent commentator already quoted presents the whole section of the two Gospels from the right point of view when he says of a fragment of it: "The truth of the story of the shepherds and the angels lies in the realm of the idea, not in that of historical reality. Regarded as reality the history loses its truth as a premise, with which what is notorious as a fact that Jesus was later unknown and unrecognized as the Messiah, as well as the entire silence of the evangelic preaching with respect to the heavenly Gospel, is irreconcilable. The want of agreement of this account with the story of the magians and the murder of the children in the first Gospel is to be explained by the fact that different wreaths of legend, quite independent of one another, were wound about the divine Child in his lowliness." †

These prehistoric chapters, as well as some other sections of the Gospels, can only be rightly apprehended when we take into account the oriental æsthetic and poetic feeling which busied itself with weaving beautiful creations of fancy into the wonderful tradition of Jesus. Truly interpreted these records cannot be until the literary sense and the historical judgment have done their work upon them. But it is not the task of literary and historical criticism to cut out and cast aside with contempt these fine creations of poetic sentiment, the productions of the love and devoutness of a susceptible race and age. Its province rather it is to assign them their true place and to estimate them at their true value as fragments of "the history of Christianity rather than of the history of Jesus." If it be true that "a religion

---

* "Offenbar unrichtig," Meyer.   † Commentar, i. 2, p. 288.

without poesy were an abortion incapable of life," then we should be warned to retain and treat these æsthetic effusions as the poetry of the first Christian century rather than as the history of Jesus, since to retain and treat them as history is to run the risk of invalidating the historical kernel itself of the tradition. Only so, too, can their spirit be appreciated and their inspiring mission fulfilled. For "the more admiration the poetic beauty of these productions of ancient Christian devoutness deserves and has found, the less is one just to their spirit when one endeavors to transform them into prose at the cost of the odor of wonder which the morning mists of the evangelic history have distilled upon them." *

The foregoing considerations establish the maxim of criticism that the evangelists' accounts of the life and teachings of Jesus must often be corrected, not only by a comparison of them with one another, but also by a judgment based upon an historical knowledge of the influences acting upon the tradition from the media through which it passed. The complete illustration and defence of this maxim would require an entire commentary upon the Gospels. But the history of commentaries shows but too clearly that only its application can put an end to the puerile harmonizing and exegetical subtleties which have so long discredited hermeneutical science. The true historical character of the Gospels is only brought to light when this principle is applied to them. Sometimes it shows the influence of a belief dominating an entire generation, as in the form given to the eschatological discourses; sometimes a design on the part of an evangelist, as when Luke makes Jesus begin his ministry at Nazareth instead of at Capernaum in order that the

* Holtzmann, Hand-Commentar, i. p. 54.

Pauline traits which he inserts may receive a greater intensity*; sometimes an ineptness, as when the same writer puts into the mouth of Jesus violent words against the Pharisees at the table of one of this sect; † and sometimes a transformation of an ethical doctrine, as when the morality of Jesus which taught a lofty contempt of reward, that one is not even to expect thanks for doing one's duty,‡ and that help should be extended without hope of anything "in return," § is disfigured by an encouragement of calculating self-interest which shall find its account in "houses, lands," etc., in a high place at a feast, in a place at the "right hand," in sitting upon "thrones," in recompense "at the resurrection of the just." The objection that this maxim is subjective, and leads to results which vary according to the caprice of the interpreter, is without force in view of the arbitrariness and caprice of the old interpretation and its infinitely varying and contradictory conclusions. The result of a century's critical investigation of the Gospels, the criticism of the present and of the future cannot abandon it, nor shrink from its thorough application. The charge touching its conclusions really lies not against it, but against the nature of the material with which it has to deal. Only through it do we learn at length the real character, and come to appreciate the worth of the Gospels as histories.

* Luke iv. 16, 24–27.
† Luke xi. 37–52.
‡ Luke xvii. 7–10.
§ Luke vi. 35.

CHAPTER XII.

CRITICISM AND HISTORICAL CHRISTIANITY.

THAT criticism tends to invalidate historical Christianity is a prevalent popular impression. But like many another popular impression, this is a popular misapprehension. A prejudice, or perhaps it were better to say a sentiment, is the root of this error. What is established, what is venerable with age, what has served noble ends, and nurtured great virtues, naturally calls forth the conservative interest, the devotion, even the zeal and fanaticism of mankind. Accordingly, when even the soberest and most reverent criticism is directed upon revered documents or institutions with the sincere purpose of reconstructing the one or improving the other, it is confronted by a sentiment which can see in its performance only a menace or a work of destruction. Against a criticism which is merely negative and destructive, it must be conceded that this sentiment is a wise provision of nature. It is not, however, until the discriminating judgment is applied to the matter that a justifiable opposition to the critical procedure can even seem to be established. Now, at the first glance there does appear, indeed, to be ground for a rational judgment against criticism as hostile to historical Christianity, for the reason that in its name many excesses have been committed, and many conclusions reached which tend to dissolve the historical contents of the Gospels by making it appear that these writings are composed mainly of myths, or of creations of the imagination, or of "tendency-" speculations. But it is evident that criticism, as a whole, can no more fairly be condemned for its excesses than science or theology, as a whole, for its errors. Besides, criticism has always tended to correct itself, exposing and repudiating the errors which have been committed in its name. Great critics have alone been found competent to deal with the most masterly perversions of criticism. So Strauss had his Weisse, and Baur his Hilgenfeld within his own school, and his Ewald and Meyer outside it. Accordingly, the history of criticism shows a tendency towards quite sober and sound conclusions, a tendency, in fact, to construct rather than to destroy, to establish rather than to overthrow, historical Christianity.

Now, since criticism proceeds upon the principle that the Gospels are to be treated as literature, as productions of men affected by the spirit which came forth from Jesus, indeed, but also by the influences which their age threw around them, who dealt with their materials in a wholly sincere and earnest way, it must seek the grounds of the credibility of the historical kernel of these writings, or, in other words, the basis of historical Christianity, in the documents themselves and in the data which history furnishes. No other course is indeed open to it, since it is one of its fundamental principles that no claims which may be dogmatically set up in favor of the infallibility of the writers of the Gospels can be allowed before they have been tested by its processes. Such claims, then, cannot be suffered to determine its conclusions. In fact, if it should admit them its occupation would be gone, its whole work superfluous. With respect to the historical basis internal to the Gospels, it has already been shown in the course of this work, how that is supplied in the Mark-hypothesis and in the hypothesis of the logia-collection of Matthew. These hypotheses may be regarded as established, if not beyond question, at least by the preponderance of critical authority. As to another series of logia originating with John and incorporated in the fourth Gospel, there is a strong probability as well as a considerable weight of critical judgment in its favor. Criticism might, then, very well rest its case upon these conclusions, and await the impartial judgment of mankind as to its friendly or hostile relation to historical Christianity. There are, however, important evidences independent of the Gospels which may properly be adduced in confirmation of the critical conclusions regarding the essential historical contents of these records.

The apostle Paul is a pre-eminent witness to the central facts which the Gospels record. For it were certainly an error to think that his claim that he had his Gospel by special revelation, that he "did not receive it from man," and that "those in reputation communicated nothing new"* to him, excludes all knowledge on his part of the leading external facts of the life of Jesus and of the substance of his teaching. Rather these words relate to his own peculiar interpretation of Christianity, the fundamental doctrinal tenets which he held, the universal mission of the religion of Jesus and justification by faith. It cannot be presumed that even before his conversion he had no information as to the character of the doctrine which he bitterly persecuted. A man of his earnestness could not have persecuted a phantom. Neither could he have been converted without evidence. However the event on the road to Damascus may be ex-

* Gal. i. 12, ii. 6.

plained, there is certainly nothing in his intense and vivid narration of it, which necessarily excluded details, that should lead us to suppose that it had no psychological antecedents, no preparation of meditation, of remorse, of conviction. Convictions he certainly had from that time, and very positive ones. He was convinced that the man Jesus who had been rejected and slain as a malefactor by the Jews was the Christ, his own Saviour and the Saviour of the world. He believed that in this great personality a new principle of life was revealed for himself and for mankind. Perhaps no stronger testimony could be furnished, has ever been furnished, to the power of that personality, to its historical reality as portrayed in the Gospels, than that this man Paul, this Jew of the Jews, yielded to it the homage of his great intellect, bowed his strong will to the man of Nazareth, became the unwearied and zealous minister of the Gospel which he had persecuted, and consecrated to it all the resources of his powerful nature, through privations, perils, stripes, even to death.

Not a few of the central historical facts of the synoptic Gospels are expressly referred to by Paul. According to him, Jesus was born of the seed of David, born under the law, was a "man," was "in the likeness of sinful flesh." He was conscious of no sin, was obedient to the divine will even unto death, and was filled with the spirit of holiness. Of especial events in the life of Jesus he mentions the last supper and the betrayal; the fact that Jesus was not comprehended by the authorities of his time, and that before them he was outwardly weak; his inner joy in affliction and his devotion to death out of love to man: his passion and crucifixion as "our passover," and the crowning spiritual event which followed it, and constituted one of the central ideas of the Pauline theology. Of some wonderful works wrought by Jesus Paul must also have known, as may legitimately be inferred from the facts that he recognized healing as among the spiritual gifts in the Christian Church of his time, and that he appealed to "signs, wonders, and mighty deeds" performed by himself as "signs of an apostle." The various gifts are to him manifestations of the Spirit which gives the word of wisdom, of knowledge, of faith, of prophecy, of healing. But to him the Lord, or Jesus, is the Spirit who now works these minor wonders in and through the believers, and also the greater wonder of changing them "into the same image from glory to glory." Though Paul stands forth in grand isolation and self-dependence in the history of the primitive Church, we learn from his writings that he was not without intercourse with men who had personally known Jesus. That he learned nothing of them concerning the prominent facts of the earthly life of his Master is in the highest degree improbable. Three years after his conversion, he tells us, he went to Jerusalem and remained with Peter fifteen days. Fourteen years later he again visited Jerusalem and held a conference with some of the apostles. His recognition by the apostles of Jesus as a missionary to the gentiles is an indirect testimony in favor of the presumption that he was instructed in the essentials of Christian knowledge and faith.

Besides an acquaintance with facts of the history of Jesus, such as that he had twelve apostles, Paul shows a knowledge of the tradition of his teachings as recorded in the Gospels. There are quotations of them, references to them, and certain accords with them in his writings. With respect to divorce he gives a free quotation as a "command" of the "Lord,"* and says that the Lord "ordained" that "those who preach the Gospel should live from the Gospel." The great doctrine of Jesus that the substance of the law is love finds an accordant expression in Paul's words that the whole law is fulfilled in one commandment: "Thou shalt love thy neighbor as thyself." The words, "Being reviled, we bless; being persecuted, we endure it; being defamed, we intreat"; the saying about faith which might remove mountains; the admonition to render no one evil for evil, should be referred to the tradition of Jesus as their most natural and probable source, especially since Paul frequently appeals expressly to "the word of the Lord" as authority for certain teachings.

The author of the Epistle to the Hebrews, who was probably a contemporary of the synoptists, presents along with some speculative traits confirmations of the tradition known to them. He speaks of Jesus as "made in all respects like to his brethren," a "partaker of flesh and blood," being "able to be forbearing towards the ignorant and the erring," himself "compassed with infirmity," "in all points tempted as man, yet without sin," offering up "in the days of his flesh" "prayers and supplications, with strong crying and tears," though a son, yet "learning his obedience from what he suffered," and "being perfected, becoming the author of everlasting salvation." From other contemporary Christian documents abundant confirmations of the essential, historical features of the personality and teaching of Jesus as they are set forth in the synoptic records might be produced. They all tend to show the transforming power of the fruitful principles of life and religion which came into the world through the

* I. Cor. vi. 10, 11.

great Teacher, "the inner law of love to God and man, which subjects all human relations to its exalting and purifying influence, and unites all who receive it in a great community of the spirit." The great spiritual transformation which this doctrine was regarded as effecting is set forth in the Epistle to Titus: "For the grace of God that bringeth salvation to all men was manifested, teaching us that denying ungodliness and worldly lusts we should live soberly, righteously, and godly in the present world; looking for the blessed hope and appearing of the glory of the great God and of our Saviour Jesus Christ, who gave himself for us that he might redeem us from all iniquity, and purify to himself a people to be his own, zealous in good works."

Criticism appears, then, on its own grounds and by its own methods to contribute to the confirmation of historical Christianity, if to establish the general credibility of the synoptic Gospels as to the essential teachings and the character of Jesus be to do this. It must be acknowledged, however, that if by historical Christianity is meant the whole body of doctrines, or a certain considerable number of them, which have been and are taught in the name of Christianity, then criticism does not give it support. If it is made to include such doctrines as the infallibility of the records, original sin, total depravity, the trinity, imputed righteousness, a vicarious atonement, and endless punishment, then so far criticism is unfriendly to it. If, however, it means that Jesus of Nazareth lived; that he was a personality of unsurpassed moral and spiritual greatness; that he taught a morality and religion founded upon the doctrine that God is the Father of men, and all men are brothers, the central, practical precept of which was love to God and man; that he lived a blameless, worshipful life of consecration and service in which his great teachings were eminently illustrated ; that he performed some works which in his age were regarded as wonders; that after an amazing and brilliant career of a few months in Galilee he was crucified at Jerusalem ; and that he was thereupon in some way manifested to those who had loved and followed him as victorious over death ; if these are the essential contents of historical Christianity, then it finds in criticism not an opposing and destructive agent, but a helpful ally. The relation which some of the important conclusions of criticism hold to it remains to be considered.

The criticism of the text of the Gospels shows that these writings were exposed to the fortune which has attended all the literary productions of ancient times ; that the autographs were early lost ; that the text was corrupted and interpolated ; that a considerable time elapsed between their composition and the appearance of careful and accurate quotations of them, during which the changes to which the text was subjected are indeterminable ; that there appears to be no reason for assuming that a regard for them as other than human productions preserved them from the perils to which they were exposed, nor any grounds for believing in a divine intervention for their protection ; that, however, alterations, corruptions, and interpolations have not, in all probability, materially affected their essential, historical contents—that is, their accounts of the great teachings of Jesus and their representation of his life and character. These results are not prejudicial to historical Christianity ; for if Christianity is properly called historical—that is, a religion which has had a history, its development belongs to the ordinary course of human affairs, and no supernatural intervention can be assumed in its interest, such as would be a miraculous preservation of its documents against the common fortune of ancient writings.

The critical study of the canon of the Gospels shows them in the stream of human history amidst a great number of other writings to which the powerful impulse proceeding from the personality of Jesus gave rise, left to make their way to public recognition chiefly by their own merits. It finds that, along with the oral tradition and these other writings, they were for a considerable time regarded as ordinary human sources of information as to the life of Jesus; that this tradition was thought by an important witness near the middle of the second century to be an authority superior to them; that down to a period which marks the lapse of nearly one hundred years from the composition of the oldest of them they were loosely and inaccurately quoted without mention of their supposed authors; that they appear to have attained recognition largely by reason of internal qualities, their historical character, and general excellence in comparison with other similar writings; that the opinion prevailed in the primitive Church that believers in Jesus were in general inspired, and that no especial inspiration was supposed to be possessed by those who wrote; that other writings than those now contained in the New Testament were then believed by some to be inspired; that not until about the end of the second century were our four Gospels ascribed to their reputed authors, and recognized as the works of specially inspired men which were to be received as exclusive or canonical sources for the life and teachings of Jesus; that the dogma of the inspiration of these writers, resting on no claim made by them in their works is to be regarded simply as a dogma which had an historical development, and admits of a genetic explanation; that the traditions current in the second century respecting the origin of the Gospels must be critically sifted, and are to be accepted only when confirmed by the criticism of these writings themselves; and finally, that the writers of that century, commonly quoted as "witnesses" to the canon, often give no reasons, or only trivial ones, for their opinions, show little or no evidence of having critically examined the matter, and accordingly furnish testimony which is to be received only with caution and discrimination. These are precisely such phenomena as one would expect to find in the natural, historical development of a religion under the conditions of the age in question; and they are rather favorable than otherwise to historical Christianity, since they show its records to have come to recognition and authority in the ordinary course of events on their intrinsic merits, and accordingly to have been able to dispense with a divine supervision to determine their selection as canonical. The question of the inspiration of their writers is not vital to historical Christianity, for their infallibility was not necessary to insure general accuracy and credibility in their works, which is all that a system of belief calling itself historical can reasonably claim for its documents. So far, then, as criticism tends to establish such an accuracy and credibility in the essential contents of the Gospels, it comes to the support of historical Christianity, and sustains its claims in the only way in which they can be sustained. For if Christianity is based upon the assumption of the inerrancy of the writers of its records, it is likely to be rejected entirely when this assumption is found, as sooner or later it must be, to be unsupported by the facts in the case.

The results of the critical study of the synoptic problem and the synoptic Gospels go to show that these writings are precisely such attempts at historical composition as one would look for under the existing conditions, which were an original Gospel and a logia-document, an abundant and varying oral tradition, writers with different points of view, Messianic beliefs, tendencies, apocalyptic expectations, a predilection for æsthetic and poetic representations, and a disinclination to critical and historical investigation. Writings so produced could not but present agreements and contradictions, correct statements and inaccuracies, historical and unhistorical elements, loose connections, transpositions, and a want of chronological arrangement. They might also be expected to contain the essential historical facts of the tradition of the life and teaching of Jesus, if we assume, as we must, the sincerity, good sense, and earnest purpose of their writers. This threefold form of the common tradition of Jesus furnishes to historical Christianity a substantial basis, which is not invalidated by the conclusions of criticism respecting the origin of apocalyptic portions of it, or with regard to the hermeneutical treatment of the Old Testament employed by the writers, or concerning tendencies and Messianic hopes. The conclusion that no one of the synoptics was immediately written by an apostle does not overthrow their historical credibility, since it is not essential to the integrity of history that it should be recorded by the original witnesses to the facts. The results of the criticism of the first Gospel place it, then, on the same footing with the second and third in relation to the sources of the history.

Since, then, historical Christianity is not based upon the immediate apostolic authorship of any one or all of the four Gospels, the criticism cannot be hostile to it, which concludes that the fourth Gospel is not the work of the apostle John. The historical ground of the beginnings of Christianity is securely established in the common tradition of the synoptics; and so far as the author of the fourth Gospel recognized this tradition by in part founding his work upon it, he has strengthened it by a confirmation which was perhaps more than half a century later than the composition of the oldest of these writings. It would probably be incorrect to say that in every instance in which he departs from the synoptic tradition he writes romance and not history, for there is no reason to suppose that the synoptists have recorded all the historical facts of the life of Jesus. But it is evident that his speculative ideas about the nature and pre-existence of Jesus and considerable portions of the long discourses which constitute the greater part of his record are not history. They cannot be made to appear to be of capital importance without the gratuitous assumption of his infallible inspiration as a philosopher and a reproducer from memory. The importance of his work is no doubt very greatly enhanced if he has incorporated into it some Johannine logia of Jesus; but its utility is not to be estimated entirely by its conformity to an historical standard, since it is not without importance for the conception of Jesus and the understanding of his personality and his tradition to know how a man of great intelligence and spirituality living in the first half of the second century apprehended him in relation to the questions of that time. With regard to apostolic origin, then, this Gospel appears to be upon the same basis as the others.

It would appear, then, in view of the results of the criticism of the Gospels which has been carried on for more than one hundred years by men who, far from being hostile to Christianity, have been and are devout believers in its inspired Founder and consecrated followers of him, that some concessions must be made to this science by the advocates of traditional opinions and interpretations, just as in other departments of human knowledge tradition has been obliged to give way to scientific investigation. Unless the insight and reason of a multitude of the greatest minds that have adorned the Christian Church are altogether perverted; unless conclusions which have maintained their ground, and are still acquiring wider recognition after having been discussed and contested for a century, are futile and abortive; unless the dogmatic assumption which takes the Gospels out of the category of historical writings is better grounded than the science of history which must include all historical phenomena in order to be a science; and unless the protestations of the timid are to outweigh with mankind the voice of the masters; then is criticism destined to have at length its rights and its empire. The maxim of criticism laid down in the preceding chapter,* applied from the point of view of historical criticism, which regards the Gospels as products of their times under the influences which proceeded from the inspiring personality and teaching of Jesus, leads to the conclusion that these writings contain unhistorical elements of various kinds. There are mistakes which result from a misunderstanding, an error of memory, or ignorance of history.† Different accounts are combined into one, or the same is given twice.‡ It is

---

* See page 335.

† The two beasts of the entry into Jerusalem, Matt. xxi. 2–5, *cf.* Mark xi. 2–4, due to a misunderstanding of prophecy, Zech. ix. 9; and the statement of Luke regarding Quirinius, ii. 2.

‡ The two demoniacs at Gadara, a comparison of the texts showing

found to be a characteristic of tradition to enhance events and effects,* and to transform parables and parabolic sayings into facts.† Spiritual are transformed into physical facts and events, as the ethical divine sonship of Jesus into a supernatural physical generation, the consciousness of this sonship and of the approval of God into an external announcement at the baptism,‡ and his internal conflict into an **objective occurrence** in the temptation. **Historical narratives are constructed to** represent what was in the consciousness of the primitive Church as to the **dignity** of Jesus and the effects which would follow **from his mission, as the** account of his transfiguration **to set forth his glory** in relation to Moses and Elias, the rending **of the veil of** the temple to symbolize that by his death **admittance to God was opened to all, and the resurrection of the saints to indicate that to the pious of old times he was the resurrection and the life.** The present is sometimes read back, so **to speak, into the past, or the** accounts of events in his life and the reports **of words of** Jesus are colored **by** a knowledge on the **part of the** evangelist of events **and institutions of his own time.** A case of *vaticinium post eventum* is furnished, for example,

---

probably a combination of Mark i. 23 f. and v. 1 f. ; the instructions to the twelve blended with those to the seventy in the tradition, Luke ix. 1 f., x. 1 f. ; and the twofold account of the feeding of the multitude, Mark vi. 31 f., viii. 1 f.

* The number of healings, Matt. xv. 30 f., *cf.* Mark vii. 32-37 ; the struggle in Gethsemane, Luke xxii. 40-45, *cf.* Mark xiv. 35-39 ; and the parable, Matt. xxii. 2-10, *cf.* Luke xiv. 16-24.

† The preaching of the Gospel is compared to fishing, and the kingdom of God to a net, Mark i. 17, Matt. xiii. 47 ; but in Luke v. 2 f. a miraculous draught of fishes is recorded. This must also pass for Luke's modified and legendary account of the calling of Peter ; *cf.* Mark i. 16-20 ; Matt. iv. 18-22.

‡ Matt. iii. 16, 17.

in Luke's detailed account of the destruction of Jerusalem.* The same writer represents the last supper as a formal establishment of a rite, following Paul's account of it rather than the simpler one of the first two evangelists,† and the formula of baptism in Matt. xxviii. 19 is of doubtful originality. The religious tendencies and apologetic necessities of later times have induced modifications of and additions to the original tradition, some of which have already been pointed out. ‡

Yet if one will consider one cannot but see that this discrimination between historical and unhistorical components, this critical reconstruction, does not invalidate the essentials of the Gospel-history. Rather the result of the process is that they are relieved in greater distinctness and grandeur. The real criticism of the Gospels, the criticism that has stood the test of a long and fierce conflict, and is sure to make its way finally to general recognition in the Church, is conservative and constructive. It establishes the kernel of the history of Jesus in an inexpugnable position. Having cleared the ground and shown the point at which Christianity must be assailed, if assailed at all, it erects around it impregnable defences. The religion which it sets forth and commends to mankind is the religion of Jesus in its original simplicity and purity. An "emasculated Christianity," if it be proper to speak at all of such a thing, is not the product of its reconstruction, but of the construction of the first century. When

---

* Chap. xix. 43 f., xxi. 24.

† Chap. xxii. 19, cf. Mark xiv. 22 f. ; Matt. xxvi. 26. f.

‡ See besides, Luke's addition to the saying about new wine in old skins (chap. v. 39, cf. Mark ii. 21 f.; Matt. ix. 16 f.), which is inappropriate to the connection, indicates the disinclination of the Jewish Christians to the new doctrine, and can have originated only in the time of gentile Christianity. Weizsäcker, Das apostol. Zeitalter, p. 390.

by the application of its own processes in a truly scientific way the excesses and errors of criticism have been corrected, the divine doctrine of Jesus stands forth clearly defined, and of his personality there emerge not only "a few ineffaceable lineaments which could belong only to a figure unique in grace and majesty," but the figure itself emerges in its majesty and grace.

This doctrine and this personality as criticism reveals rather than beclouds them have never been approached, and will never be surpassed. Goethe has truly said: "Intellectual culture may ever advance, the natural sciences may grow in ever broader extent and greater depth, and the human mind may enlarge itself as it will, no progress will surpass the grandeur and moral culture of Christianity as it shines forth in the Gospels." * No appreciation of the teaching and the moral greatness of Jesus is, perhaps, clearer and more acute than that of reverent critics, as testify the words of one of the most learned and sagacious of this class in modern times: " Is it seriousness or is it a word when one calls this virtuous, God-allied human life the noblest blossom of a noble tree, the crown of the cedar of Israel? In a withered age a full, satisfied life, in the midst of ruin a structure, among characters undone an upright and a strong, among the godless and abandoned a Son of God, among the mourning and despairing a joyful, hopeful, giving soul, among sinners a saint; in this contradiction to the facts of the time, in this prodigious exaltation above the oppressed, the low, the level conditions of the century, in this transformation of stationariness, retrogression, death-sickness into progress, health, power, and the color of eternal youth, in this conspicuous demarkation, finally, of his performance, his purity and

---

* Letzte Gespräche mit Eckermann, iii. 373.

his nearness to God even from the new, endless centuries, which *through him* have overcome stationariness and retrogression, he makes the impression of **mysterious loneliness, superhuman wonder, divine creation.**" *

Historical criticism is not opposed to the doctrine of a providential revelation, like that given in Jesus Christ, under the conditions of human development and the limitations of human nature. It does not exclude God from history, but finds it no wonder that, since he has designs to work out in man, exceptional manifestations of his revealing spirit should betimes appear. That in an historical period when the course of events seems to have prepared a place for him, when the world was waiting for transformation, and many were ready and intent to catch the accents of a divine voice, a personality should appear charged with the powers of a new life and bearing a great revelation, is a result to be looked for in the course of providential dealing with men. The moral and spiritual superiority of Jesus places his personality and teaching beyond the invention of his age, and attests their historical truth. He was, indeed, so far in advance of the spirit and temper, the insight and intelligence, of his time, that it is no wonder that his early followers looked upon him as a phenomenal creation, a Son or a Word. In an age of the supremacy of formalism he discarded forms, teaching that not in Jerusalem and on Gerizim alone was the Father to be worshipped, but wherever a human soul would come into spiritual communion with him. In the midst of tyranny and oppression he taught that all men are brothers. Surrounded by cruelty and indifference to human suffering, by scornful caste and pride of rank and race, he preached the Gospel of helpfulness and mercy.

* Keim, Geschichte Jesu, iii. 662.

To Phariseeism, ostentation, and self-righteousness he set
forth the doctrine and the example of humility. Hemmed
in and pressed upon by a spirit of self-seeking, whose
dominant passion was temporal power, he made the
unique manifestation of self-devotion in history, and
wrought his life into the foundations of a kingdom not of
this world. Reared in the traditions of a people who
worshipped God as a national Divinity, he transcended
the greatest of its teachers and seers in the revelation of
the Universal Father. In a time-serving generation he
carried his uncompromising fidelity to duty to the pitch
of absolute self-sacrifice. His patience and his sufferings
have evoked the wonder and the tears of thousands, and
enshrined his memory in the heart of mankind. The cross
on which he died has become a great spiritual symbol to
the ages, and the crown of thorns which tortured his
brow the adoring faith of men has transformed into the
diadem of universal, endless spiritual dominion. " He
has laid an eternal rock," says Renan, " foundation of the
true religion ; therefore he deserves the divine rank; an
absolutely new idea made through him its entrance into
the world ; we are all his disciples and his continuators."
As a spiritual interpreter of human nature he has, indeed,
never been surpassed, never equalled. As an embodiment
and manifestation of whatever is noblest, purest, and
tenderest in man, he stands unrivalled among the great
religious teachers of the ages. Other personality so
morally fruitful, so abounding in intensity of spiritual
power, has never appeared in history. In him all that is
most godlike and most human was united in harmony,
and found consummate expression. His life is at once
the enigma of the centuries and the solution of their
problems. In the universality of his religious genius, in

the scope and sureness of his ethical insight, in the depth of his sympathy and the breadth and lucidity of his understanding, in the intensity of his sufferings and the completeness of his victory, he was the true Son of Man. Tempted in all points, and assailed by the powers of sin and the ferocity of enraged and brutal men, he held with a firm grasp the sceptre of spiritual ascendancy which shall never depart from his hand. It is no reluctant and stinted homage of words which criticism pays to this greatest of the divine messengers to man; but its supreme homage is paid to him by its reverent and fearless work which, delivering his personality and his teachings from the misconceptions of ages, places them in true perspective and bold relief for the instruction and inspiration of mankind.

INDEX.

A

Abbot, Ezra, on the paschal question, 237; on Basilides and the fourth Gospel, 229
Abbott, E. A., on synoptic problem, 137
Alcuin revises the Vulgate, 25
Alexandrine, manuscript, 9; church, the, and the canon, 113–116
Allegorical interpretation, the method of, employed by the evangelists, 311 f.
Anicetus and the paschal question, 235
Anonymous, the Saxon, on Pauline traits in Luke, 301
Apocalyptics, Jewish and Christian, affinity of, 273
Apocryphal books of Old Testament silent as to person of Messiah, 260
Apocryphal Gospels, quoted in Ignatian Epistles, 59; and Justin's memoirs, 66
Apollinaris on the paschal question, 236
Apostolic age, condition of, unfavorable to formation of canon, 33, 34; tendencies in, towards formation of canon, 35
Application or interpretation of Old-Testament passages by the evangelists, 307
Arnold, Matthew, on Papias and the fourth Gospel, 225; on the fourth Gospel, 230; on tradition, 232; on the geographical knowledge of the author of the fourth Gospel, 243; his criticism of the "tendency"-doctrine, 291

Athenagoras and the canon, 96
Augustine, his theory of the relation of the synoptics, 125
Augusti on the canon, 31
Autographs of the Gospels, early perished, 1, 2; how written, 3

B

Barnabas, Epistle of, in relation to the canon, 45–48; his allegorizing, 46; does not quote our gospels, 47; his καθὼς γέγραπται, 47
Bartholomew, legend of, in reference to first Gospel, 177, 178
Basilides in relation to the canon, 80
Bauer, Bruno, 319
Baur, on Eichhorn's hypothesis, 136; on Gieseler's hypothesis, 141; his historical criticism of Gospels, 144; on Marcion's Gospel, 146; his conclusions on date of Gospels modified in his own school, 146; on historical character of fourth Gospel, 219; on Justin and the fourth Gospel, 227; on term Son of Man as used by Jesus, 268; on triumphal entry of Jesus into Jerusalem, 295; on "tendency" in the first Gospel, 296
Bezæ, Codex, remarkable for glosses, 17
Biography of Jesus, want of material for, on the part of the evangelists, 325
Bleek, on the paschal question, 234; on the hermeneutics of the evangelists, 313
Bunsen on the canon of Muratori, 99

357

C

Canonical and classical, 30
Canonicity, idea of, 28, 29; not established by councils, 30; independent of supposed inspiration, 31
Canon of Gospels, study of, 27–117; nature of history of, 27; summary of results of critical study of, 345
Carpenter, J. Estlin, approves "tendency"-criticism, 292
Church, hostile to revision of the text, 24; and the canon, 32, 108–113
Clementine Homilies, the, in relation to the canon, 74–78
Clement of Alexandria, complains of changes made in text of Gospels, 7; regards Hebrews as work of Paul, 113, note; quotes Barnabas and Clement of Rome as apostles, 113; his distinction of canonical and uncanonical writings not clear 113; account of composition of Gospels, 114
Clement of Rome, his Epistle in relation to the canon, 41–44
Clement V., Pope, forbids addition to Matt. xvii. 49, p. 15
Colani on Messianism, 259, 271
Conception of Jesus, the miraculous, 331 ff.
Copies of Gospels made in second and third centuries have perished, 5
Copying, hypothesis of, to explain the synoptic problem, 125–130
Copyists, errors of, classified, 12
Credner, on Justin's quotations, 72; on the Gnostics and the canon, 84; on quotations from the Old Testament in the first Gospel, 180; on the interpretation of Is. ix. 1, 2 in Matt. iv. 14, 15, p. 309
Criticism, the true, historical, 255; conservative conclusions of, 319, 351; maxim of, 335; and historical Christianity, 337–355; proceeds on the principle that the Gospels are to be treated as literature, 338; confirms historical Christianity, 343 f.; homage of, to Jesus, 355

Cureton published fragments of the Gospels in Syriac, 25

D

Daniel, book of, its object and date, 259
Davidson, on the "order" of Mark's Gospel, 163; on Papias' testimony as to Mark's Gospel, 163; on date of Mark's Gospel, 172; on relation of Luke to the logia and to Matthew, 201; on Eusebius' testimony to the fourth Gospel, 225; on the reading "Bethany" in John i. 28, p. 243; on "tendency" in Luke, 302
Delitzsch on the synoptic problem, 150
Demoniacs first recognize Jesus as the Messiah according to Mark, 154
De Wette, on relation of synoptics, 126, 143; on the fourth Gospel, 143
Diestel on types, 316
Dillmann on the book of Enoch, 260
Diognetus, Epistle to, and fourth Gospel, 50, 231.
Dionysius of Corinth and the canon, 93
Discourses of Jesus in fourth Gospel, 215
Discrepancy between first and third Gospels in the prehistorical portions, 204
Divination, historical, 300
Divisions in early Church hinder formation of canon, 39
Divorce, Mark's reference to Roman custom regarding, 165
Dogmatic changes in text, 18, 19
Donaldson, on Athenagoras, 97; on canon of Muratori, 101
Duplicates in Matthew, 185, 188

E

Eichhorn, on development of canon, 32; his hypothesis to explain relation of synoptics, 130–138; on the fourth Gospel, 134
Enoch, book of, its Messianic features, 260

INDEX. 359

Epiphanius, on a Hebrew Matthew, 178; on the fourth Gospel, 230
Eschatology of Gospels discussed, 254–290, 335
Esdras, fourth book of, **its Messianism,** 262
Ethical teaching of Jesus modified in the Gospels, 336
Eusebius, on canonicity, **30**; on Epistle of Barnabas, 45
Evangelists, first **and** third, **in relation to** Mark, 203
Ewald, his hypothesis of formation of synoptic Gospels, 148; his attitude towards "tendency"-criticism, **147**; on ἐκεῖνος in John xix. 35, p. 239

F

Falsus in uno, falsus in omnibus, **not** applicable to Gospels, 329
Fantastic elements in Jewish apocalyptics, 259
Feeding of multitude, duplicate accounts of, 168, 185; Weizsäcker on, 328
Fig-tree, the barren, Mark's account of, as indicating **a** tendency to think parabolic **words into** parabolic acts, 167
Figures of speech, Jesus' use of, in reference to the future, **278**
Formula of quotation from **the Old Testament used** by the evangelists **as indicating a** purpose to interpret, 307
Fourth Gospel, see John.
Fritzsche on telic use of ἵνα **by evangelists in quoting from Old Testament,** 307
Fulfilment **of** prophecy as understood by author of first Gospel, 308; sought by evangelists as result **of** new hermeneutics of Old Testament, 327
Future of Old-Testament **prophecy,** 258

G

Genealogy of Jesus in Matthew, **192**; in Luke, 204

Gieseler on synoptic problem, 138–142
Glosses, origin of, 17; **when words or** sentences are to be **regarded as,** 20
Gnosticism, **78**
Goethe, eulogy **of** Christianity, 352
Gospels, originally without titles, 3; **not** protected by reverence from errors of early copyists, 4; division of into chapters, etc., 11, **12**; writers of, do not claim inspiration, 31; results of study of, as literature, 118, 209; synoptic, limitation of their historic material, 120; problem of their agreements and dif**ferences,** 122; not histories in the strict sense of the word, 219; right point of view for study of, **255**; as histories, 318–336
Griesbach, his hypothesis **on relation** of synoptic Gospels, 126–130
Guard of soldiers at grave of Jesus, 184

H

Harmonizing of Gospels as effecting changes in the text, 14; puerile **expedients of, 335**
Harnack on canon of Muratori, 99, 101
Hase **on** composite character of fourth Gospel, 249
Hebrews, Gospel according to, and Matthew, 179; Epistle to, author of, confirms the synoptic tradition, 342
Hegesippus, memoirs of, in relation to the canon, 63
Hengstenberg on the paschal question, **234**
Hermas, **the** Shepherd of, date and relation to the canon, 48
Hermeneutics, the, **of the evangelists, 306–317**
Hilgenfeld, on the Ignatian Epistles **and the** fourth Gospel, 59; on Justin's quotations, 72, 73; on the Clementine Homilies, 77; on the canon of Muratori, 99; his hypothesis of **the relation** of the

synoptics, 147 ; on authorship of third Gospel, 208 ; on an original Matthew, 296 ; on the paschal question, 237

Hippolytus on the Gnostics, 81

Historical interpretation, 300

Histories, the Gospels as, 219, 325

Hitzig on the Danielic vision of the Son of Man, 259, 267

Holtzmann, on the restoration of the Itala, 23 ; on the synoptic problem, 124, 140, 157 ; on Eichhorn's hypothesis, 135 ; on an original Mark, 151 ; on priority of Mark, 153 ; on Papias' testimony as to Matthew, 174 ; on the historical and legendary, 328 ; on the poetry of the prehistorical narratives of first and third Gospels, 335

I

Ignatius, Epistles of, in relation to canon, 33

Immer, on textual criticism, 20 ; on types, 316 ; on eschatology, 285

Ἵνα, used as telic particle in quotations made by evangelists from Old Testament, 307

Inspiration, not claimed by evangelists, 31 ; Justin Martyr on, 67 ; not thought in apostolic and post-apostolic ages to be special, 39, 42 ; not attributed to evangelists in middle of the second century, 175

Intercourse between churches, want of, in post-apostolic age unfavorable to formation of canon, 38

Interpolation of text, charges concerning, 6 ; in Mark xvi. 9–20, and John v. 4 and vii. 52–viii. 12, p. 17 ; the great, in Luke, 156, 205

Interpretation, allegorical, used by the evangelists, 311 f. ; the, of teachings of Jesus required by conditions of first century, 331

Irenæus, on the Gospels of the Gnostics, 81 ; quotes Shepherd of Hermas as inspired, 95 ; writings of, in relation to canon, 102–106 ;

appeals to prophecy to confirm Gospel-accounts of miracles, 115 ; gives fantastic reasons for accepting the four Gospels, 103, 104 ; his testimony to miracles in the second century, 115 ; on the first Gospel, 177, on the third, 206

Isaiah, the second, point of view of, 258

Itala, early Latin version of Gospels, 22

J

Jachmann on the Shepherd of Hermas, 49

Jacobsen on relation of Matthew and Luke, 152

Jerome author of Vulgate-version, 24

Jerusalem, judgment on, and the Parousia, 254

Jesus, his appearance after resurrection, according to Matthew and Luke, 123 ; discourses of, in Matthew and Luke, 123 ; his announcement of himself as Messiah, in Mark and Matthew, 154 ; conception of, in fourth Gospel, 212 ; his confidence in the success of his cause, 254 ; his relation to Jewish Messianism, 263–270 ; his spiritual apprehension of the kingdom of God, 264 ; his attitude towards the popular Messianic titles, Son of David, Son of God, 265 f. ; his apprehension of his Sonship, 266 ; in what sense he regarded himself as Messiah, 270 f. ; at Cæsarea Philippi, 270, 272, 286 ; impression made by his personality, 322 ; his teachings intended for mankind, and not for Jews only, 331 ; known by his contemporaries as the carpenter's son, 332 ; his moral and spiritual greatness, 353 f.

Jewish Messianism, 256–263 ; attitude of Jesus towards, 263 ff.

Jews, attitude of fourth evangelist towards, 224

John's Gospel, probably known to author of Ignatian Epistles, 59 ;

INDEX. 361

discussion of, 210-253; prologue of, 211 f.; relation of, to synoptics, 214; discourses of Jesus in, 215 f.; accounts of miracles in, 216; sources of, 218 f.; relation of to Pauline ideas, 219, **222**; subjective character of, **221**; historical evidences as to, **224**; whether cited by Justin, **226** f.; conclusions regarding external evidences, **231**; authorship, **238** f.; point of view of that of second century, **242**; composite character of, 249; logia of Jesus in, **252**, 339; date of composition, **252**; eschatology of, 288 f.; interpretation of Old Testament in, 309 f.; genuineness of, not essential to historical Christianity, 347 f.

John the apostle supposed to have settled the canon, 31; character of in synoptics incompatible with his authorship of fourth Gospel, 240

John the presbyter, on Mark, 61, 162

Justin Martyr's Gospels, with reference to the canon, 65-74; and the fourth Gospel, 226 f

K

Kahnis on synoptic problem, 150
Keim, on date of second Gospel, **172**; on date of first Gospel, 196; on sources of fourth Gospel, 219, **220**; on the passover question, 237; on synoptic eschatology, 255; on the Parousia, 281, 287; on Pauline traits in Luke, 301; tribute to Jesus, 352

Kingdom of Jesus, spiritual nature of, 330

Köstlin, on Marcion's Gospel, 88; on place of composition of Luke, 208; on historical character of synoptics, 322

Koppe, his hypothesis as to synoptics, **115**

L

"Last days," thought to be near, in apostolic age, 34

Legendary narratives in Gospels, 183, 331 f.

λόγια, discussion of meaning of, as used by Papias of Matthew's writing, 174; κυριακά by Matthew, 36

Logia of Jesus in fourth Gospel, **252, 339**

Logia-source, used by authors of synoptic Gospels, **156, 166, 186, 200**; how sayings of Jesus were contained in, **158**; preferred by author of first Gospels to other sources, **189**; used by first and third evangelists, **190**; how used by Luke, **203**; importance of the fact that it was in writing, 320

Lord's prayer, changes in text of, 14

Luke, author of third Gospel, **197**; revised eschatology of Mark and Matthew, **274, 278**; his Pauline "tendency," and the historical character of his Gospel, **331**

Luke's Gospel, relation of, to the logia and Matthew, 156, **157, 202**; dependence of, on Mark, **159, 199** f.; sources of, **191** f., 204 f.; discussed, 197-209; and the logia-source, **200** f.; Pauline character of, 206; "tendency" of and relation to Paul's Epistles, 206, 300 f.; historical point of view of, 207; written last of the synoptics, date, 208 f.; account of overthrow of Jerusalem in, 209; not a merely dogmatic composition, 305

M

Mangold on relation of Matthew and Luke, **152**

Manuscripts of Gospels, earliest existing, **5**; account of principal, 9-11

Marcion, corrupts Luke's Gospel, 6; his collection in relation to canon, 32; canon of, 85-90; acknowledged only Pauline writings, 86; his Gospel, controversy on, 87 f.

Mark, as epitomator and copyist, 126; his relation to Peter, 161

Mark's Gospel, priority of, to other synoptics, 153; discussed, 161-172; vivid style of, 162, 169; testimony of Papias regarding, 162; relation to first Gospel, 165; relation to logia-source, 166; and the oral tradition, 166; contains legendary expansion of oral tradition, 168; linguistic usage, 170; object of, 171; time and place of composition, 171; historical character of, 322 f.

Mark-hypothesis, the, as developed by Weisse and Wilke, 143 f.; Meyer on, 148; Weiss and Holtzmann on, 151

Marsh on Eichhorn's hypothesis, 137

Martineau, on the paschal question, 238; on Jesus' Messianic claims, 285 f.

Mary and the miraculous conception, 332

Matthew, author of "Oracles" of Christ, 36, 173

Matthew's Gospel, numerical symbolism in, 152; dependence on Mark, 153; difference from Mark as to announcement of Messiah, 154; discussion of, 173-196; sources of, 186 f., 192; not originally a Hebrew Gospel, 177 f.; and that according to Hebrews, 179; as an apostolic composition incompatible with Luke's record, 179; an independent composition in Greek, 180 f.; quotations from Old Testament in, 180 f.; not work of an eyewitness, 183, 185; relation to logia, 188 f.; place and time of writing, 193 f.; "tendency" of, 195, 293; point of departure, 297

Melito of Sardis and the canon, 95

"Memoirs of the Apostles," Justin's, 65-74

Messianic expectations of Jews, 255 f.

Messianism in Jewish prophets and apocalypses, 256-262; as a source of "tendency," 329

Meyer, his hypothesis on the synoptics, 148; on the legend of the shepherds and the angels, 334

Miracle and allegory, 328

Multitude, feeding of, duplicates of, 167; fed numbers of, in Mark and Matthew, 167

Muratori, canon of, 98-102

Mysticism of fourth Gospel, 244

Mythical theory, reaction from, 328

N

Nazarene, the, and the "Branch," 183

Nazareth, how mentioned in first Gospel, 333

Nice, council of, settled paschal controversy, 235

Nösgen, on the synoptic problem, 150

Norton, on Epistle of Barnabas, 46; on Ignatian Epistles, 56; on Justin's quotations, 74; on Eichhorn's hypothesis, 137; on oral tradition as solving the synoptic problem, 142

Numerical symbolism in the first Gospel, 152, 195

O

Old Testament, the, in the Gospels, 306-317; read in a new light by Jewish Christians, 327

Oral canon, the, 36

Oral proclamation of Gospel, fragmentary character of, 323

Oral tradition, early, and the canon, 37; hypothesis of, to explain the synoptic problem, 138-142; perils of, for the evangelists, 320

Organization, want of, hinders formation of canon in post-apostolic age, 38

Origen on text of the Gospels, 7, 8; his testimony to canon, 114-116; first to distinguish Gospels and Epistles as "accepted" and "doubted," 114; his statement

of tradition as to composition of Gospels, **115**; distinguished Gospel of Nazarenes from that according to Matthew, 178
Original Gospel, hypothesis of, **130**–138
Overbeck on Pauline traits in Luke, 301

P

Palestinian-Jewish exegesis, 312
Pantænus on first Gospel, 177
Papias, testimony of, to canon, 60; did not know a Gospel by Matthew, **180**; canon of, 224; relation to fourth Gospel, 225
Parabolic sayings thought into parabolic acts by Mark, 235 f.
Parousia, Mark's record of discourse on, not from oral tradition, 157, **164**; as set forth by Luke, 209; in synoptic Gospels, 255; sayings regarding in the Gospels examined, 278–284
Paschal question and the fourth Gospel, 233 f.
Pauline-Jewish controversy, the, 39; ideas in fourth Gospel, 219, 223; traits in first Gospel, 294, 300
Paul, occasion of his Epistles, 34; Epistles not written for future ages, 35; claims no especial inspiration as a writer, 35; allegorizes Old Testament, 35, 314; appeals to tradition of "words of the Lord," 36; indifferent to history of Jesus, 36; on the Messiah as judge, 284; his use of typology, 314; a witness to the facts of synoptic history, 339; conversion of, 339
Peschito, early Syriac version of Gospels, 22, **25**
Peter, call of, as reported by Matthew and Mark irreconcilable with Luke's account, 123; confession of, 265, 270
Pfleiderer, on Mark as a "tendency"-writing, **168**; on Mark's reference to the overthrow of Jerusalem,

172; on Pauline traits in Luke, 301
Philo as an allegorist, 313
Polycarp, Epistle of, in relation to canon, 51; on paschal question, **235**
Post-apostolic age in relation to the canon, 37
Pragmatism of first evangelist, 298, 330
Predilections, personal, hinder formation of canon in post-apostolic age, 37
Prehistorical narratives of first and third Gospels want verification, 332
Presumptions as to canonicity not accepted by criticism, 31

Q

Quartodecimans, the, in paschal controversy, 235
Quirinius, Luke's account of census under, unhistorical, 334
Quotations from Gospels, in second century, **7**; not made by Clement of Rome, 23; question as to Justin's, 65–74
Quotations from Old Testament, formula as applied to Gospels, 43, 48; by first evangelists, 180; by evangelists considered, 306–317

R

Readings, various, classified, 12; arising from attempts to reconcile evangelists with one another, 14; arising from attempts of copyists to reconcile an evangelist with himself or with facts, 15; which remove difficulties, suspicious, 21
Renan, on Pauline traits in Luke, 301; eulogy of Jesus, 354
Reuss, on conflicts in early Church with reference to the canon, 40; on Epistle of Barnabas, 46; on Gnosticism and the canon, 81; on Marcion's Gospel, 88; on copying hypothesis, 129

Revelation, the, and the fourth Gospel, 232 ; historical criticism not opposed to, 353
Réville, on Papias' ignorance of first Gospel, 180 ; on legends in first Gospel, 185 ; on date of first Gospel, 196
Ritschl, on date of Clementine Homilies, 75 ; on priority of Mark, 155

S

Sanday on the Clementine Homilies and the canon, 77
Schenkel on the eschatological problem, 254
Schleiermacher, on Marcion's Gospel, 87 ; his theory of composition of Luke, 198
Schürer on paschal question, 237
Schwegler, on Epistle of Polycarp, 51 ; as a Tübingen critic, 147 ; his extreme tendency-criticism, 292
Scriptures ($\gamma\rho\alpha\phi\alpha\acute{\iota}$) first applied to Gospel-writings, 95
Semler, on the canon as a growth, 32 ; on Marcion's Gospel, 87
Shepherds and angels, story of, ideal, 334
Simon Magus in Clementine Homilies, 75
Sinaïtic Manuscript, 9 ; omits many spurious readings, 19; and Vatican, agree in majority of readings, 19
Source-criticism, growing favor of, 319
Spiritual transformed into physical facts by tradition, 350
Storr on synoptic problem, 125
Strauss, his mythical theory, 143, 146 ; on the oral tradition of sayings of Jesus, 157 ; his services to Gospel-criticism, 327
"Supernatural Religion," author of, on Justin's quotations, 74 ; on Clementine Homilies, 77
Symbolism, of certain Gospel-narratives, 184 ; numerical, in first Gospel, 152, 195
Synoptic Gospels compared with fourth Gospel, 118

Synoptic problem, with reference to integrity of synoptic text, 5 ; discussion of, 118–160 ; importance of to hypotheses of origin of Gospels, 124 ; theories for solution of, 125 ; results of study of, 347
Synoptists, their use of the same limited material, 124 ; their Messianic beliefs, 272 f.

T

Targums, the, their Messianism, 261
Tatian, Diatessaron in relation to the canon, 91 ; knew fourth Gospel, 230
Tayler on fourth Gospel, 211
"Tendencies," dogmatic, in the Gospels, 291–315
"Tendency," as affecting first Gospel, 195, 293 ; as affecting historical character of Gospels, 329 f.
Tertullian, on the heretics and the Scriptures, 81 ; his uncritical acceptance of tradition, 107 ; testimony to canon, 106–108 ; on third Gospel as ascribed to Paul, 106
Text of Gospels, 1–27 ; witnesses to, 6 ; original, cannot be restored, 26
Text, summary of results of criticism of, 344
Textual criticism, some principles of, 20 ; has to do with human phenomena, 26
Theophilus, and the canon, 97 ; his $\pi\nu\epsilon\upsilon\mu\alpha\tau\acute{o}\phi\rho\rho\iota$, 98 ; first to ascribe fourth Gospel to John, 230
Time-order often disregarded in the Gospels, 185
Tischendorf, on textual criticism, 20 ; on date of Clementine Homilies, 75
Tradition of Jesus, modified by the media through which it passed, 325 ; characteristic of, to enhance events and effects, 350
Tregelles on canon of Muratori, 99
Tübingen critics, on Justin's testimony to fourth Gospel, 226 ; their doctrine of "tendency," 291

Tübingen school, modifications in, 319
Types, none in Old Testament, 315 ; **an invention** of a false exegesis, 316
Typology, in hermeneutics of evangelists, 311 f. ; true meaning of, 315

U

Uncial manuscripts, 9
Uncritical acceptance, of Gospels by Irenæus, 103, 104 ; of tradition by Tertullian, 107
Unhistorical features of Gospels do not invalidate historical, 329 f.
Universalism of Paul surpassed in fourth Gospel, 241

V

Valentinus and the canon, 82–85
Variants, 12
Vatican Manuscript, 9 ; **omits many** spurious readings, 12
Vaticinium post eventum, 172, 350
Versions of Gospels, 22
Virgin-birth of Jesus erroneously derived in first Gospel from Is. vii. 14, pp. 182, **297, 308**
Virginity, perpetual, **of Mary,** doctrine of, causes dogmatic **change** in text, 19
Volkmar, **on Marcion's Gospel, 88 ;** his "**tendency**"-interpretation of Peter's **miraculous draught** of fishes, 292
Voss, recension of Ignatian Epistles by, 54
Vulgate-version of Gospels, 22–24 ; revised by order of Charlemagne, 25

W

Weiffenbach **on Jesus** before the High-priest, **281**

Weisse, author of Mark-hypothesis, 143 ; **on** the Mark-hypothesis, 166
Weiss, **on quotations of Gospels by** Clement **of Rome, 44 ; on the** Shepherd **of Hermas and the canon,** 50 ; **on hypothesis of copying, 129 ; on Matthew's logia, 151 ; on Mark and the logia, 158 ;** his reconstruction of the logia, 190 ; on Luke's relation to logia and Matthew, 204
Weizsäcker, **on historical** character of fourth Gospel, 220 ; on apostolic and unapostolic elements in fourth Gospel, **249 ;** his arrangement of synoptic narratives in **groups** of "doctrinal tenets," 328
Wendt, on Mark and the logia, 157 ; on relation **of** Matthew and Luke, **152 ;** his reconstruction of the logia, 190 ; on composite character of fourth Gospel, 249
Westcott, on the preservation of the text, 22 ; on "Words of the Lord" as oral **canon, 36 ; on** Justin's quotations, **74 ; on oral** tradition, **142**
Wieseler on the paschal question, 234
Wilke, on the synoptic problem, 144 ; on the Mark-hypothesis, 166
Winer on **formula of** quotation from Old Testament used by evangelists, 307

Z

Zechariah, prophecies of the "**Branch**" by, 258
Zeller, as a Tübingen critic, 147 ; on Papias and the fourth Gospel, **225**

www.ingramcontent.com/pod-product-compliance
Lightning Source LLC
Chambersburg PA
CBHW030744250426
43672CB00028B/393